Eight Pathways of Healing Love

ISBN 978-0-9857666-0-3

Bella-Tierra International
Rocky River, OH 44116 USA

Books available at: www.amazon.com or www.eightpathways.com

Cover and Pathway images by: Francene Hart - www.francenehart.com

PLEASE NOTE:

In this book, we provide examples from our many years of experience of working with couples. All names used in this book are fictional for confidentiality purposes and examples provided are for educational purposes only. Any reference that may sound familiar is unintended.

Eight Pathways
of
Healing Love

Your Journey of Transformation

Thank You and Welcome to Pathways of Healing Love Series!

With over 50 years of combined experience in working with individuals, couples, families, and groups, authors Philip Belzunce, Ph.D and Lalei Gutierrez, Ph.D. are holistic and energy psychologists and life, relationship, diversity, and wellness coaches, and are board certified polarity practitioners. They teach, train, lead workshops, and provide seminars both locally and internationally.

Philip and Lalei are available for lectures, conferences, speaking engagements and personal coaching in person, via telephone or Skype. They can be reached through their websites, www.phillalei.com and www.spiritcenteredcoaching.com 216.712.6192 EST.

This book, the first in the series has been a labor of love. We hope you gain valuable insight to guide you in your relations with others. The paperback print book with Pathways A through H is available at www.amazon.com. Kindle format of Pathway books individually or as a paperback book, Pathway A through H are available at www.amazon.com. To enrich and deepen your journey of transformation, a video download and/or DVD of *Eight Pathways of Healing Love - Movement Meditation*, is available at www.eightpathways.com.

Eight Pathways is also available in paperback and Kindle at Amazon and as individual e-books or whole book for download at eightpathways.com:

Introduction
Pathway A: Pathway of Affirmation and Awakening
Pathway B: Pathway of Being and Balance
Pathway C: Pathway of Connection and Communication
Pathway D: Pathway of Development and Discovery
Pathway E: Pathway of Evolving in Experience
Pathway F: Pathway of Freedom and Responsibility
Pathway G: Pathway of Gratitude and Grace
Pathway H: Pathway to a Higher Purpose of Love

The **Pathways of Healing Love** series is continually evolving for your transformational journey. Please check back with us for more discoveries on the **Pathways - *for your continuing Journey of Transformation***.
- ❖ Pathway I
- ❖ Pathway J
- ❖ Pathway K
- ❖ Pathway L

**LIKE US** and Follow Us on Facebook

Table of Contents

Table of Contents 5

Foreword 6

Our Dedication 8

Acknowledgements 9

What People Are Saying 12

Glossary 16

Introduction 18

An Overview... 23

Discovering the Pathways.. 34

Pathway A: Pathway of Affirmation and Awakening 38

Pathway B: Pathway of Being and Balance.................... 52

Pathway C: Pathway of Connection and Communication............ 62

Pathway D: Pathway of Development and Discovery 95

Pathway E: Pathway of Evolving in Experience............... 139

Pathway F: Pathway of Freedom and Responsibility 165

Pathway G: Pathway of Gratitude and Grace 201

Pathway H: Pathway to a Higher Purpose of Love 229

Closure and Summary... 254

Epilogue 260

About the Authors... 261

References & Suggested Readings................................... 262

Foreword

I am a firm believer that people are brought into our lives for a purpose. When I met Philip Belzunce and Lalei Gutierrez over twenty years ago, I had no idea the incredible influence they would have on my life. Because of their wonderful resonance, I decided to pursue their help during the more difficult and tender experiences of my life, including the death of my father and other profound transformations such as illness and divorce. It can be difficult to find genuine assistance during such transformative times, and it is clear to me that Lalei and Philip have been brought into my life for precisely that purpose. Each has a unique approach to personal healing-expanding mere psychology into holistic, energetic, and spiritual realms.

When you have the intention to heal, transform, and shift your old, outmoded forms of consciousness, it's important to work with people who share your philosophy and who resonate with your own energy. It's also important to find someone who is compassionate and caring, yet also directive and probing. The right balance of investigation and encouragement can break through stuck energy, heal old patterns, and bring guidance for new direction.

Lalei and Philip have blessed me with all of these qualities and more; and now they bring their wonderfully healing and practical techniques to you in this book. The principles in their book, **Eight Pathways of Healing Love**, are simple but profound. They help to take both the individual and the couple on a journey of personal awareness and growth. They offer skills in communication, balance, meditation, affirmation, and so much more. The skills described herein can be engaged in by the individual with dramatic effect—but when a couple pursues these activities with a shared intention, it can bring profound peace and harmony, not only to each individual but to the relationship itself.

This is something that Lalei and Philip know a great deal about. In recent years I have had the great good fortune of becoming friends with this wonderful couple. In that capacity I've been able to witness something rare indeed, a relationship built on mutual respect, tenderness, and a spiritual bond that is a living example of what we all can achieve.

If we are brought together for a purpose, then the purpose behind our romantic partnering must be one of the most important of our lives. It's not just for companionship, sexual intimacy, or even financial security, although all of these are important factors in the loving relationship. Yet a deeper purpose and meaning threads itself through our most intimate relationships. It speaks to personal evolution and self-mastery—and even spiritual enlightenment—for each party involved.

This is the depth of relationship that Lalei and Philip have themselves, and it's the type of relationship they offer in the pages of this book. They bring their practical wisdom to the most common-place and the most difficult issues we face with our partners, and they offer advice that goes to the heart of the matter. They show us that the spirit-driven relationship doesn't have to be weird or unachievable. In fact, this is the most practical and beneficial approach that we can take. It stems from a clear recognition of each partner's value and identity, and it expands to a shared intention to experience all of the vagaries of life with mutual caring and an intelligence that comes not from the head, but from the heart.

The intention of this book is clear, the growth of love for one's self and one's partner, and the evident changes that come to enhance such a loving lifestyle. This expansion of love and compassion blesses the individual, the couple, the family, and the whole world. Lalei and Philip remind us that we are on this journey of love together—and no matter what state our relationship may be in at the present time, we can still bring healing, growth, and appreciation to our partner and ourselves. This journey of loving partnership is an important priority, for it is in the essence and energy of real love that we find our soul's intention and deepest expression.

As you read these pages, open yourself to the spiritual nature of the loving relationship and see how truly fulfilling your love can become. Take the *Eight Pathways of Healing Love* together, and your relationship results will be profound. May you be blessed on your journey now and forever.

Sandra Anne Taylor
New York Times *bestselling author of* **Quantum Success**
and **Truth, Triumph, and Transformation**

Our Dedication

Over the years we have been asked for a collection of our experiences and wisdom that we have gathered together in our journey, both as individuals and as a couple. The culmination of what we have learned has brought us to write this book and it is full of the many WONDERS we have discovered along the way.

We would like to heartfully dedicate **Eight Pathways of Healing Love** to our mother, Rosie, with whom our journey of Love began. To our children: Paolo, Tisha, and Jin and their spouses, Lisa, Joey, and Tina. And to our energetic and beautiful grandchildren: Lorenzo, Alexa, Alfonso, Ari, Isaac, Sydney, and Seville, who help us view life with wonder and make us smile.

We also dedicate this book to all our families, brothers, sisters, cousins, nieces, nephews, and all our relatives, too numerous to name, and that live in so many different places, we are ever so grateful to them for being in our lives.

We would like to give our deepest thanks to all of you, for the unique ways you have enriched our lives in being part of our past, our present, and our future earth journey.

And lastly, to all individuals, couples, families, and communities, who are on the quest for **Healing Love**, this is our gift of love to you!

Living Life with Love, Peace, Joy, and Gratitude,
Warmly,
Phil and Lalei

Acknowledgments

The writing of the **Eight Pathways of Healing Love: Your Journey of Transformation** has been a journey in itself through many phases of creation. There are so many people, in body, energy, emotion, heart, mind, soul, system, and spirit (BEEHMSSS™, which we will discuss at a deeper level throughout the book) relation to whom we are deeply grateful, for they have been a part of this writing and creation process.

Looking out our window we call to mind the journey of the **Eight Pathways**. We see the autumn leaves dancing in the wind in symphonic rhythm and our hearts are warm and full with thanks. It is the oneness of all this that has made this Book possible.

We thank Marci Leibowitz for being with us throughout our three year writing journey, for your commitment and dedication to see this writing project through the ride of its ups and downs, starting as the Ten Pathways of Healing Love to its edits as **Eight Pathways** for this writing. Marci's gifts of heart intuition together with her creative embodied connection with the pulse of the reading community has helped us focus and to take the flow of our divergent thinking processes to an organized format for writing. We are grateful, Marci, for your guided questions and your immense patience that helped clarify and translate our communications from an interactive, facilitative teaching and training format, to readable and understandable form for readers. We thank you for keeping us focused and to the task. Our regular meetings were truly helpful.

We thank Lisa Riopell-Gonzalez for your thorough and detailed editing of language, grammar, and copy and for the happy and much needed breaks with Whiskey, Braego, and the farm.

We thank Tricia Leonard, Ginny Gutierrez, Gwen Klapperich, and Jasmine Massions for being readers, for sharing your experience of reading the material, and for your helpful suggestions and critiques that helped shape its presentation.

We thank Paolo Gonzalez for your authentic and unbridled feedback, your enthusiasm, and creative development of the DVD video on the Pathways movement meditation and to Paitoon (PT) Punturungsi for bringing **Eight Pathways of Healing Love** to the www.phillalei.com website.

We thank Lyn Kelley, our coach, who supported us in our processes and helped us maintain our focus on our action steps towards accomplishing our goals.

We thank Krystina Rymsky, our amazing personal assistant, office and project manager, for your valuable help in the final stages and the many details of final edits and book presentation. Your grounding, calm, and organizing presence that brought the **Eight Pathways of Healing Love** to the finish line, is a true gift for us.

We thank our friends Rosanna Zavarella, Roger Hess, Lynne and Jim Kweder for our dialogues, discussions and togetherness, living our commitment to Healing Love in our lives. It is truly wonderful to have kindred spirits in embodied presence in this earth journey.

We thank the Gestalt Institute of Cleveland, Wes Jackson, Les Wyman, Debra Dunkle, and Karen Fleming of the Couples and Family Program; Jim Kepner, Tom Cutolo, Michael Clemmens, Donna Berwald, Jackie Lowe Stevenson, Denise Tervo, Jody Telfair, and Will Heindel of the Working with Physical Process Program; Lynne Kweder, Frances Baker, Dan Jones, Vikki Winbush, Barbara Thomas, Rosanna Zavarella and the faculty of the Gestalt Training Program; our teachers, Frances Baker, Len Hirsch, Sonia and Ed Nevis, Carolyn Lukensmeyer, Elaine Kepner, John Carter, Ansel Woldt, Virginia Satir, Carl Whitaker, Jay Haley, Chloe Madanes, and the many whose significant impact in our professional and personal lives for over 30 years, that have influenced our work in the community, our unique presentation, and for the integration of material for Healing Love Pathways in this book. We value our personal-professional growth as a dynamic transformative process in our learning and training community. We thank all for the love and I-Thou connections in being part of 'Evolving in Learning' how to learn from experience.

We thank the Masters Program in Diversity Management at Cleveland State University, Deborah Plummer, Lisa Gaynier, faculty, students, and alumni, whose dedication to the appreciation of diversity on the many levels of system, has become a force for transforming the separations of institutions of "ism" to engagements of evolution, impacting unfolding system shifts and changes. Your mission for being gives Hope for the world to be one of **Healing Love**.

We thank Ron Casselberry, naturopathic mentor and friend, for the complementary world of naturopathic medicine.

We thank Alexandra Pierce, for her consultations in heightening our awareness of planetary shifts and influences on the world climate of relational consciousness shifts.

We thank the Ohio Institute of Energetic Studies and Bodywork, Mary Jo Ruggieri; our Tuesday Healing Group and our Lady of Guadalupe prayer group; Tom Leonhardt, Carolyn Horvath, Bill and Pattie Wisniewski, Federation of Christian Ministries and CORPUS; Mantak Chia and the Universal Tao Institute; and our alternative, energetic, metaphysical, spiritual, polarity, chiropractic, natural health, and healing friends. We thank the holistic process of our life journey and the diversity of our connections that contribute to **Healing Love**. We feel truly grateful to be in this amazing time on our planet. So many healing individuals are here now, on the many levels of relationship, to assist in the Healing of our Planet Earth.

We acknowledge and thank each other. It is so heartwarming to do this book with one another, as a partner, spouse, colleague, friend... for it is a testimony of the many years of our own work of **Healing Love** together and this is our contribution to the many relationships, couples-families, groups-communities, that have touched us.

And most of all, we thank the ALL-THAT-IS, Universal Intelligence, Higher Power, Healing Force, Energetic Field, Source, and the GOD Presence in All Creation, Whose powerful vibration is...

...Infinite Love.

What People Are Saying...

"Drs. Phil and Lalei are well known for their perceptive and careful couples work. This book, ***Eight Pathways of Healing Love: Your Journey of Transformation,*** provides a practical structure for couples to learn more about themselves both as individuals and as a couple. What a marvelous addition that will help couples to move at their own pace and gain insight into how they function together. I highly recommend this book."

~Frances Baker, Psychologist
Cleveland, Ohio

"This brilliant workbook for couples is a unique contribution from a very talented couple who are grounded in the reality of two intertwined lifetimes of experience with one another and the hundreds of couples with whom they have worked professionally. Drs. Phil and Lalei's experience and understanding of the underlying struggles in every committed relationship and their deep spirituality shine through in every paragraph. Use of this guide will deepen and enhance any relationship, no matter how recent or longstanding. This book is designed as a guide for every couple who seek deep fulfilling intimacy with one another to explore and enrich their relationship. Couples seeking the help of therapists and counselors will find this workbook useful in delving beneath the surface of their issues with one another so that they can bring fresh insights into the therapy setting, making their therapy more productive. Therapists and counselors will find this book useful as an adjunct to couples therapy, assisting the couples to identify underlying issues which have created problematic patterns in their relationships, and the therapist to work more productively with those patterns. Overall, this guidebook is an incredibly useful and beautifully spiritual contribution to those in committed relationships and the therapists and counselors who work with them."

~Lynne M. Kweder, M.P.A., G.P.C.C.
Faculty, Gestalt Institute of Cleveland, Inc.

"In their book Dr. Gutierrez and Dr. Belzunce generously share the inspiration and wisdom which they have gleaned from their own long-term coupleship, and from their experiences as master teachers and consummate clinicians. In a wonderfully insightful and authentic manner they engage us to consider how we too can create and maintain relationships that are both lively and fulfilling."

~Victoria R.Winbush, PhD, Faculty Coordinator
Gestalt Institute of Cleveland, Inc

"Staying open to our partner takes work and awareness. There are far too few guides and coaches available for the process. If you go slowly into this opening with the loving guidance of Phil and Lalei, you will be richly rewarded. They talk the talk and walk and walk wisely."

~ Roger N Hess, Ph.D.
Clinical Psychologist and Couples Therapist

"Through this book Drs. Belzunce and Gutierrez offer us their insights gleaned from their years of experience being a successful couple, as well as working with struggling couples, and multiple ways to develop our own wisdom and apply it in our uniquely painful and confusing situations. This is not a book to read once and put away. It is a guide to pick up any time we are lost or stuck. This book will not tell you what is wrong with your relationship (you already know what it is). It will tell you how to use what is right to make it better than you could ever have imagined."

~K.L.Carlson, Advanced Practice Nurse
Cleveland, Ohio

"For any couple, young or old, who wish to transform their relationship into deeper, more fulfilling levels, **Eight Pathways of Healing Love** is a highly effective and wonderful resource. It is written by two gifted and well-respected professionals who personally live these pathways and who have dedicated themselves to providing guidance to a multitude of couples in a most genuine and compassionate manner. **Eight Pathways of Healing Love** is written in the manner in which Dr. Lalei and Dr. Phil live their lives, with a nonjudgmental stance, a generosity of Spirit, hopefulness, and above all love for humanity. They acknowledge the interrelated dimensions of being and discuss Spirituality in profound and meaningful ways. Couples can move at their own pace and are supported throughout their journey of transformation. This book is powerful, insightful, filled with wisdom and is a true gift to all who seek to develop meaningful relationships."

~Carmela Palmentera, Ph.D.
Clinical Psychologist, www.palmentera.com

"Being true to oneself while remaining committed to a loving relationship is a journey that is often underestimated and misunderstood. This book offers gems of knowledge and skill for how to navigate and grow our relationship. The **Eight Pathways of Healing Love** provides crucial ingredients for how to love. Lalei and Phil are masterful guides in healing love."

~Rosanna Zavarella, Ph.D.
Psychologist and Transformational Healer

"I've worked with Phil and Lalei for five years and known them for over ten. They have unique and special gifts. One of their special gifts is seeing the diversity that exists in their clients and helping them to honor and to leverage the "I" and the "Thou" that makes up a successful and loving "WE." I highly recommend this book."

~Lisa (Tong) Parola Gaynier, MA
Director, Masters Program in Diversity Management
Developing Culturally Competent Leaders Who Can Lead and Sustain Change

"As a couple we have had the rich gift of the guidance and support of Drs. Gutierrez and Belzunce for over 25 years of our marriage and raising our family. They have modeled through their own relationship, as well as encouraged us to find the unique patterns and rhythms, wounds and healing of our own couple-ship. We have learned to be there for each other, to identify our patterns, and to explore new choices for healing, growth and love. May you also find these gifts as you begin the *Eight Pathway of Healing Love: Your Journey of Transformation*."

~Alex Tomoff, CPA, Professional Counselor
~Karen Tomoff, Professional Clinical Counselor, Rocky River, Ohio

"Working with Drs. Gutierrez and Belzunce in our own journey toward healing love has been wonderfully creative, affirming of what we know already, recognizing our ability to learn together and to open to the transforming energy of the universe. The Pathways are tools for our lifetime together as a married couple, and we will be glad to have them at our fingertips in this book."

~Lea Mahan, United Methodist Clergy, www.wellingtonfumc.org
~George P. Bohan, Consultant, www.chagrinriverconsulting.com

"Phil and Lalei's book is a beautiful illustration of the *Eight Pathways* by which we can travel closer to the Source of all things within our relationships. The pathways are a spiritual roadmap for us to increase our awareness while at the same time nourishing and healing our hearts and souls through truly loving one another. Through our conscious relationships we can more fully open to the Divine Love within ourselves and each other."

~Lynn Williams, Ph.D., Psychologist

"As my favorite teachers at the Diversity Management Program 12, Drs. Phil and Lalei shared some simple yet wise tools on how to learn about one self and develop relationship with diverse others. With the willingness to dig deep into the many layers that makes us who we are, we discover, get to know and love ourselves and are better able to appreciate, work with and love others. The *Eight Pathways* serve as a guide in developing a healing relationship with oneself and with others with enough universal love for all. Sounds simple? Aren't most beautiful and valuable things simple?"

~Ljiljana L. Bobinac, MA
Cuyahoga County Board of Developmental Disabilities

"I highly recommend the *Eight Pathways of Healing Love: Your Journey of Transformation* to couples who want to strengthen the core of their relationship. It is through the process of "conscious evolution" or knowing and transforming oneself that meaningful relations with a significant other take place. To unite with another human being in wholeness, love, and respect requires effort in the spiritual, emotional, psychological realm. Phil and Lalei provide a recipe for couples to come together with kindness, understanding, and compassion."

~Jeanette Velez, MA, CDP, Physician Liaison, Manger of Physician Relations
Euclid and Lutheran Hospitals, Cleveland Clinic Health System

"We are blessed to have Lalei and Phil as friends. Their presence and professionalism are a source of inspiration. They have helped couples grow as persons and thus bless each other in their loving relationship. Our lives and relationships are transformed by the giving and receiving of healing, redemptive love. Phil and Lalei, in *Eight Pathways of Healing Love: Your Journey of Transformation,* invite us to rediscover our relational journey of healing love and experience an on-going deepening love in our relationship."

~Bill and Pattie Wisniewski
Married Priest Couple, Ravenna, Ohio

"My husband and I were honored to have Dr. Phil Belzunce as the officiant at our wedding. Both he and Dr. Lalei were instrumental during our pre-marriage counseling process, to guide and support our working through much of the drama associated with family gatherings prior to our ceremony. The result was that we entered our marriage with a stronger connection and commitment to each other and to our families. This book takes the reader completely through that process, and is the next best thing to having them in the room with you! Whatever stage you are in your relationships, *Eight Pathways of Healing Love* will help you discover what you seek from those around you."

~Gwen Navarrete, Writer, Speaker, and Corporate Trainer

"Phil and Lalei have been our friends and colleagues for many years. Their gentle, conscious, non-judgmental, affirming, healing presence comes from their soul(s). The *Eight Pathways of Healing Love: Your Journey of Transformation* embodies what they have lived and continue to live."

~Tom Leonhardt & Carolyn Horvath
Coordinators, Federation of Christian Ministries

15

Glossary

These are some of the terms we use throughout the Pathways Series, which may be unfamiliar or new to many of you. In our effort for clarity, we have defined the words in how we are using them in the Pathway Series and which may have a variation in meaning, process, and practice in the Pathways. We appreciate your input or any questions you may have for clarification of terms as we use them.

- **Affirming** - Your ability to positively appreciate yourself and your partner. A relational skill involving attending, acknowledging, awaring, and appreciating.

- **Attune** - As an attuning skill of calibrating internally one's senses to be receptive, as in listening with one's inner ear to the other, and responding in a heartfelt and connective way.

- **Awaring** - As a skill of being in awareness in the present of here-and-now felt sensations and verbalizing one's awareness of present felt sensations.

- **BEEHMSSS**™ - Refers to the **B**ody-**E**nergy-**E**motion-**H**eart-**M**ind-**S**oul-**S**ystem-**S**pirit. Our holistic and integrative approach incorporating a perspective, a process, and a practice for personal and relational transformation and the well-being in our evolution to wholeness.

- **Co-create** - To create together in a collaborative fashion, whether aware or unaware of their participation in their co-created experience.

- **Couple** - A two person system, which could be a husband-wife, partners, spouses, siblings, parents, co-worker, your significant other, your marriage, your partnership, your sibling relationship, your friendship, your companionship, your colleagueship etc.

- **Dialogue** - As a living skill of exchange, connection, and interaction (different from debate) that involves communicating understanding, empathy, support, sharing awareness with presence, authenticity, and response-ability in a mutually reciprocal manner.

- **Embody** (embodied) - To be fully present in your physical body with your mind, heart, and being, for example, having a felt sense of one's spirit within one's body, in one's embodied presence to the other, in a connective way to oneself, in the relational context of the present moment.

- **Foundational** - As in a foundation or the beginning process for building upon or enhancing skills.

- **God** - the universal energetic field (called by many names such as: God, Buddha, Nature, Mother Earth, Tao, Spirit, Allah, Krishna, Jehovah, the Universe, the Force, the Source, Energy, the One, the All, etc.).

- **Relational (System Skill)** - The skill or ability to orient within your relationship on the two-person dimensional exchange or interaction evolving out of the social context of the relationship (ie. The marriage context is different from the co-workers context).

Introduction

The life of human beings… does not exist in virtue of activities alone
That have something for their object…
This and the like together establish the realm of I-It…
But the realm of I-Thou has a different basis…
When Thou is spoken, there is no thing.
Thou has no bounds.
~Martin Buber

Eight Pathways of Healing Love has been lovingly co-created from the encouragement of many wonderful people, but there is one experience we want to share with you that was the beginning of our writing journey. It all began several years ago…

We were on a plane trip from Cleveland to Guadalajara, Mexico and overheard a lovely young couple in their mid-20s discuss their fears about marriage based on their various relationship role models.

"Why even get married, when it will just end in divorce? Honey, do you honestly know of any marriages that have lasted?" exclaimed the young man. "A wedding is just a big expense and a big party. Logically, it is not a great way for us to start our lives together, beginning our marriage on credit, if we do it the way folks expect it to be done."

"Well, I would want to have this love that we have last a long time…and a wedding ceremony is a once in a lifetime memorable event. But you are right, what guarantees are there? It's so scary to think that relationships simply do not last," replied the young woman.

"How can you tell who is really happy? What DOES it take to make love last?" asked the beautiful, young woman who with a deep sigh, rested her head on his shoulders. "I dream of having a happy relationship with a loving husband and happy family."

"It might sound rather pessimistic, but look around us, my dear, our relationship has lasted three happy years, much longer than many of our friends who have gotten married. It seems that marriage really dooms love. With all the heavy expectations, somehow people change after they get married, and are filled with disappointments."

"Do you think you will change?" asked the woman.   "Why am I beginning to feel that I do not like where this discussion is going? I wish we could have someone to talk to about all of this, because it is really important to me."

"Well, look at it this way; we are going on this vacation to a wonderful place. We have this present moment, so why ruin it, by thinking about how we are going to make this last? Let's just make this journey to Guadalajara and enjoy," responded the young man while caressing her hand.

"Oh...you're right."

"And honey, if I were ever going to marry anyone, it would be you. You know that. It is just as scary for me. I know most of my family and friends are divorced. Those who do stay married are always fighting or have settled into having a miserable relationship. Though my parents have stayed together, they are not role models for me. Sometimes I wished they had separated, because the house was so full of tension. Not a day passed without them arguing. I stayed away and vowed to myself that if that is the kind of marriage that I was doomed to have, I would not have it at all."

"You are so pessimistic." She responded.

"You are right. I hate it when people say "Like father, like son." I surely would not want to treat someone I love the way he treats my mother," he retorted. "Sometimes I am afraid that I might."

"My parents do not fight. But they don't do anything together as a couple; they always are focused on us. One time I asked them why they did this and they replied, "Our joy is our kids... and besides, fun is for young folks." My parents always tell us to live at home as long as we want. My brother and sister have moved out of state and I'm left, the last child at home. I can't wait to leave after graduate school. I worry about them and yet I feel so responsible for them..."

"You have such a compassionate heart and that is what I love about you. But you do need to live your own life. Not go straight from your parent's home to our getting married."

"You're right... Well, we are on our own journey, you know. I just need you to know that I would love for our lives to be different from our parents. I like it how we can talk, laugh, discuss and share just about anything. I sometime wonder whatever happened with my parents... It is like their kids became their entertainment committee. I never saw my parents talk to each other like we do." "I know, I feel the same way," said the young man as they both drifted into dreamland.

This was only the beginning of our journey with this young couple.

We ran into them again at Rio Caliente in Guadalajara, Mexico where they excitedly introduced themselves, "I am Mark and this is Sophia, my soon to be fiancé. We have noticed you and you seem like a very interesting couple. Are you guys married?" We simply smiled and nodded.

One morning we walked up the mountain trail with this couple and noticed the trail was magnificently studded with glistening obsidian rocks reflecting the sunlight. We were fascinated with the sheer beauty of it all and felt drawn to pick a few of them up on the trek down. Our leader described to us that we were on a volcanic mountain that spewed molten lava that had quickly cooled and crystallized into rock formations.

As Sophia picked up a stone, she exclaimed, "I just read about these rocks! Did you know that these rocks repel negativity? Its healing effects actually go back into past lives, including healing ancestral and family lines. It is a protective stone, releasing old loves and provides support during change. It is such a powerful and creative stone."

Turning to us, she added, "It also said that it grounds the soul and spiritual forces into the physical plane, bringing them under the direction of the conscious will. It can draw together scattered energy and promote emotional release."

Selectively picking up these rocks, we marveled at their dark, shimmering beauty and shared the wonders of our own felt sensations holding them in our palms. Laughter and delight sprinkled our enjoyable climb together.

The next day Mark joined us at the lithium pools, exclaiming, "I must tell you guys, I want what you have in your relationship! You say you've been married for many, many years! You are the only couple that I have met so far that seems genuinely happy. How do you do it? I had lost faith in marriage, with all the divorces that I see around me, yet when I think of my life without Sophia, it would be so empty. I am just so scared that marriage may ruin what we have. I hope I am not hounding you. I am a researcher for a health magazine and I have been looking for couples with a healthy relationship. This is such a powerful vacation for us! This place is magical; it is making me examine, what is really important to me in my life. The people, the environment, the spa, the organic food, meeting you both – it all gives me hope."

Mark went on further to say: "You guys need to write a book to help folks like us. I feel like I have failed in my past relationships, as I was married once before. Luckily we did not have any children. I have done a lot of reflecting and soul-searching since then, but have not done any counseling. I have read a lot of self-help books that has really been my form of therapy."

As Sophia came to join us at the lithium pool, she jumped in, "Notice how people are all smiling and happy here...it's the lithium. It makes us all feel light!"

"I think you guys need to prescribe to the folks you counsel, to come here every year and swim in these warm waters...and enjoy the hot caves. We were there earlier today and I felt my body cleared of all the toxins."

Phil chuckled with laughter, "Oh, you just gave yourselves a prescription for your cellular memory together." Mark retorted, "What do you mean?"

Phil replied, "We observed that many couples forget when they marry, the Pathways which they have taken that brought them to the center of their love."

Sophia chimed in, "Oh, you mean, that we must remember the good feelings that we have here, to really feel it in our cells and bring this into our life. By us telling you to prescribe it to your clients, I am really giving myself a prescription of how we can support ourselves in our own relationship!"

"I totally get it!" said Mark. "I would love coming here regularly. It would be a great break for us. The key is to give ourselves permission to do this, so we can break away from the regular grind of our lives. Somehow married couples seem to lose something.   Maybe it takes conscious commitment to maintain an awareness to preserve and grow our love in marriage, which is probably easier said than done..."

"Mark tends to see the difficult side of life, and I tend to be more optimistic," said Sophia. I guess that is why we complement each other. He allows me to lighten him up."

"She lets me bring her back to reality. It's good for now because we are romantically in love, but what will happen when we marry?" To Sophia he said, "Will you resent me when I try to bring you back to reality and I won't let you lighten me up? There's something there for us to explore, together."

We also shared with them that we believe a key ingredient to maintaining a vital and healthy marriage is to be in the present 'marrying' or 'merrying'.

As we retired to our cabins, we reflected on the discussions we had with Mark and Sophia and the many other couples that had joined us in the discussion. There were folks from all over the world - Canada, Europe, South America, Israel and Asia. To be in a place where everyone was focused on healing relationships and the role it plays in the healing of our planet: the energetic convergence was amazing! As we listened to everyone's journey of love, a resonance filled the air with compassion and understanding, guiding us to understand how we could help couples co-create their own journey of Healing Love.

When we returned from this wondrous vacation, we noticed that our practice and life carried on and the resistance to writing set in as the demands of our life took over.

Spirit has been relentless and generous in reminding us, through our dreams at night, through our clients and students, who often tell us to write, and also through our children who remind us that they wanted a resource to refer to and that before we die, it was important that we put our legacy of work into written form and to make it accessible to the international community.

Eight Pathways of Healing Love is our fullest expression of the trust that the energy of Love carries us through, as there is no perfect way to get started or to complete a book or a relationship, other than to take it as…

Your Journey of Transformation through Healing Love…

An Overview of Our Journey and an Invitation Into Your Own Journey

In embracing unconditional love you surrender all emotions and thoughts
That separates you from wellbeing and harmony.
This is the essential commitment in transformation and it must be
renewed every day.
Love is a daily celebration of aliveness and permission to go deeper.
~Richard Moss, M.D.

Please Make Yourself Comfortable and Join Us

We warmly welcome you here in this place and time. We are so excited to be here with you, to invite you into your own journey of transformation! This book is our deepest soul offering to you. We want you to know that the information in this book is from what we have learned along the way in our own personal journey as a couple but also from our work with numerous individuals and couples for several decades.

We have deep regard for the amazing power of love which we observed with people in their search and desire for true and fulfilling love in their lives. As love grows and enhances us, we are moved and inspired. As love's presence embraces and affirms, it heals and transforms us in profound ways and on so many levels of life.

Why Now? **What drives people who desire happiness, success, and growth to explore?**

As technology advances, we have become aware of the increasingly speedy pace with which technology impacts our relationships. While access to knowledge for almost anything one wants to know is readily available, we find that this knowledge through information alone is limited. Further, when this knowledge is used without awareness, relational skill, and spiritual maturity, our human dramas of repeating patterns has just taken on a greater complexity.

We find that it is through our connectedness to others that deeper human needs can be met. We then begin to wonder whether the increased use of technologies in order to speed up communications, has reduced our time and space for the deeper understanding of others and for making our meaningful connections. Human interactions, in many respects, have unfortunately become relegated as a *commodity in matters of time and money*.

While technology does bring the world closer for us to witness and be informed about our human struggles and accomplishments, it is through our physical-emotional-energetic-mindful-heartfelt-soulful-system-spiritual connectedness within ourselves and with others that we can meet our deeper human needs.

Repeating Patterns

We see many individuals and couples who want to transform their 'inherited' repeating patterns that want to face their challenges, and harness the opportunity that is unleashed by the power of technological innovations. These individuals, by aligning within and becoming more aware, their opportunity for evolving deep into Love's essence and their transformational growth, they now gain the skills to be a healing presence to themselves and to others in the world.

As you 'slow down' to heal from within and by heeding the 'call' reflected in the pain of the repeating patterns of...

- loneliness, emptiness and a loss of SELF (**S**piritual, **E**nergy, **L**ove, **F**oundation)
- missing intimacy
- communication and understanding difficulties
- frustrations in working through conflict of differences

...you can choose to evolve in your relations to yourself and to others, by *"being the change you want to see in the world." (Gandhi)*

As we exercise the power of our intentions for **healing love** in our world, we choose to explore and learn from our life experience. Through our exploring, we gain an awareness of our repeating patterns of relating that has become passed on to us from one generation to another - from our families, social models, and our culture. We then come to realize how some of these repeating patterns are the *unconscious enactments* of our survival beliefs that are couched in:

- Assumptions
- Biases
- Customs and Habits
- Expectations and Prescriptions
- Roles and Rules
- Secrets

Some couples share with us that they experienced a moment in their lives where they had a glimpse of that 'perfect time of being in love', where they felt a wholeness that brought them to deeper commitment. Soon, however, the inevitable happens. They find themselves repeating survival coping behaviors propelled by their 'secret' yearning and the belief that they need to protect themselves from feelings of insecurity, loneliness, guilt, shame, fear, hurt, and anger. Even though their repetitive patterns perpetuate their need for survival in the midst of the 'inevitable' wounding of human souls, their deep yearning for an affirming, nourishing, unconditional, wholesome and healing love still persists.

And, NOW, even as humanity advances technologically, the possibilities for our relational evolution is within our INNER reach...IF WE SO CHOOSE to be aware...

...they are imbedded in the course of our relational journey, real-life crises, adversities, and challenges...they are the opportunities for our emergence to the healing of our human heart.

How we heal is our choice.

> *For all of us here on this earth, it is a journey of love.*
> *It is a journey home to the Source of All Love.*

We offer you **Eight Pathways of Healing Love** to accompany you on your journey. In this book, we share our insights and discoveries, as well as provide you with the tools, supports, and resources that will assist you in both understanding and appreciating your own transformational journey.

Our Journey

Discovering the **Eight Pathways of Healing Love** has been a journey of transformation for us. It was and is an emergent, living process and practice that has evolved from our own search to heal, deepen, strengthen, and enhance our ability to love and be loved.

Affirming the premise that 'we are all spiritual beings having a human experience' and that there is a higher purpose to our relationship, began for us when we **both** made the commitment to our individual development as well as to our development as a couple. By making this commitment, we have given ourselves the charge and the space to learn what the higher purpose of our love is and how we can be a healing presence to each other.

We all have family and cultural generational histories that run through our DNA. These have positive and negative complementarities that can both support and hinder love.

> *Our commitment is to not allow complacency or neglect to erode*
> *The beautiful garden that we have been given.*
> *Our commitment is to be co-creators of the love we desire.*

The Couples Journey

Generally, couples come together based on a mutual attraction process. It is often difficult for them to describe what attracted them, other than the identified valued qualities that they recognized in the other.

This is nature's way of bringing two people together. This connection allows for the preservation of the human species. But beyond propagation, human beings need connection with another human being in their intimate quest for knowing the Divine that resides within themselves.

Through our life journey, our intimate quest is driven by our desire to fulfill our deepest, secret and/or pressing needs. Whether consciously or unconsciously, we further seek a significant relationship to help meet our basic needs:

- To love and to be loved
- To see and to be seen
- To hear and be heard
- To value and be valued
- To feel whole and complete

While it is expected and believed that the most wonderful arena to have these basic needs fulfilled is marriage, and it is in this healing love relationship between two people that transformation of these basic needs can occur.

Please Note: We may address the relationship between two people as a marriage, 'couple-ness', partnership, or a significant relationship. For the purposes of this book we shall refer to this significant two-person system as a 'couple'. You may apply it to your marriage, your partnership, your sibling relationship, your friendship, your companionship, your relation, etc.

The Challenges of the Couples Journey

Often, after a period of time after two people have chosen to become intimate or to marry, they wake up one day and say in disbelief, "Who is this person I married? (Sound familiar?) This isn't the same person I fell in love with. Things have changed and I am not the same person I was when I married. Who am I now? What happened to me and why am I feeling this way?"

As challenges surface in a relationship, the human ego survival needs rapidly emerges and the individuals tend to instinctively grab onto or hook each other to survive, projecting their invisible maps or movies in self-preservation.

The harder they try by blaming, shaming, criticizing, stone-walling, withdrawing or ignoring, the harder it becomes to save and sustain their love. That is when we see couples that come to counseling exhausted, some ready to leave or divorce. Others come holding a glimmer of hope that perhaps their love can be saved.

Because the emotional pain is uncomfortable, couples want to get rid of the pain and stop struggling. The challenge and the surprise for many couples are to find the seed of health in the intention behind the struggle. Instead of repeating the old patterns of self-blaming or blaming the other, of distancing and pursuit, or not talking and exploding, couples learn how to struggle in a healthier way.

Sometimes the struggle involves clarifying expectations of themselves, the other, and the relationship. We found that unsaid expectations, assumptions, and yearnings lead to break-downs and disappointments.

There are a few models of healthy practices that teach us how to work through struggles in a way that grow the relationship in loving ways. Paradoxically, drama and struggles gone awry are seen as the norm, which become glamorized and are unconsciously and repeatedly passed on.

Feeling Stuck and the Opportunity for Growth

Paradoxically, as a couple is willing, the very process in which the Universe teaches us to deepen and heal love, is imbedded in the 'stuckness' of the painful challenge. It involves awakening to the invisible undercurrents that they continue to re-enact. Many continue to replay these invisible tides in their interactions, finding themselves swept in the undertow and spiraling into the sink hole by doing more of the same and hoping to have a different result. They sink deeper into frustration, trying to enforce their desires on themselves and on the other.

Some have given-up or given-in to their fight. Some come to counseling either blaming themselves or blaming their partner for the failing relationship. And, there are some who realize that they need to learn new skills in loving and to have the courage to turn their challenges into opportunities for growth and learning.

By becoming conscious of how their cultural and family survival dramas can replicate in their dynamics as a couple, partners learn to appreciate and examine together how their current choices promote healing and growth. With these skills, resources, and awareness, partners can learn to interrupt unhealthy systemic patterns that have been passed on from generation to generation.

Did you know that the divorce rate in first marriages is 50%? When people enter into a second marriage we see the divorce rate jump to 79% due to previous unfinished business and patterns such as blaming and negative ways of relating to each other. Some regret that they did not learn the first time around. However, the Universe is kind and patient with us, allowing us to heed the call to healing love. The Universe provides us with opportunities to learn through our human mistakes and transform ourselves to become beacons for healing love in our world.

For us, we noticed that when we encountered difficulties in our own relationship, we felt the desire to discover an enlightened way. Our awareness heightened as we began to notice how we were doing the same 'fight' over and over again, and hoping for different results. We acknowledged our contribution to how our pain was our co-created experience.

We asked the questions:

- How deeply must a relationship sink before a couple stops, looks at themselves and each other and acknowledges they are falling into a sinking hole?

- Why is love just not enough?

- How can we stop and heal this pain?

- Why are our reactions so triggered by innocuous incidents?

- Is it possible to reconnect like we did or in ways that feel even better?

- What are some resolutions that will work for us?

- What is the higher purpose of this challenge?

The Experience of 'Pearl-Making'

Are you familiar with how pearls are made? A grain of sand gets into an oyster shell and friction occurs, thus forming a pearl. Thus, in intimacy, pearls are also formed in the depth of the ocean of the significant relationship.

When a couple can stay in the deep of their relationship, to witness how the sand comes in to irritate by friction, then they can learn the process and the practice of 'pearl making' in their own lives.

These are some important, elemental processes for 'pearl making' in an intimate relationship to occur. These are:

- To have courage to slow down
- To give time, energy, and attention
- To breathe and harness the inner supports as grounding, centering to be present in the NOW within oneself and with the other's space and pace
- To co-create safety to hold their vulnerability in each other's company and honor their confidence
- To share present inner experience and be a presence to each other's sharing
- To suspend judgment and right-wrong thinking
- To value taking turns chartering their couples' maps of the inner 'truth' reality experience more than factual reality
- To monitor their BEEHMSSS^{TM} (body-energy-emotion-heart-mind-soul-system-spirit) resources and functioning of their tools and skills
- To co-create and discover their unique way of "pearl making"

As the couple practices together these elemental processes, they are co-creating their environment for transformation, thus allowing strands of wisdom, compassion, and empowerment to strengthen their relationship. They draw to them a circle who support and who are attracted to the 'pearls' that they are, and will want to know what their secret is in 'pearl making'.

Growing your Garden

An intimate relationship is like a garden. In the beginning of the couples' relationship, their garden is fresh, beautiful, and new as they picture it. Then after a while, the raw materials come into fuller view: rocks, stone, clay, debris, weeds, wild grass, wild herbs, wild flowers, wood, trees, and shrubs, some perennials...and is not quite as you pictured it. Their intimate garden requires some work, sometimes a lot of work!

Each of us has the choice to learn how to grow our intimacy garden. For example, the garden may have a pile of manure in it. For manure to become fertilizer, it has to be poked, tilled, and turned. The fertilized ground of a relationship becomes rich with a vibrant harvest as couples tend their garden together, by utilizing appropriate tools, sharing their landscape maps and designing and co-creating their relationship landscape. Couples can then enjoy the harvest of their relationship and relax in its beauty and light and savor all the living experiences in their garden.

We love offering this metaphor to couples. We ask them to visualize, draw, and co-create their garden individually and then share it with each other. We have them bring meaningful objects to their garden and tell their story. We ask them to share and illustrate with each other what they see their garden growing into and the kinds of "blooms" they would enjoy.

One magnificent example we have is of a couple in their 60's. After 35 years of marriage, they decided they needed couples counseling. They talked of their many challenges that they had overcome but one secret surfaced: bringing their marriage to a critical place. A 34-year-old daughter 'materialized', looking for her father. While the wife was aware of the affair her husband had while overseas serving in Vietnam, painful memories and a discovery that her husband had been sending financial support to the daughter he left behind, shook the trust they had rebuilt. This couple took the garden metaphor and roto-tilled their 'relationship backyard garden' and turned their relationship landscape (and even their home backyard garden) to reflect their healing partnership.

Eight Pathways of Healing Love

History is replete with wounding and traumatic experiences, whether experienced directly or passed on by a significant wounded other. Significant relationships such as marriage, a partnership, a commitment whether verbalized or not, carry with it baggage from past wounding memories of relationships that can be activated. Whether we are aware of it or not, we find relationships desiring to heal ourselves, with safety, belonging, acceptance, mattering, respect, kindness, support, peace, joy...all aspects of love. However with unawareness, these past, unhealed wounding experiences are seen in the "dramas" of unproductive arguments and mutual blame.

In working on our own relationship and with clients, we discovered there are *Eight Pathways* that a significant relationship, such as a couple, takes to discover healing love.

1. Affirmation and Awakening
2. Being and Balance
3. Connection and Communication
4. Development and Discovery
5. Evolving Through Learning How to Learn from Experience
6. Freedom and Responsibility
7. Gratitude and Grace
8. Higher Purpose of Love

Eight Pathways of Healing Love Model

We will describe the Eight Pathways for you in depth in the chapters to come! During your explorations of the Pathways, we invite you to reflect on which Pathway you are currently on in your relationship with yourself and with your partner. We will also share the challenges and obstacles that present themselves along the way, and provide you with process options to develop the skills needed to assist you in integrating your Body, Energy, Emotion, Heart, Mind, Soul, System, and Spirit. **From here on, we will call it the "BEEHMSSS™" process.**

Creating the Healing Love Relationship

When partners understand and integrate the skills of loving one another, a 'third reality' is created. This 'third reality' is an alchemical combination, such as hydrogen and oxygen that produce water. Water is not hydrogen, nor is it oxygen. A couple's third reality emerges as the two people co-creating their own reality; alchemy emerges that turns their relationship to either gold or to lead.

The importance of mutual attraction, of touching each other's soul is to learn how to support, sustain, enhance, and grow love within oneself and within their healing love relationship. We believe that this becomes the best foundational model and security that can be offered to children. It is not about having parents taking care of the children alone, but creating an environment of conscious and skillful loving for the entire family!

It is about being able to shift our perspective to understand the elements involved in being a healing partnership. When couples are willing and commit to being a part of a healing relationship, new dimensions and directions open. We see people learn how to laugh at their imperfections and see their baggage in a different light. They learn to examine their challenges from a place of compassion and appreciation, being both vulnerable and struggling with differences. They can grapple with and hold multiple realities and beliefs that seem incompatible.

In learning the process and skill practices of healing love in each Pathway, you will discover options of 'pearl making' and choices so that you can manage your automatic reactions and shift to responsive interactions. With consciousness, choice, and BEEHMSSS™ practice, we activate our cellular memory cells to strengthen neural pathways of our inherent *healing connection to the Divine Love presence* as part of our daily experience.

By daily living these principles, we now enjoy the ripple effects of healing love in our journey! We have co-created a relational energy field that sustains, nourishes, strengthens, and magnetizes our love through daily practices involving body, energy, emotion, heart, mind, soul, system, spirit, (BEEHMSSS™) well-being.

We humbly accept that we are the transforming generation of our extended family. We know healing love is the greatest gift we can give to one another. This transforming 'revolution' of healing love begins within oneself and with every couple when they each commit to be a healing love partnership. It is the sacred legacy of healing love that vibrates and generates a peaceful world that we can collectively give to our children and generations to come.

The greatest force and tool we have to heal our world is Love. What an amazing experience it is to know that we can start the healing partnership right here and NOW with ourselves and with our significant relationship, our partner, or our spouse.

We all have the freedom to choose, to be part of an energetic matrix of
Healing Love in our world.

Please take a moment to join all of us who love from this energetic matrix.

Our Intention

Join us in visualizing and affirming the energy of love for couples everywhere! This deep intention for healing love shifts our DNA and cellular memory so couples everywhere can activate their spiritual connection to the Universal Source of All That Is Love!

We hold this space of appreciative consciousness with:

- A sense of awe
- An attention to the power of the moment
- An opening and embracing the magnificence of the unknown
- A shift of ordinary perceptions into higher awareness

We commit to:

- Embodying the magic and miracle of Spirit.
- Holding in our microcosmic universe the macrocosmic Love that is here for all of Humanity.
- Believing in the depths of our being that Love, Peace, and Joy is a Radiant inner experience vibrating in the energetic matrix of Healing Love that here NOW embraces you and I, we and us, each one and together, all together Humanity and the Universe.

The Joyful Commitment

To be in an intimate partnership is both a very strong bond of love and at the same time, a very fragile bond. To be in a healing love partnership involves choosing to commit to one's own growth as an individual and to co-create a loving, kinder, gentler, empowering, compassionate, healing world for ourselves and others.

As 'spiritual beings having a human experience', whether we are aware of it or not, the Universe is kind and patient in the belief that humanity will someday understand that struggling is part of the University of Love.

The learning process invites each and every one of us to participate in co-creating healing love in our world.

Our part is to declare "YES" to:

- The struggle
- Accept the invitation to go beyond our comfort zones
- Reach out to others

- Touch the parts of ourselves that can be intimately known and embraced with Healing Love

Think of the beauty of a butterfly. Now, think about how the caterpillar's struggle in the cocoon is inherently important in its metamorphosis to become a butterfly. There is a higher knowing within this caterpillar, struggling to create itself into the miracle of a butterfly.

This energy and potential is available for all of us – **to create what we truly desire.**

Discovering the Pathways!

*"The consciousness of loving and being loved
brings a warmth and richness that nothing else can bring."*
~Oscar Wilde

Welcome to the *Eight Pathways of Healing Love!* We are so glad you are joining us on your path to discovering **Healing Love**!

Here are some guidelines so you can get the most from using this book.

To deepen your understanding of each Pathway, we will

1. Define each Pathway
2. Explore the challenges and value of each Pathway
3. Provide you with the skills required to transform in each Pathway
4. Show you how we work through the Pathways in our own life
5. Explain how we work with couples
6. Offer processes that will help you move through the challenges

To begin your journey with us, we invite you to reflect on the following questions and jot down your responses. This will help you begin to clarify and focus so you can more easily receive all the riches that are in store for you!

It may also be helpful for you to refer to your answers as you read through the book. We encourage you to write your reflections or any questions or insights that arise.

My/Our intention in taking this Course of **Eight Pathways of Healing Love**

_____

A Journey in Transformation is

_____

The Heart and Soul of my relationship is

_____

The most pressing dilemma/issue that we are facing in our relationship is

_____

My secret yearning is

_____

At times I feel

_____

At the end of my life journey, I would like to look back and be able to say that I

_____

My parents/family believe that a significant relationship

_____

I believe that a significant relationship

_____

I feel stuck relating when

_____

On my life journey I am

_____

I would like to

_____

What is great about us is

_____

The part I play to co-create what is best is

_____

What is most difficult for us is

_____

The part I play in co-creating what is difficult for us is

_____

While we present the **Eight Pathways of Healing Love** sequentially in the following chapters, we have found that the Pathways must not always be taken linearly and in order, in the healing love process.

Rather, we would encourage you to notice the Pathway you are currently on. Whether we are aware of it or not, by the very nature of being in relationship you will be in or on a Pathway. Observe what is going on for you and your partner. What are your patterns and processes? Your issue themes and dilemmas? Notice where you are stuck. Also notice what Pathways bring you ease and support.

It is possible that you and your partner may be on different Pathways in your individual journeys and as a couple you may find it useful to shift to a path where you can meet and join. It is also possible that you will notice recurring dilemmas, themes or areas where you feel stuck that could be problematic, uncomfortable and/or charged. By learning about other Pathways, you can begin to explore other options for you and your partnership in the process of your transformational journey.

In relationships, whether we like it or not, we are challenged to move beyond our comfort zones, and to grow and discover more of our possibilities and stretch ourselves. By doing this, you connect to the very heart and soul of your relationship.

Wherever you are in your relational life journey, we welcome you to take any of the **Pathways of Healing Love**, either sequentially or according to what draws you. You can begin by taking any of the Pathways A to H.

We invite you to enjoy Your Journey of Transformation through all the
Pathways of Healing Love...

PATHWAY A: PATHWAY OF AFFIRMATION AND AWAKENING

"The goal of the path is to transform awareness from separation to unity. In unity, we perceive only love, express only love and are only love."
~Deepak Chopra

The First Pathway is that of Affirmation. This is your ability to positively appreciate yourself and your partner, i.e., the recognition of yourself and partner on a profoundly foundational basis. When you are in a place of affirming, the very condition of affirmation puts you into a place of giving and receiving.

The Rich Value of Affirming

Affirmation has great value in an intimate relationship because when two people can come from this space, it lays the foundation for open communication. If someone is worried that they will be criticized or judged, they will not feel safe. To be able to move through the Pathways together, partners must feel safe, otherwise, the relationship will be unfulfilling: either both parties do not get their needs met or the relationship ultimately ends.

Affirming one another is a daily choice. Many times it seems fleeting or elusive as we deal with the daily grinds of life. Based on our experience, an ongoing commitment to affirming each other allows us to carry on a journey that brings us light, passion and the beautiful sweetness of joy. This continues to sweep both of us, filling us and transporting us to inner places beyond our imagination and making life worth the trouble of living.

But here's something most people don't know: You don't only affirm the *good* things. How can that be?

Lalei explains:

*"I think one of the things that sustained us is affirming the hard (or negative) stuff, as well. I remember back to when your parents died. It was an amazing time of solitude for you, and there were moments there when I wondered where you were. It is much easier to be in a positively affirming space with others where there is some distance, for me. With my significant relationship, I was deliberate in choosing to stay in the affirmation of **What Is**, which was the 'is-ness' of your grieving. I noticed that by doing this, it opened a space for you to share your grieving with me. It is much easier to affirm what we project as the good or easy stuff, and it is much harder to affirm the struggles and the challenges. By affirming all, we value and affirm life."*

The Challenges of Pathway A

For many, the challenge of Pathway A is that as humans we tend to focus on what's not there or what is missing.

> *"Our relationship is like a gardener's microclimate. If the conditions are right, we together and each will healthily grow. We will attend to nurture the ground to the best of our abilities."*
> ~Mike George

Our Conversations

Phil: *"I discovered more and more of myself in meeting Lalei: as feelings of personal power and personal joy. I felt seen, heard and loved. A big part of my inner being opened to a journey within. My consciousness awakened to see things in different ways, to examine old beliefs, to explore the wonder of the universe within and around us. Each day of our friendship unfolded yet another discovery. I felt and feel alive."*

Lalei
"When I reflect on the events of my life and what was going on within me, I am aware of my intense search for meaning and purpose for the painful losses that shook the ground of my being. What mattered most to me was developing friendships that supported and stimulated growth of my whole person. What stood out most about Phil was his genuine friendship, his affirming laughter, his spirituality and ability to appreciate my empowerment. I experienced the impact of my presence and felt seen, heard, valued and respected."

Phil

"I believe that whether it is about an easy or hard subject, it is important to express the truth. When you expressed your caring for me when my parents died, you were expressing the truth from your point of view. Your doing this helped me heal, simply by you being there with me and speaking your truth. It also gave me the space to speak my truth."

Lalei

"I remember one of the earliest instances where affirming truly stretched us. We had a real struggle because I wanted one thing and Phil wanted another. I wanted to go on this long trip in the car by myself, driving rather than flying, to a conference. I wanted him to trust me that I could do this alone by myself, taking this long drive. I wanted him to trust that I was going to take this long journey to face an inner need for my own growth and my own empowerment. It was scary for us because I could come back not being connected to him, I could come back different. I remember how Phil affirmed his own fear. I did not want to hear his fear. I wanted to hear his belief and trust and I only wanted to hear his support. I needed to affirm out loud my own challenge to take this task and go. My selfishness at that moment was a struggle. I knew Phil was coming from a place of protectiveness as he wanted me to go with a group of people. However, I needed to connect with the warrior woman in me.

"The field was big enough for us to stretch the boundaries of our relationship. I said to Phil, 'If you are afraid that I am going to leave you by going to this conference, I want to affirm to you that our relationship is so big that going there will only enhance me more and have me love us even more because I will do something that is so important for me.' It was then that I noticed Phil chose to practice affirming, 'I am allowing this to be difficult for me in this moment and I trust in you because I know your courage and I know you will do what you need to do for yourself."

How We Work With Couples

When we work with couples, we ask them how they met and what attracted them to each other. In triggering their memories of what initially pleased them and drew them to each other, we invariably notice their shift in energy to tender, affirming, attending vibration, eyes connecting, feeling moved, laughter and lightness. They draw upon the positive energy of affirming the beginnings of their relationship. They recall their common ground; that which is good and great about them. Their collective cellular memory of their attraction (Pathway of Affirmation) is reignited. They recall how by being in love, they attended, acknowledged, and appreciated each other.

Since most relationships replicate what is in the culture, Pathway A process skills fade into the background and into unawareness. For some luckier couples, something happens to awaken them to the realization that something has gone wrong.

To help couples delve into this Pathway, we encourage them to explore the answers to some initial questions:

How did you meet each other? What drew you or attracted you to each other? As you think of your beginnings, what pleased you about your relationship?

And, as you might expect, the answers tend to reflect the similarity of the human condition:

> *"We met in college…high school…at work…in a bar…we ran into each other literally had an accident…we were introduced…on the internet…on a blind date…in church…we were dancing partners…"*
>
> *"Physical attraction…intelligence…we could talk about anything…we laughed and had so much fun…we believed in the same things…we helped each other through the most difficult time in our lives…I liked how he is with children…she had ambition and challenged me…he organized my life…we had amazing mental telepathy, it was easy as we were on the same page…he is a person of his word…she listened and made me feel so important…"*

Often these questions conjure up memories that can shift a couple's thoughts and emotions to an affirmative time in their journey. We notice a change in eye contact, facial tone, fuller breathing, and warmer body language. These cellular memories recall the glow of being in love and sends waves of exhilaration through the brain.

Remembering brings into context their earlier experience of attending, affirming, acknowledging, appreciating and how the juices of attraction magnetize the draw for them to come together, be together, work together, live together and want to share the rest of their lives together.

Sarah's Story

"Well, Dr. Phil, it was so much easier for us to be together then. "David and I used to enjoy doing things together and we could talk about almost anything. Then he started to spend so much time in the office and would come home so exhausted, the kids would be asleep and he would go in front of the television and fall asleep. I would feel guilty about wanting to talk with him, because he would be so irritated and would say that I was so demanding of his time. That would hurt me so much because all I really wanted was to connect and receive attention. After so many years, I decided to stop wanting to talk with him, so that I would not hurt. I started talking to my friends. He thought everything was cool because I stopped hounding him about talking. Now he is surprised when I said that I do not have any more feelings for him."

David's Story

"Before the children came, I loved how Sarah and I were just the two of us. We were really close then. Now, every time we talk, it's about problems…it seems that we cannot get away from it. It seems that it is never enough. The children are growing up and we have their many needs to meet. Plus we have aging and ill parents and there is so much to attend to there, as well. My work is focused on solving problems all day, so when I come home, I just want peace. I try not to burden her with all that. I believed that we were OK because the children are all doing fine and we are a good team because we are surviving well and have all bases covered. Now she tells me that she has no feelings for me and I do not understand."

Lalei: *"Sarah and David, as you tell us about the beginning of your relationship, we notice you both say how you enjoyed being together, how you felt close, tell us more."*

Sarah

"He was my best friend. It was so easy for me because my heart felt warm. When we talked it was as though nothing else mattered because we were so focused on each other."

David

"We handled so much together. She was there when my mother became really ill and died. It was only with her that I could talk about my sadness. She listened and I felt comforted. It was really hard for the whole family losing our mother. Right now in thinking about that, I have so much Gratitude that she is in my life, and I am so afraid now that I am losing the person I love the most."

Practice Skills for Blossoming in Pathway A

There are a variety of skills required in each Pathway. Let's begin to explore some of the specific skills of the Pathway of Affirmation and Awakening.

> *"What, where and how we attend, impacts what we grow*
> *What, how and when we acknowledge, enlivens what matters*
> *What, where and how we appreciate, moves and touches*
> *What, where and how we affirm, liberates and heals."*
> ~Phil Belzunce, Ph.D.

The Four-Part Foundational Practice Skill of Being In An Affirming Stance

Activating affirmation with energy involves our awareness and appreciation of how we are Now attending in the Present moment:

- To oneself (I, me and myself)
- To each other (you)
- To the partnership (we and us)

As couples take on an affirming stance, this foundational practice skill involves four parts:

1. **Attending in the Present** involves your inner self supports to attend. This may involve placing your feet flat on the ground, aligning your spine and centering within oneself. You

go into a neutral place within, noticing your breathing as you experience the natural flow of inhalation and exhalation. As you are attending within, you may notice your felt or intuitive senses.

Attending in the present to your partner involves seeing, hearing and listening to your partner with your senses, your heart, your mind and your spirit.

Attending in the present also involves noticing and experiencing how and what movement, dance, or interaction that is happening.

The key in attending is to <u>slow down</u>, <u>breathe</u>, and be a witnessing presence and to suspend moving quickly to make judgments or interpretation of your sensations, observations, and experiences. When you move quickly into interpretations or assumptions, you are either in the past or in the future and have just left the present moment. However, you can be an attending presence to yourself and notice your own interpretations and assumptions and how that affects how you feel in the present.

To us, the practice of attending can be a meditational process of slowing down to 'smell the flowers' and witness the 'awesome' presence of the moment as we are in nature and with animals.

2. **Awareness in the Present** is closely aligned with attending as you are aware of yourself attending, aware of your partner and of the both of you. You can be aware of the links and associations, assumptions and interpretations you are making to what you are attending to in the present.

3. **Acknowledging in the Present** involves verbal acknowledgement of what stands out for you in attending to yourself, to your partner and/or to the both of you and/or your awareness of attending. Acknowledging also involves staying in the present to notice the impact of sharing in the relational field of the both of you and your relations with others. For example:

   "I see you wrinkling your nose, I too am aware of a smell in the air."

   "I am aware of listening fully to what you are sharing with me."

   "I am aware of being so moved to tears with the movie we just saw. May I share my awareness and reflections with you?"

   "I am aware of how we hung in there together through it all and I am aware of a warm feeling in my heart."

"As you and I shared our experiences of overcoming the sudden loss of our son,
I could hear a pin drop in the silence of the whole room."

4. **Appreciating in the Present** involves both a verbal and a non-verbal acknowledgement of your awareness of what is presently being attended to. This last piece is a skill and an art that deepens the foundations of the Pathway of Affirmation. Appreciations affirm as new when acknowledged in the present, even though the event itself may have past. For example:

"I am aware of running a movie in my mind of the dinner we had last Sunday and how much fun I had. I am appreciating the fun that I am laughing all day just thinking about it."

The Practice Skill of Speaking the Truth

By building on the Four-Part foundational skill of affirmation, the practice skill of speaking and acknowledging inner truth is a way of affirming what is, whether painful or joyful. This practice has helped us nurture and expand us, both individually and together to be our best friends, as well as our being a couple. The practice of affirming our truth to ourselves and to one another has allowed us to flow into affirming those around us in a skillful way.

The Practice Skill of Strengthening Affirming Muscles

Over time, you develop an inner trust and the undercurrent of affirming creates even more value in your relationship, even though truth might be bumpy and prickly. For us, we needed to learn that the affirming process is not necessarily easy all the time. We have learned that if we were to tell or share something that we know would be difficult for the other to hear, we also need to state and affirm the value or the strength of our relationship.

In this practice skill of strengthening affirming muscles, sometimes we want to take short cuts, and assume that affirmation should be felt. We had a couple assume that when they lecture, label, think for each other, it is a way of showing that they care and appreciate each other.

It is often the interpretation 'short cuts' one gives to what is attended to, that can cut at the roots of one's foundation and close opportunities for growth of the relationship. A shortcut that erodes at the foundations of Affirmation is unchecked short cut 'habits' of:

- Assumptions or unchecked interpretations
- Conclusions or generalizations drawn from assumptions
- Labeling ourselves or our loved ones assumptions and conclusions made

Unconscious and fixed labeling makes us think that we know the person by the labels we give. It stops affirmation and gets in the way of discovery. It encourages partnerships to go numb.

Can you think of members of your family or friends whose lives seem to be carved out of the labels they were given and called themselves? We were amazed with a couple who were in an unhappy marriage and whose children referred to them as Mr. Screw-up and Mrs. Perfect.

Reflect on this: Are you aware of labels that you give yourself or each other? How is it helpful or not helpful to your Body-Energy-Emotion-Heart-Mind-Soul-System-Spirit (BEEHMSSS™)?

So for example: Many couples may notice some body language shift in their partner and quickly go into saying, "What's wrong?" This shortcut can be effective, if the couple is in alignment with each other. However, most couples are caught in a habitual way of talking about 'right and wrong' which often leads to immobility and negativity. Rich elements such as curiosity, interest and discovery become tucked away and the alchemical ingredients that foster intimacy and growth are left to rust.

Recall our earlier example, where the couple David and Sarah took the 'short cut', each coming up with a 'fix' to the loss of their closeness. When Sarah affirmed how she appreciated David for being an excellent provider and David affirmed how he noticed Sarah giving him a lot of space to decompress from his stressful work environment, they created a positive place to start together as they re-entered the Pathway "A" of Affirmation. Sarah affirmed her loss of feeling because she had to 'suppress' her feelings of missing her best friend. David acknowledged how he too missed the times they had together; just the two of them without talking about problems. They both affirmed the beginnings of their fun together and acknowledged how they co-created their present state of having an undernourished relationship. Such awareness was empowering for them. David appreciated Sarah for the jolt 'of having no more feelings for me' she gave him. Sarah appreciated him for listening and setting the appointment. They both affirmed that they needed to get back on track to heal their love.

The Practice Skill of Co-Creating Your Environment of Affirmation

The practice of creating an affirming environment involves:

- Naming the internal or external context
- Having a mindful intention
- Allowing a positive attitude of the heart
- Offering a process of how we use our energy
- Practicing collaboratively in accord with all the above

Here is an example of Lalei initiating the *practice* of creating an environment of affirmation.

> *"Phil, I have thoughts and feelings about taking the long trip to visit my mother (an internal context about an external event). My intention is to gain some clarity about my*

dilemma (mindful intention) I love how you allow yourself to be my sounding board when you listen and reflect to me what you hear me saying (attitude of the heart). I know just talking about it with you will ease me. I will appreciate knowing when is a good time for us to talk (practice for collaboration.)"

As you co-create together the environment for affirmation, you both activate remembering what was attractive in your coming together. Cultivating your affirmation environment generates your appreciation processes to grow and connect to the spiritual source of loving energy from your Inner Selves that can be activated in a shared present.

Phil
"My intention in affirming is to connect with the 'Thou-ness' of Lalei; to come to her with respect and acknowledgment of her presence in my life. In practicing the skill of affirmation, I intend to create a field of receptivity, where I participate in sharing and listening. When we affirm each other from within ourselves, we create an energetic field shared between the two of us. In this affirming environment, we know that we can have a lot of room to be ourselves. We can check out our perceptions, share our experiences, our beliefs, thoughts, our struggles, our feelings, our dreams and goals. We can discuss and dialogue. Being in an environment of affirmation is nurturing and allows room for healing, growing and thriving. Our senses are alive and open. In this affirming Pathway, I see the wonder of you and I and all of the small details in our life together.

"When I think back to an intense affirmation time, like when I was grieving my parents, I knew that the affirmation you shared came from the fullness of your love for me as well as your self-care practice. Your affirmation gave me permission take time to journal my grieving. I must admit that now in looking back, our overcoming makes everything really magical."

The Skill of Affirming the Tension

Choosing to co-create an environment of affirmation provides a big enough safe field to be able to hold tensions and stresses that occur.

In our history together, we have supported the heightening state of affirming one another. We allowed ourselves to look at our feelings and then to look again to state and restate them again as we need to. *Slowing Down to* speak the truth of our experience, we begin to embody an affirming stance that allows both to just be with WHAT IS NOW and be able to relax into whatever situation we were in that moment. Paradoxically, the tension eases and the situation shifts.

After we affirm our tension and our differences, we have a conversation affirming how we moved through the process together. We look back and reflect on what we have learned, so we can strengthen our foundational bond even more by looking at how we have met the challenges together.

The Message of Pathway A

The message of this Pathway is to cultivate our mutual attraction, strengthen the foundation of our healing partnership and to allow the Divine to have a central place in our relationship. We take this as connecting with the 'Thou-ness' within ourselves and each other. Whether the significant other relates or thinks in 'It' (treating each other as things) terms, we attract more of who we are in them as we connect to their 'Thou-ness'. As a couple embodies their affirming presence within themselves together, the energetic field created radiates an affirming presence to others. That presence is the Divine affirming presence that is embodied in the whole 'Thou-ness' of the couple together.

We say, 'yes' to life in a bigger and fuller way. We cheer each other on!

> *Wow that was really a hurdle to move through.*
> *We are in two different arenas.*
> *Let's hang in there and see how it unfolds!*

From this perspective, we approach the journey of Pathway A as a living, energizing and affirming process, and practice.

> *"The practice of intimacy is a mindfulness exercise in which your purpose is to be open and honest with your partner and to pay scrupulous attention to him or her. Willfully appreciate this person, whether you are together or not. Appreciation is a doorway into the heart."*
> *~Frank Andrews, Ph.D., The Art and Practice of Loving*

As you practice the **four-part affirmation** exercise (attending, awareness, acknowledging, appreciating) and build with affirming practice skills of sharing your inner truth, strengthening affirming muscles, co-creating an affirming environment and affirming the tension, you together expand your capacity to be fascinated with the simple and the complicated things of life and relationships. You open to experience the wonder of your enriching capacity to affirm and appreciate all of your life together.

When we stop ourselves from being in a state of affirming or appreciating, we can unconsciously revert to a state of "stuck-ness," which is reflected in frustrations, restlessness, boredom, unease, dissatisfaction or criticism of ourselves and one another. The illusions of the world become seductively "interesting" and we rely on what we call 'quick fixes'. Quick fixes can become bigger than who we are.

For example, computer games, too much work, shopping sprees, over-eating, over-achieving are all common fixes. At the extreme, this form or negation can bury the earlier glimpses of affirmation to a place where what seems normal and spontaneous is, in fact, a way of relating that is dis-satisfying and dis-affirming. If this becomes the endpoint, it could derail our senses and our capacity to continue the growth of being in awe and wonder of one another and of the amazing universe that is to be discovered within. Couples and partners fall into the unconscious "programs" which are pigeonholes, i.e., expectations with automatic ways of interacting.

> *"The unconditional love that spring from the heart has both a receptive side –*
> *affirming ourselves and appreciating others as they are and letting them touch*
> *us –and an active side – going out to meet, touch and make contact."*
> *~John Welwood, Journey of the Heart*

What we know is that affirmation begets affirmation. It is this process that feeds and nurtures the heart of the relationship. It is now claiming, within the heart, **Healing Love.**

Four-Part Affirmation Practice Exercises

Take turns practicing these exercises. Allow yourselves to practice without expecting to feel spontaneous. As with learning any new skill, it takes practice before anything becomes a part of you. Give yourselves room to practice imperfectly. The quoted statements below of individuals who have done this practice are examples.

1. **Attending in the Present**

   With Yourself: Attending with the Inner Smile

   Begin by either closing your eyes or letting your eyes be softly open. Let your lips curl up as in a peaceful smile. As you breathe, allow your eyes to soften and your lips to relax as you prepare to attend within to yourself.

   Attend to placing your feet flat on the ground as you smile within to your feet. Notice your breathing, as you experience the natural flow of inhaling and exhaling. Let your exhalation go to your feet and to the ground.

   Attend as you align your spine and visualize smiling within to your spine as you breathe to your spine.

   Scan your body from top to bottom, attending within to your sensing of yourself. Attend with an inner smile to your organs, your heart, your lungs, your liver, your kidneys, your spleen, your intestines, your stomach.

   Attend and breathe with an inner smile within.

   Notice your experience of attending within to yourself. Notice and be present within now.

2. **Awareness in the Present**

<u>Affirming Your Awareness of Attending</u>

Take turns practicing with your partner: Let your inner smile radiate from within you. Attend with awareness. Stay close to what you observe with your senses not what you interpret.

Verbalize your attending with awareness.

- yourself
- your partner
- both together

Partner A verbalizes what, where, how you are attending.

Partner B listens and attends within to how you are receiving being.

Examples:

With yourself: "Right now, I sense my heart beats."
"Right now, I am attending to aligning within."

With partner: "Right now, I am aware of your presence."
"Right now, I notice your smile as you speak."
"As I attend to easing the tightness in my neck, I notice you watching me."

With both together: "Right now, I see us sitting together and I am noticing that I like looking into your eyes."

Share with each other your experience of practicing this exercise. How it was for you to practice affirming your awareness of attending? How it was for you to practice being on the receiving end?

3. **Acknowledging in the Present**

<u>Affirming by Acknowledging Your Awareness</u>

Take turns acknowledging your awareness of what has your attention.

Examples:

"I acknowledge that I see you here with me."

"I am aware of fumbling for words to acknowledge how moved I feel right now."
"I hear you right now and I acknowledge that I am attending to listening."

Share with each other your experience of acknowledging and receiving your partner's acknowledging of their awareness of themselves and of you.

4. Appreciating in the Present

Affirming by Appreciating Yourself and Partner's Acknowledgment, Awareness and Attention

Take turns appreciating in the present your practice of attending with awareness and acknowledging yourself and each other.

Examples:

"I appreciate your acknowledgement of my listening right now."
"I appreciate the two of us taking this time to attend to ourselves in this way."
"I appreciate that we are taking this time to attend to this practice."

Take turns to share your **present inner truth experience** of Pathway A practice. Affirm your inner truth for right now.

Examples:

"For right now, I am aware of how uncomfortable and non-spontaneous this practice feels for me right now."
"I am feeling positive and hopeful that I am learning to do this practice."

Allow yourself to affirm the goodness of the experience, wherever you are. Let yourself notice that as you cultivate this practice on a daily basis, for yourselves, for each other, for your family...how you are co-creating your foundation of a healing love relationship.

Examples:

"I affirm me, I affirm you, I affirm us."
"Right now, we are co-creating our foundation together with affirming attention, awareness, acknowledgment, and appreciation."

You can also affirm yourselves nonverbally...with a hug, handshake or an affirming nod.

SUMMARY HIGHLIGHTS OF PATHWAY "A": AFFIRMATION AND AWAKENING

1. Affirmation is a foundation that nourishes and supports the growth of a significant relationship.

2. Affirmation practice skills involves:
   - Co-creating an environment of affirmation
   - Embodying an affirming stance
   - Speaking and valuing inner truth experiences
   - Affirming the tensions in challenging experiences
   - Strengthening affirming muscles

3. Affirming is a four-step foundational process involving the practice of:
   - Attending to yourself, each other, and the "we/us" experience in the **now**
   - Acknowledging yourself, your partner, and the "we/us" experience
   - Opening to present awareness of yourself, your partner and the "we/us" experience by checking in and clarifying your perceptions and assumptions with the other

     "I am aware of being really concerned about your health"
     "I noticed you turned your chair to look the other way when I brought up my concern."

   - Appreciating yourself, your partner and your "we/us".

4. The stance of Affirmation is a daily, deliberate and intentional practice. Couples who create an affirming habit ask each other to share an affirmation they have for their day. This energetic shift creates a way of sharing that activates, stimulates and strengthens the foundations of the healing partnership through Pathway A.

5. As couples co-create an environment of Affirmation, they become more present, living in the moment so each event, experience and struggle allows them to deepen into the journey of growth and transformation.

6. The art and skill of Affirmation is to attend, acknowledge and appreciate yourself and your partner without interpretation or judgment.

7. Activating Affirmation with energy involves being aware of how we are attending in the present moment.

8. Unaware interpretation 'short cuts' that become habitual patterns can 'sap the juice' from the roots of one's foundation of affirmation and close opportunities for growth of the 'TREE' of your healing love relationship.

9. When one moves into an affirming stance, one becomes grounded, centered and aligned within the spaces of themselves.

10. Affirm…Affirm…Affirm where you are, how you are experiencing right **NOW**.

PATHWAY B: PATHWAY OF BEING AND BALANCE

"There are no choices that are really a detour that will take you far from where you're wanting to be because your Inner Being is always guiding you to the next and the next and the next. Don't be concerned that you may make a fatal choice because there aren't any of those. You are always finding your balance. It's a never ending process."
~Abraham Hicks

Introduction

As your intimate life progresses over time, your relationship unfolds into the Second Pathway -- of **Being and Balance**. This Pathway involves the ability to bring to balance seemingly discordant aspects of yourself and your partner's needs and experience in the struggle for a harmonious relationship.

This Second Pathway can be the most challenging Pathway for couples as their needs, identity, values, goals and styles surface in a way that bumps, collides, irritates and bristles around the second year and intensifying through their seventh year of relationship. The opportunities for enrichment are great as couples practice processes learned in Pathway A. They learn from the push, pull, 'bump' and balance of their polarities which are complicated by adversities and challenges of their inner and outer life.

The Shifting of Roles

In previous generations, the designated roles of the intimate partners were clearly defined. Balance in the relationship was set based on who took care of particular responsibilities. Traditional relationships were more instrumental for survival. For example, with our parents, the husband/father was the provider and protector and the wife/mother was in charge of nurturing relationships and maintaining the home. There was balance by acting in accordance with the terms of these territories. The focus was cooperation for the 'highest' good and survival of the family as prescribed by traditional values.

Present Generation

Over the last few decades, a major shift towards fulfillment, intimacy and actualization of the self have become the focus. As meeting survival and security needs are much more accessible to both men and women, the quest for personal fulfillment and meaningful relationships have become propelling desires. Many couples partner or marry to fulfill these intimacy needs and find themselves faced with some important complicating external factors:

- Juggling many 'significant' demands to fulfill changing roles and accomplishments
- An increase of substitute needs for a Loving Presence, such as security, unconditional love, approval, acceptance, freedom, recognition and respect
- A fast-paced changing environment with little down time

We see now many dual career couples trying to negotiate their lives who are torn between the responsibilities of caring for their family, working and trying to find time to nurture their relationship to each other as well as caring for themselves.

They are seeking to balance the need to have quality time for themselves as a couple: time for their children that have needs according to their developmental stage and/or special needs; time for themselves to relax; time with their friends and some time for retreat to sort out their inner struggles and connect with their own spirituality. Along with this come demands of their jobs/careers, caring for elderly parents, extended family and involvement with church, community and society. Their socio-economic, health, educational and community supports resources and expectations can influence the couples' ability to have a balanced response. As the couple loses their center of balance, they get caught in the mindset of 'having so many balls in the air to juggle'.

Why Is Balance Important In Relationships?

Phil:

"Balance is the fundamental spiritual law of the universe. All things in nature and in the universe exist in balance. This fundamental law is dualistic. We have the sun and the moon. We have night and day. We have up and down, left and right, hot and cold, the bright and dark. We see this interplay of polarities in all levels of creation."

"There is no growth for couples unless they know how to manage their differences and learn how to view themselves as a whole system, as individuals and as a couple."

"Managing differences means learning the skill of negotiation. Negotiation is like a seesaw. The couple sits on the two ends of the plank and the fulcrum, the center of the seesaw is the balancing point. In order to keep the momentum going there must be constant movement, but most importantly, there must be a connection between the two people playing together. The same is true with couples."

"We agreed long ago that our connection is what is most important. Whether we agree or disagree, our intention is our connection. This has to be of primary importance for partners."

Working Out Issues

In the early years together, many partners find it relatively easy to be in agreement. Around the second to seventh years of marriage, this can change for a variety of reasons:

- Feeling that their partner has changed, they are each no longer the same person.
- The one who is giving becomes weary and stops giving to take care of him or herself, while the person who was given to observes the change in the other and may think that their partner has now become selfish and feel abandoned. The one who was given to or felt they were in charge may end up feeling weighted, trapped, burdened or bored. We then see that one or both may go into oblivion thinking they are in harmony.

In the following Being and Balance Exercise there are questions that you may explore to deepen your sense of being and balance. You may do these alone and share them with your partner. We have listed the questions for you.

"All couples have a choice to engage in the ancient struggle of fighting or discover the present art and dance of Being and Balance."
~Phil & Lalei

Being and Balance Exercises:

Reflections Questions:

1. In what areas of your life do you feel a need for balance? How is your choice of partner bringing balance to you?

2. Can you see your partner's 'gifts' or 'style of being', as a mirror to your underdeveloped side bringing you to balance? Describe.

3. How can both you and your partner support each other to continue developing your underdeveloped sides? Give examples.

4. How can you support each other to bring balance to yourselves together and individually?

5.   Create a Couple's Balance Chart (Note: you'll need a flip chart to complete this process.)

    It is important that when filling out this chart, you move into an inner mode of observation rather than interpreting and judging your own and your partner's responses.

    a)   Please indicate the percent of time spent on each activity.

Activity	Alone	Together
Physical		
Nutritional		
Financial		
Emotional Intimacy		
Family		
Leisure / Play		
Growth & Development		
Social Supports		
Career / Work		
Spiritual		

b) Which areas do you feel in balance? Which areas do you feel out of balance?

c) Which one of you attends to which areas?

d) When are you in Harmony and Balance?

e) In what areas do you feel you need support individually and as a couple?

f) How do you perceive co-creating collaboration together? And in what areas?

g) Experiment and share with each other using the process from Pathway "A":

The Four-Part Affirmation Practice of Attending, Awareness, Acknowledging, and Appreciating. (see page 48 in Pathway A)

Take turns affirming your experience of sharing this exercise of Being and Balance. Acknowledge and appreciate yourselves.

h) Allow yourselves to savor the goodness of your experience, wherever it is at the moment, as a start.

Conscious Verses Unconscious Choices

In appreciating, managing and growing through their differences, couples learn how to make conscious choices and create balance which enhances them together. By becoming aware of their contribution to the co-creation of imbalance, they are able to help themselves notice their re-enactment of old, automatic patterns.

Can you think of a situation where you notice yourselves re-enact automatically together? Usually the outcome is one of dissatisfaction, for one or both. If one partner loses, both lose.

Pathway B - Seven Practice Skills

There are Seven Practice Skills that couples can employ to consciously manage their differences. As with any practice, it is important to know that practicing these skills, may not necessarily "feel good", comfortable, easy, or even spontaneous. Practice, practice, practice with awareness, affirmation, and appreciation that you practiced...and be in the present process of practicing and expanding your skills.

1. The Practice Skill of Grounding

This involves being embodied all the way down to your feet, and feeling the balance of your left and your right side with both feet on the ground when standing or when sitting. This practice is important to feel supported within your body as you affirm your unique strengths and diversities to be able to really develop the following six skills. Practice the following first.

Focus you attention down to your feet and feel your connection to the earth/ ground. You may imagine your breath from your belly pushing down as you exhale; growing roots into the earth: thick, strong healthy roots to the center of the earth. Let any tension release through the roots to the earth. Let the earth absorb your stress and tensions. From the center of the earth, draw up creative energy, inhale, and let the roots bring you nutrients and energy to flow up your legs, spine, organs, all the way to your arms, neck, and out the top of your head. Imagine yourself as your tall tree with branches filled with energy toward the sky.

2. The Practice Skill of Positive 'Bumping' – Clean Fighting

There is great skill in learning to positively fight. Many couples are afraid to fight, terrified to reenact past experiences: especially if their parents modeled violent or abusive fighting without resolution.   If they learned that fighting is bad because they've only seen it go to extremes, then they need to learn how fighting can be healthy.   People often fight the same way their parents fought and they may find a partner to complete these roles and repeat their fighting patterns. If partners know how to fight clean and well, they can actually balance and become enriched by their differences.

3. The Practice Skill of Accommodating

The second skill a couple needs to learn is accommodation. It is a wonderful skill when partners consciously choose this as a loving and gifting practice and when there is a balance of accommodations. Some accommodations begin as an uncomfortable stretch of a loving gesture for one to another. The practice of accommodation involves balancing all three parts of the couple's relationships where all three parts are attended to, affirmed, acknowledged and appreciated in the experience of accommodating as a present moment gifting experience.

Many couples have difficulties learning the art of attending to all three parts: oneself, the other and both together, in taking turns between being the accommodator and the accommodated. Accommodation becomes unhealthy if this is unconscious: particularly when it is an automatic expectation on oneself or the other and they are stuck in a growing resentment of having 'no choice but to accommodate' for some kind of peace in their relationship.

4. The Practice Skill of Avoidance in the Service of Connecting

Sometimes, couples manage their differences by consciously choosing to avoid issues that create unhealthy tension for the sake of allowing the partners to diffuse. If there is a topic that is extremely hot and partners are easily triggered, they can choose to avoid discussion for the moment. Once they have had some time for self-reflection and space for their emotions to settle, they can then talk about the topic or issues.

We made it a practice to make an appointment with each other for our 'hot topics' and gave ourselves a time and date to work with it. Avoidance was in the service of our having all our other positive connections and honoring the hot topic with its accorded time for work. We looked at it like an 'in grown toe nail that hurts'. Avoiding an 'in grown toe nail for a long time and repeatedly would only exacerbate the issue. So when we would repeatedly be stuck, we made an appointment with a third party, attended a workshop or go on a couples or individual retreat to help us get unstuck.

We believe that if people cannot handle high emotions, it is better to choose to avoid at the moment. However, this is a temporary decision. Avoidance becomes a compounding problem when it is the couple's primary and automatic way of dealing with their difficult issues that seem 'unresolvable'. The stuck energy involved in repeated avoiding can stunt couples' growth and eventually bury their love under a 'heap of more constipated resentment'.

Under some circumstances, a couple cannot move forward in dealing with their hot topics together. This is particularly true if there is a 'tale' to what is being avoided. Sometimes one of them may take the lead and deal with their part of the 'stuckness' through personal growth.

Their couple's growth happens when they can re-group and the other partner follows with their own growth as well. With their personal growth, they can learn how to 'bump' and stretch each other with their difference in a renewed way. The art and skill of healthy avoiding becomes their choice in their Pathway of being and balance.

5. The Practice Skill of a Wide Angle Lens

Often people carry their own perspective which they see only through their own lens. It is as though they are saying that there is only one right way to look at things and verbalize "If you would only see it my way, you will know that I am right."

When you learn to widen your lens, or perspective, you begin to see and incorporate each other's perspective and vantage points. A wide-angle lens incorporates each of the couple's perspectives. It is being able to see yourself and your partner and see the interconnectedness of who you both are and what you are perceiving and sharing. Practicing the change from a narrow lens to a wide-angle perspective helps the partners shift from focusing on the 'either-or' struggle to a 'both-and' way of holding their multiple realities. It is no longer win-lose or win-win. It becomes 'growth-growth'. When couples use a wide-angle lens, they can see all kinds of interconnections that create intimacy and love.

We worked with a couple - she is very artistic and he is very sports-minded. For a long time they fought about how they could share their time and have common ground. She wanted to do the things that are meaningful to her, that would expand her creative horizons like going to the theater, museums, etc. She wanted her husband to be interested in doing the same things. She would tell him he is uncultured and if he would just do these things with her, it would be fun for them. He, on the other hand, tells her that she needs to care for her health and get active physically. She does not enjoy physical things and does not appreciate undue attention to her body. He suggests she should play softball and volleyball: these are activities he enjoys. One can only imagine the intensity and pain of these fights. For a long time they were stuck as they both insisted that the other should do what they enjoyed.

Ultimately, she accommodated him and went to all his softball games. She started as a spectator and has given up her artistic endeavors to satisfy him. Of course, he felt very pleased with her for her taking on physical activities and becoming more physically fit. However, they are stuck. She says, "I don't know who I am anymore, I have lost my passion, I have lost my creativity" and blames him because "we have done everything he wants." He, on the other hand, reacts by saying, "I am helping you be involved, to be healthy and for us to have healthy friends. What is wrong with you, why are you complaining?"

As they learned about having a Wide Angle Lens, their awareness shifted to acknowledging that they both have a piece of their health as a whole couple. They realized that they each focused on their own version of what feels healthy for them. To bring balance to themselves together, they needed to widen their lens and explore their emotional-mental and spiritual aspects.   This was uncomfortable for him as this was his underdeveloped side. He acknowledged her passion for the arts but did not appreciate being labeled as 'uncultured'. They worked together on Balance wherein there is room for each of their passions and their openness to creating room for developing their shared interests.

6. The Practice Skill of Balancing the Poles

What may feel balanced or 'normal' for an individual, when viewed by the other partner, may be seen at an extreme pole, particularly when couples polarize.

Identify your middle ground, individually and as a couple. This is where you can agree to meet in the middle. This will determine some freedom for both parties, rather than making one adjust to the other so it becomes a 'win-lose' where one gives in. Sometimes the middle ground may be that you take turns 'giving in'. This process can shift, so checking in for balance within one's self, the other, and together as a couple, is significant for being in balance. It is always important to feel some freedom and some movement.

There were many years that we struggled around our different orientation to 'time'. We polarized around our concept, meaning, value, approach, expression and attention with 'time'. This issue took us up and down the **Eight Pathways**, which we shall clarify for you as we go along.

Lalei:

"I was very attracted to Phil's reliability. Whatever he said, he did. If he said, 'I will be there at 7,' he was there. If he says I will give you the draft on that day, he does. He was so orderly, scheduled and predictable, which was so different from my Dad. My Dad made promises he didn't keep. So I was really appreciative and attracted to how Phil was dependable. I felt loved and grew in trust as he kept his word."

"Phil's early training in his family and in the seminary emphasized order, timeliness, discipline and dependability. He was attracted to my ability to be timeless, to be in the moment awed by the beauty of nature, lost in a book or in an interesting conversation. Like my mother, I could forget time altogether engaged in a creative project to its completion, or be in a place of meditation and quiet and realize later how much time has passed."

"Eventually, Phil's concept of time threw me off balance. My being in the moment caused him to feel anxiety about being late. Individually, we were each fine. Our struggle was exacerbated when we began to see the other's style as taking away our sense of self. We tried many tactics in our struggle to try to get the other to come to our side. The very quality that initially attracted us to each other became repulsive."

"We would become irritated and angry with each other, controlled by each other's need to do it their way as the correct way. We found ourselves pathologizing the other's style -- I would call Phil 'rigid' so that I would not have to be 'ruled' by his concepts of time, and Phil saw my being in the moment as 'disrespectful' of other's time. When we did that to each other, there was no way we could influence each other, let alone be open to any change."

"As a couple, we had to learn to balance our different time orientations. We continue to have to view our differences in time as poles and as possibilities, learning from one another about how to balance what we now call 'time structure and time flow' as a couple."

7. The Practice Skill of Holding Tension and Relaxation in Balance

If strings on a guitar are too loose, when you play it nothing happens and you won't hear anything. If the strings are too tight when you strum it, they break. If the strings have just the perfect amount of tension, there is music.

The same is true with the balance between intimate partners. Finding balance in relationships is like playing a guitar or on a seesaw: there is always dynamic movement. If two people stay connected with one another, there can be movement, joy, and fun. The seesaw itself becomes playful and tension can bring music. However, if any one person in the couple does not want to play, then there is no balance on the seesaw and there is no music.

SUMMARY HIGHLIGHTS OF PATHWAY "B": BEING AND BALANCE

1. This Pathway involves the ability to bring to balance seemingly discordant, diverse and polar aspects of yourself and your partner's needs and experience in the struggle for a harmonious relationship.

2. The opportunities for enrichment are great as couples learn from the push, pull, 'bump' and balance of their polarities which are complicated by adversities and challenges of their inner and outer life.

3. Balance is the fundamental spiritual law of the universe. All things in nature and in the universe exist in balance. As couples view themselves as a whole system comprising of them as individuals and as a couple and manage their different parts they move to be in balance as the conscious choice process.

4. In appreciating, managing and growing through their differences, couples learn how to make conscious choices and create balance which enhances them together.

5. There are seven practice skills that couples can employ to consciously manage their differences:

    1. Skill of Grounding
    2. Skill of Positive 'Bumping' and Clean Fighting
    3. Skill of Accommodating
    4. Skill of Avoidance in the Service of Connecting
    5. Skill of the Wide Angel Lens
    6. Skill of Balancing the Poles
    7. Skill of Holding Tension and Relaxation in Balance

PATHWAY C: PATHWAY OF CONNECTION AND COMMUNICATION

"A human being is a part of the whole called by us universe, a part limited in time and space. He experiences himself, his thoughts and feeling as something separated from the rest, a kind of optical delusion of his consciousness. This delusion is a kind of prison for us, restricting us to our personal desires and to affection for a few persons nearest to us. Our task must be to free ourselves from this prison by widening our circle of compassion to embrace all living creatures and the whole of nature in its beauty."
~Albert Einstein

Introduction

Pathway C is about the balance between connection and conflict. Human beings desire the depth of connection, the joining together so that we can discover ourselves as individuals and who we are as a couple. The balance between connections and conflict allow us to grow; it is circular and feeds the couple.

While connection is core to our survival, well-being and growth, how we communicate becomes difficult as we perceive disconnection and conflict over differences with our valued and significant other. We filter connections and how we communicate according to our view of the world, beliefs, life experiences and culture. Many of us are genuinely confused as to what connection *really is,* while trying our best to connect from our own vantage point or our own agenda. When efforts of connection do not work, the other is made to be 'the enemy' to be feared, the 'patient' to be fixed, or the 'non-believer' to be convinced or punished; again from our own vantage point.

We believe this is one of the primary contributors to the fact that so many of us are experiencing isolation, anxiety and depression. We would like to shed light from a **BEEHMSSS**™ (**B**ody-**E**nergy-**E**motion-**H**eart-**M**ind-**S**oul-**S**ystem-**S**pirit) way of **connection** and how you can experience connection in your significant relationship or intimate bond.

Importance of Connecting

Did you know that humans are not born with the knowledge or skills to connect? These are actually learned attitudes and developed behaviors through interaction with significant relationships in their environment.

The early environments and formative years have the biggest impact on humans' ability to connect. If the basic needs such as feelings of safety, love, belonging, respect, value, mastery, and growth are stunted or traumatized, one's ability to connect may be challenged. This then shows up in one's significant relationships. The complex quality of such connections in one's early or previous environments create the complexity of hidden yearnings that propel us to join with a significant other; to be partnered, coupled or married.

The Pathway of Connection is learned and experienced throughout a couple's lifetime. All couples will experience connection and disconnection. You will feel like you can be present, attend and listen to each other and then you feel your connection blocked or dissipated. That's the natural order of the fragile bond of the couple relationship.

Sometime in the life journey of a significant relationship, the routines of daily life, work demands, pressures and stress bring couples and partners to re-enact their issues with each other. This happens particularly after the romance phase wears off.

Large-scale issue, e.g., familial, social, economic, cultural, political, religious and various "isms" passed on through generations, find their way into couple/partner interactions, whether they like it or not. The space for couples and partners to take the time to **BE** in connection has been crowded by the noise of over-stimulation from the fast pace of the technology fueled twenty first century. Often, the relationship is the place where such stresses of life get 'dumped', with the unexpressed expectation to be automatically healed, loved and whole.

When couples come to us for couple's work, they usually are in different levels of awareness in their connection and communication processes:

- Some couples consciously know they are not connecting
- Some couples know something is wrong, and do not know what the problem is
- Unaware of their loss of connection, they may say they need to communicate better

As we listen to couples' original connections, we have also heard of their experiences of a sense of déjà vu - a spark of recognition like they are meant to be together by destiny. Delving deeper to gain clarity into their connection, couples are able to transform their challenges to where learning, growth and peace occur.

We have become aware that significant relationships form and connect to fulfill purposes of soul growth and development. It is in the Pathway of Connection that couples are challenged to face the nuances of their soul journeys in their connection processes over the phases of their lives together.

> Martin Buber describes the art and skill of be-ing love, sustaining love and radiating love. He describes the connecting link between couples as their sacred partnership with the Divine, the Eternal-Thou, as the relation between humans and God is an 'I-Thou' relationship. Relationships between humans alone are frequently an 'I-It' relationship in which one and/or the other are seen and treated as objects of thought and/or action.

As connection awareness and skills are learned and practiced, they become the vehicles by which to negotiate through the rest of the other Pathways. Connection is the Pathway by which we learn to meet with our whole self with BEEHMSSS™, as it were. This is the Pathway to connect us with: our inner selves, the Thou in each other, and with the Divine Spirit that is present in the couple/partnership.

The richer, deeper, fuller, and wider our Pathway C capacities become for connection, the more likely individuals and couples are then able to handle the challenges of all the following Pathways in their life journey.

Activating Connection

There are ways for couples to learn to activate their connection. Interestingly enough, once a couple develops their inner skills and can reconnect within, they can:

1. Identify when and how they are and are not connecting
2. Identify their contribution to *how* they know **they are and are not** connecting

Once you become conscious how you both prevent connection, you can choose to do something differently or you can choose to do more of the same. Incorporating foundational practices of Pathway A, you can affirm how awareness is a huge skill unto itself. You become empowered in your chosen co-creation of healing connections together; whether spiritual, soulful, cosmic, companion, learning, parental, emotional, or physical.

For example, Marcia grew up in a family environment where feelings were not allowed. Her need for validation was met by intellectual pursuits and achievements. She fell in love with Jason, who validated her accomplishments and supported her intellectual pursuits and career goals. Jason's parents sacrificed a lot for their children's education. Jason's family gathered regularly in celebrating educational accomplishments as means to survive a 'harsh, rejecting' world. Secretly, Jason feared rejection and did his best to make others feel good through the fruits of his business since he knows the pain of rejection all too well. He felt so blessed to have found Marcia to love and be loved.

As Marcia's accomplishments and career obligations increased, Jason became uncomfortable with his experience of their disconnection. He anticipated Marcia's impending rejection. His connection style mirrored his parent's self-sacrificing love. What was functional in Jason's family did not work to connect with Marcia, who closed-off and became distant. Withdrawing to work long hours was her automatic connection style to feel validation. They became stuck in repetitive exchanges that mutually co-created more disconnection.

They wonder how they as couple or partnership can bring back the sense of soulful connection they had. Discouraged that no matter how much they had tried, they recycled in more disconnection. They state their goals for couple's work as: to re-kindle their connection, to understand themselves and each other, to have better communication, to be enriched by their differences and to forge a spiritual path to bring greater meaning into their life journey together.

So their question is: How can they re-connect? What ingredients within themselves could be tapped and accessed to contribute to their connection?

Often, after the 'honeymoon' phase of a relationship, the couple or partnership awakens to experiences of dissatisfaction, disillusionment, or disappointment. This is a normal process in the journey of the significant relationship.

> *"The truth is that our finest moments are most likely to occur when we are feeling deeply uncomfortable, unhappy, or unfulfilled. For it is only in such moments, propelled by our discomfort that we are likely to step out of our ruts and start searching for different ways or truer answers."*
> ~M. Scott Peck, The Road Less Traveled

Relationship Connection Styles and Communication Patterns

There are six different connection styles in a relationship. Our connection styles emerge in our family of origin and cultural environment to meet our needs and to survive. If our connection styles, though automatic, unconscious and survival driven, become unhealthy and entrenched, they do not support us in meeting our deepest needs in our intimate and healing love relationship.

Our styles of connection are learned ways of relating and communication to survive childhood. Harville Hendrix asserts that we tend to be attracted and fall in love with one of our parents and become the other parent as unaware couples yearn to fulfill unmet needs of childhood. Because the drive to fulfill unmet needs is strong, romantic love that brings couples to find their complementary 'loved other' carries with it an underlying energy so compelling that we hear couples stories surmounting 'great' odds to connect and be together.

Other explanations into the mysteries of significant relationship connections, from metaphysics, astrology, spiritual, cultural and human relations studies point to how unconscious connection styles and communication patterns are recreated and passed on throughout generations of family histories with the hope that the next generation will find real love, joy and peace. More often than not, the underlying forces of survival connection styles have perpetuated traumatic exchanges that bring about anxiety, depression, divorce, abuse, illness, addictions and even violence within families.

In our own work as a couple, we have taken this journey of Pathway C and continue to delve in its underlying mysteries through varying forms of therapy, coaching, healing and beyond to soul and spiritual work. In becoming aware of the transmission of trans-generational patterns in history and cultures and its impact on family and couples relationships, our deepest desire for peace, love and joy in our world meant that transformation began in what we can each control...and that is within ourselves.

> *"In our every deliberation, we must consider the impact of our decisions on the next seven generations."*
> *~The Great Law of The Iroquois Confederacy*

Even though their connecting becomes dissatisfying, couples bump up against their *resistance* to change and fulfill their *desire* for peaceful, loving and joyful connections. It is truly heartwarming when couples use that energy that 'compelled' them to connect and overcome their own inner adversities to bring themselves to a level of awareness, discovery, healing and transformation.

When couples come to appreciate the positive intention and the genealogical/cultural/familial underpinnings of their unconscious, stuck, and repetitive patterns, their choice can involve attitudinal shifts and practice skills in learning together, conscious ways of fostering healing connections in their communication. We help couples gain awareness of their process as well as explore the BEEHMSSS™ processes of connecting that are both satisfying and healing.

It is important to understand your connection styles individually and your connection style as a couple. If your connection style does not get you what you desire and you are not getting your needs met, then there may be something you each and together are contributing to prevent this. You'll want to become aware of whether you want to continue with your connection style or change it.

For instance, if a couple desires closeness and affectionate expressions such as hugging, but they maintain a stance with their arms closed and folded over their center while they blame each other for how the other is unaffectionate, cold and distant. Together, their connection style prevents affection.

Personally, their own connection style to maintain a closed-off stance to others could have a survival function. The benefits may be that they learned to be self- sufficient emotionally and therefore protecting themselves from getting hurt. Another benefit may be that they learned to be cautious and figure out the other so as to not get rejected when reaching out.

Now in their relationship, it is problematic because their habitual and automatic 'choice' is to close-off while at the same time expecting the other to reach out and be affectionate.

It is important to discover and affirm the survival function of your connection style. It is also important to affirm how your habitual connection style is currently contributing to your present 'stuck-ness' together.

We asked this couple to affirm the survival value of their closed-off stance to each other and create together a compassionate ground for their healing partnership, as well as safe container for their exploration of avenues of connection that supports their growth.

Types of Connection Styles

We have observed six types of connection styles in couples that seek our guidance. Understanding your style can help you understand your strengths, challenges and process skills needed to enhance connection.

1. **Holding Back Couples** hold back their thoughts, feelings and actions with each other because they are often afraid of offending the other or getting hurt. The more vulnerable they feel, the more they hold back. Their strengths involve carefulness and caution in approaching each other. They are sensitive to the other's feelings. As they feel restrained, their conversations with the other are often going on inside their heads.

   At their best, their connections are measured, well thought out, and designed not to hurt and avoid conflict. Their expressions are muted, toned down, brief with a lot in between the lines. Much can be left unsaid for the other to figure out. Their energy is constricted and their actions are generally not spontaneous.

In their presence, there can be an aura of caution in the air with long silences as part of their conversations.

Pathway C Practice Skills to support and develop connection for the Holding Back Couple includes:

- Exploring safety for their sharing and self-expression
- Exploring their positive intention for holding back or not talking
- Exploring what their worst fears might be if they were to not hold back
- Exploring what they imagine would be the best outcome of their holding back
- Exploring what they want for themselves and how they want to feel in their relationship, aside from holding back

2. **Projecting Couples** tend to assign responsibility to the other for their feelings or experiences. You will frequently hear them using those terms such as "You make me feel _____." They can be consciously or unconsciously blaming each other using "You are..." statements.

It is easier for them to project their assumption or interpretations of what the other is saying, doing, will say and will do. They tend to believe their assumptions as true, thus, they base their reactions on it.

Their couple strengths may involve their creativity, their ability to empathize with each other and their ability to intuit the other's thoughts and feelings. They can visualize and imagine both positive as well as negative things. When they are expressing their creativity, they can be passionate and excited about their shared project and get along very well.

As a couple, their challenge is the speed of their conversation, as they tend to talk over the top of each other. It is difficult for them to take ownership for their inner feelings and contribution to their being mired as their focus is external on their partner.

Pathway C Practice Skills to support and develop connection for the Projecting Couple includes:

- To Breathe and to Slow themselves Down
- To attend to where they are looking (BEEHMSSS™) and acknowledge what has their attention
- To own their assumption or interpretation of it
- To check their assumptions out with the other
- To connect within oneself, and notice what is going on within (BEEHMSSS™); what was evoked in them, and when ready, to share

3. **Distracting Couples** tend to talk about everything else but themselves. This couple's style of connecting is a round-a-bout, humorous, and in a joking manner - particularly when the conversation comes close to connecting with their feelings towards one another or what is going on inside of them or between the two of them that is uncomfortable. They tend to love to party, have fun talking and laugh as they are distracting themselves. Since they can't talk about anything serious, you don't know where you stand with them, or they with each other. Couched underneath satire or jokes is what they really want to say but they aren't really saying it. If they stop they have to deal with their uncomfortable feelings of hurt, anger or sadness or their innermost thoughts.

Pathway C Practice Skills to support and develop connection for the Distracting Couple includes:

- To gain awareness when and how deflection behaviors, i.e. humor, supports and when and how it hinders their connection
- To breathe, slow down, and notice shifts of inner experience and acknowledge their own shift
- To breathe, slow down, notice, and acknowledge shift in the other with attending skills
- To co-create safety and support to check in with each other and take a moment to connect with what they really want to say or share
- To be able to stay with present experience of satisfying intimate connection and hold off deflection

4. **Numbing Couple** is usually a couple who lives in their heads. They are intellectual in their connection and numb to their feelings. They can't feel in their body what they experience in their mind. They can look at facts and value being objective. They can be opinion driven and have analytical judgments often with professed objectivity. They come up with intellectual concepts and models for problem solving and plan ways of going about it. Their great intellectual prowess may be that they are well read. When there is crisis, they look like they manage well as it is hard to tell what they feel.

The problem in being excessively cognitive is that these couples live above their neck. Often times if you look at their body structure, their head and body is off balance. Energetically, they live in their heads and their body serves only to carry their head around. When uncomfortable feelings come up, their eyes glaze over or they start yawning. Deep down, they are really scared of emotions and may have been in families where emotions meant danger. Self-talk of "Be rational...Be logical... and Be reasonable..." are mottos and ways of thinking that they have taught themselves to survive.

Pathway C Practice Skills to support and develop connection for the Numbing Couple includes:

- Co-creating a place of safety
- Grounding, breathing and centering self-support skills
- Creating couple supports that provide healing alternatives to numbing to painful thoughts, emotions and memories
- Affirm positive value of their survival skill of rationality
- Explore what they would want and how they want to experience connecting with more of themselves in a safe and healing way

5. **Righteous Couple** is usually a couple who wants to do the right thing. They follow 'rules', such as what experts say is the right way, the rules of their religion and tradition(s). They believe that the only choice is the 'right' choice, not *their* choice. Often you will hear them using phrases such as 'ought to' and 'have to' with each other.

   These are very conscious, dependable, reliable and responsible people. They are good citizens and make sure that everybody else follows the rules. They keep things on schedule and get things done.

   However, they tend to see everything from a righteous stance and their thinking is black/white and right/wrong. They struggle to see gray and cannot see the 'technicolor' of life experiences.

   Their pain emerges when what they think is right and should be, is NOT. And they usually wonder what they did wrong, or how the other did wrong to cause the situation.

   Pathway C Practice Skills to support and develop connection for the Righteous Couple includes:

   - How to see different perspectives and know the difference between the inner <u>subjective reality</u> of perception, experience, and meaning-making and the <u>objective reality</u> of *fact*
   - How to hold more than their one way of experiencing or perceiving
   - How to decipher between a 'should' and a 'want'
   - How to slow down to have a sense awareness of being on the giving and on the receiving end of their righteous connection style
   - How to notice when their righteous style is helpful and when it hinders connection

6. **Self-Growth Couple** is a newer phenomenon, with the up-swing in recent years of personal growth and self-development. This is a couple who value their growth, both personally and professionally in their lives. They know how to meet their needs in self-sufficient ways. They support each other's growth in their work lives and make a lot of room in their relationship for work and career commitments and individual endeavors related to learning and success.

Their challenge is scheduling time for their relationship, since they go out-of-balance related to their professional or career gains. These couples tend to see each other as service, support and enhancement to their personal/professional/spiritual development and growth. They may often postpone having children and if they do, place demands on themselves and each other to juggle the many commitments they have in order to meet them.

This couple sees their relationship as yet another job to complete and can be impatient with themselves and each other to stay in there and work it out. Often intelligent and quick, they expect that what they read and know can easily be translated in their relations. Their challenge is in being patient with themselves to allow their growth to deepen and take stronger roots. They value supports related to their progress and feedback that strengthens them as a couple. This is a couple who seeks couples work in order to deepen their connections and take themselves as the learning laboratory for their work in the world.

Pathway C Practice Skills to support and develop connection for the Self-Growth Couple includes:

- Seeing and appreciating themselves as a couple system of three parts: me, you, us/we as **'the whole is greater than the sum of its parts'**
- Gaining appreciation of the process and practice involved in developing their 'we/us' systems perspective throughout the *Eight Pathways*
- Balancing their time and attention between me, you, we/us and we/us/them
- Practicing for couples' BEEHMSSS^{TM} awareness and inner development harnessing the richness of their diversity and unity
- Developing and strengthening their alignment with their Higher Purpose as a place for joining their relationship

Examples of Connection Styles:

Jeff and Anita: Holding Back/Numbing Connection Style

Jeff and Anita looked at each other, as though to cue themselves that it was OK for Anita to describe their present situation. "When work demands required Jeff to spend so much time working, he would come home so exhausted. I had a long day with the kids and would be exhausted as well. The children would be asleep and I would have dinner ready for him. He would pick up his dinner and go in front of the television, eat, watch sports and then fall asleep. While I love being with our children, which we agreed together was needed while they are young, I would feel guilty about wanting to talk with him. I would be looking forward to some connection with my husband all day, she tearfully expressed. He would say that I was so demanding of his time and so needy. He just could not see that I need him to connect with. After so many years of trying and telling him that we need to work on our relationship, I felt so lonely and alone. Then, I decided to take care of myself by getting my needs met and joined a support group of women. I found work that I could do from home, since I think the

71

kids still need me. I stopped myself from wanting to connect with him so that I would not hurt, be disappointed, get angry and feel lonely so much. I just stopped myself from feeling. Jeff thought everything was cool because I stopped hounding him about talking. Now he is surprised, when I said that I do not have any more feelings for him."

Jeff, while quiet most of the time, as he listened to Anita, had a sad demeanor. "I had tried to explain this to Anita that before the children came, we were just the two of us. We were really close then. When we talked, I loved to listen to her because we did not talk about problems. Now, every time we talk, it would be about problems. Somehow, I always felt that we cannot get away from it. The three children are growing up and we have their many needs to meet. Plus we have aging and ill parents, and there is so much to attend there too. My work is focused on solving critical problems all day that when I come home, I am so exhausted that the last thing I want to do is talk. I just want peace. I try not to burden her with all the problems I deal with all day. When she would insist that we talk, and I would tell her what is going on, she would get worried and that is the last thing I need."

"So talking just does not solve problems. We had peace the last few years when she became more involve working from home and having time with her friends. I believed that we were doing OK because the children are all doing fine. I thought we are a good team because we get the jobs done efficiently. Now she tells me that she has no feelings for me, and I am so sorry that I did not understand that it was so important for her to talk. I hope we can work this out."

Joe and Joyce: Projecting / Righteous Connection Style

Joyce and Joe presented that their communication is off and that they find it difficult to understand each other. They would easily go into an argument almost about anything. Joe indicated that there is an imbalance between them. "She has this big family, plus 5 children of her own. Somehow, everything I do is not enough. I have gone out of my way for her and her children and she is still not happy. With Joyce it is all about her and her family. My words do not count. I have no say. She does not listen to me. I try to fix the problem and that would even set her off even more. I just do not understand why she likes to "wallow" in all those feelings. For me it is cut and dry. She should not feel bad because other people have it worse in the world. Her problems are so small compared to the rest of the world. She should just be happy. There just is not anything right with her. I told her that she should get a hold of her feelings and just get over it. I used to be able to tell her that everything will be right and she would be OK. Now I say the same thing and she blows up at me."

While Joyce saw Joe as the more stable person in their life as a family, 'Nothing ruffles him and I am beginning to think he has no feelings. He is just all head. When I talk and cry, he says I should pray and have more faith. He is right that since Mom died, I have been wondering about death and where she is. He should understand because he lost his mom some years back. He does not understand that my mother was the best parent ever and we were so close. I say to him, people are not computers that you switch on and off. I do not understand how he could be so cold at times. He said that I should be over it in a week...that it would be good for me to be occupied so that I would not wallow in all those feelings. He said I should be glad for mom because she is now at peace. He thinks he is being helpful but he is not. He just does not understand that I do so much for him, the kids, the house, our parents...and all I want is some empathy not his lectures."

The examples presented above were couples who were committed to the Process of working through Pathway C of Connection. We shall take you through the process and practices, exercises and skills they developed and gained in Pathway C.

Connection Practice Process Skills

A. Linking Processes in the First Three Pathways: Affirmation-Being Balance-Connection

An important first step in working Pathway C involves acknowledgments of one's current situation the way things are right now. Perhaps, what may be affecting their sense of dissatisfaction has to do with how their life has become so out of balance individually and as a couple, and how their attempts at resolution in Pathway "B", have brought them both to feeling stuck.

Couples will often tell us that the issue that brought them to us is that they want to communicate better. When asked, how they would know that they are communicating better, most often, their replies would involve statements as: "We would feel understood, appreciated and connected. There would be ease in our communication. We would be able to share without feeling anxious, without feeling frustrated, without feeling hurt and angry. Our resentment will lessen, we would feel hopeful, there would be trust and safety between us, and we would feel good and re-connected. We would feel joy, love and peace."

Let's talk about the various ways that communication occurs so you'll understand how reconnection occurs.

B. The Channels and Layers of Verbal and Nonverbal Communication

As couples develop their sense of their connection, they become aware that their communication occurs on both verbal and non-verbal levels all the time.   Verbal communication is the actual content of what the partners are saying to each other in their words discussing their topic, issue, stories and feelings. More than 60% of communication is non-verbal that accompanies their verbal communication. Often what is non-verbal is the *How* by which the *What* is being delivered. This is often out of their present awareness; but can have a powerful *impact* on their connection.

Awareness of Ways of Expressing the Connection

Occurs in a variety of ways including:
- Tone of voice and loudness or softness
- Inflection
- Gestures and movement
- Facial and eye expressions
- Body language
- Posture
- Vibration
- Embodied presence
- Gut and intuitive responses

Verbal and non-verbal re-connection occurs when both parties can begin to slow down. This gives everyone the chance to breathe, connect within, attend, listen, and express themselves in congruent and connecting ways.

We call this the **Triune Connection:**
- Connecting with oneself
- Connecting with the partner
- Connecting with the Spirit of **them both**

When this Triune Connection occurs, the energy in the air is full and meaningful for both them, individually and as a couple.

Awareness of Energy Channels of Expression and Receptivity of Connection

We all have our own preferred 'wireless' energy channels of expression and receptivity. You may want to check in with yourself as to what your preferred energy channel is and what your partner's is. This is important because in order to connect you may need to know how to switch channels in order that your partner will receive your communication. Otherwise you may have two people talking, and to an observer, you can see that they are talking about the same thing; but to them, they seem to be repeating themselves because they are wondering whether they are connecting. Check in with yourself as to which channel you tend to use in your expressions and what channel you use to receive communications. Also notice that when under stress how your preferred channel becomes even more acute.

- **Visual or Seeing Channel** – involves seeing, images, pictures. This person see nuances of seeing and imagination. The words are plentiful, quick, and descriptive. The words used to express are visual words, such as: "See… Look… Imagine… Looks to me like… Picture… Show me… Illustrate… I can't see it…etc."

- **Auditory or Sound Channel** – involves hearing, sounds and nuances of sound, including hearing what is not being said. They love to be in conversation and listen to each other. "Hear... Listen... Speak... Tell... Talk... Sounds like to me... Sounding off... Tone... Loud...

   Yell... Scream... Tell me...etc." are often terms used to describe the experience of one who uses the auditory channel.

- **Sensing or Kinesthetic Channel** – involves feeling sensations, touch, doing, moving, action and includes the use of words of action such as: "Do it...Let me do it... Move...

   Actions speak louder than words...I can touch it...My gut sense...Fix...I want to know what to do...

- **Digital or Sequential Channel** – involves thinking, figuring, analyzing and processing. The words to express and receive are "logic...figure out...time frame...I am processing it...This is my analysis of it..."

Exercise: Energy Channels Awareness

1. Pay attention to what channel you use to express yourself and what channel you use to receive from your partner. Notice what words you tend to use. Notice the non-verbals that accompany your words.

2. Do the same for your partner. It is possible that you may have more than one channel? Keep a log.

3. Experiment with switching channels to connect with your partner. Notice what happens when you use the words and the non-verbals and their channel to connect. What is your experience?

   Practice with awareness – and **notice how you impact your connection**.

Skill of Present Awareness of the Layers of Connecting

The first layer of connecting is <u>within</u> oneself: what and how one is experiencing in the present moment.

The purpose of being able to connect with oneself is to become present, clear and attuned with what is happening *within oneself* on one's own internal levels. You allow yourself to be present and connected within as you meet your partner. The clearer you are within yourself the clearer your connection with your partner can be. As you are clear within yourself, you are better able to assist your partner's clarity by allowing them space to become clear without your getting in their way by working your agenda through them.

Process Exercise: Take time alone, right now, and connect *within yourself*.

A. At this moment:

My physical sensation(s) is/are ....

My emotions and feelings is/are ....

I have a need(s) ....

I want/do not want..

I desire ....

My energy is ....

I am thinking thoughts of ....

I have images and memories of ....

I am experiencing ....

My assumption(s) is/are ....

My intuition is ....

My gut sense tells me ....

I am reflecting on ....

I have an insight ....

I dream ....

I hope ....

I envision ....

My goal(s) is/are ....

Right now, I ....

B. Take turns sharing with your partner. Let yourself listen to your partner without discussing or questioning. Practice being present, connecting within and with each other.

C. Now, share your awareness and experience of listening and being present and connecting in this way.

The second layer of connecting is in the <u>interaction</u> with your partner.

This is being in and attending to the process of connecting between each other, such as: engaging, conversing and dialoguing – 'where am I, where are you, where and how are we being with each other'. Here the couples focus on their process of interactive connecting with each other.

Process Exercise: Interaction with Partner

Take 3 balls to represent: yourself, your partner, your coupleness. Label each ball. (i.e. 3 balls: 1 ball represents 'me', 1 ball represents 'you' and 1 ball is 'us'). Take turns practicing alternating holding any of the balls and speak from that ball. This gives you and your partner a place to know where you are putting your attention as you interact and share with each other. You can experiment doing this verbally (speaking) and non-verbally (movement).

Take any of your responses to the Process Exercise shared Within Self and Within Partner. Notice which layer you are speaking from and attending to.

Examples:

- Self (holding 'me' ball) "At this moment, I am aware of feeling exhausted and I have thoughts that I will need a break after these holidays are over."

- Other (holding 'you' ball) "I heard you share that you are aware about feeling your exhaustion. Please tell me more as I had a gut sense about what you just shared."

The third layer is to be able to connect with the <u>both-and-together</u> of them – their couple system or unit.

This is the layer of – 'where are we with us together?' Why this is important is that this can be taken for granted by the mere fact of being a couple. In going to the next step, which is "Where are we with us together as a couple?" allows the couple to affirm and be aware of themselves as a system (team, unit, bond) larger than themselves individually.

Example:

- Couple (holding 'us' ball) "We took the time together to talk this over and I feel good about us listening to each other. I feel connected to me, you and us."

Sometimes both parties are connected to themselves, but miss their bonding to each other. The flip side of this can also occur where they focus only on their connection as a couple and do not allow themselves to be connected with themselves individually. Their bond becomes primary and the individuals lose who they are. It is always a balance where all three layers (self, other and us) are involved in the process of making 'gold' in a healing love relationship. This alchemy of each individual and all of their own evolving wholeness, along with their evolving wholeness as a couple is what we call - their *Sacred Partnership with Spirit in their Healing Love.*

Refer back to Pathway B, where we talked about the balance between your sense of yourselves as individuals and your bonding as the couple, allowing for both the individual's expression and the couple's expression. When two people are each feeling empowered, they can connect individually, as well as a couple. They give each other space for individual connection, as well as give themselves the opportunity to connect as a couple. This is an on-going process and practice of deepening connection.

Value of Communication Processes and Skills in Facilitating Connection

As humans, we are social beings and, as such, we cannot **_not_** communicate.   All human interactions are communications, whether verbal or non-verbal.

As couples seek counseling, coaching and/or support, they are encountering the adversities and challenges of Pathway C: the Pathway of Connection and Communication. They have tried to communicate on their own and are stuck doing more and more of the same while hoping for satisfying connections.

Once couples acknowledge their **'stuckness'** (a repetitive pattern or process that is unresolved) this is the beginning of their gaining awareness. They affirm, "Our communication is a problem because we are entrenched in misunderstandings and fights that are unresolved." We validate their awareness and help them understand how this is a normal challenge in the couple's journey of Pathway C. For some who are ready, it is an awakening to their awareness of how their challenges in communication and conflict are opportunities for reconnection with the Soul and Spirit of their relationship.

Interestingly, most couples know to communicate if it is about talking. Often, many are not aware of 'HOW' their process together for connection and for disconnection is made. The Journey through Pathway C involves ways of the BEEHMSSS^{TM} connection processes that bring satisfying communications and healthy, creative, and enriching conflict resolutions.

As couples become aware of **How** their communication contributes together in co-creating their present satisfaction or dissatisfaction, they open to possible options to explore. When they take corporate ownership of their part in their process and individually commit to be conscious learning partners, they grow and deepen their connection as a healing love partnership.

Challenges and adversities of miscommunication and conflicts that lead to disconnection are paradoxically INVITATIONS to take their soul journey of healing love to know the DIVINE connection within, waiting to be tapped.

Practice Process Skills for Connection

Listening Practice Skills

It is important for couples to know how they listen to each other. Before moving on to the process and practices, take the time to do the following exercise, **Reflection on Listening** on the next page.

Exercise: Reflection on Listening

Do you know *how* you tend to listen? Do you know *how* your partner's tends to listen? Place an **(x)** as you take note of yourself and rate with 5 as Always and 1 as Not at All. Take note of your partner as well. Place an **(o)** as you take note of how your partner tends to listen and rate with **5 as Always** and **1 as Not at All**.

"I, me"		Partner
___	Physical sense: Sight, Sound/Tone, Smell, Taste, Touch	___
___	Intuitive or gut senses	___
___	Feeling emotions expressed in words and body language	___
___	Listening to inner feelings of empathy	___
___	Focusing on a specific *for what* is of personal interest	___
___	Selective listening as confirmation of one's agenda	___
___	Something in my mind to say back	___
___	Association to a memory, experience or a solution	___
___	Figuring out internally what is meant	___
___	Vibration or energy in you, in them, in both, in the field	___
___	Looking for what inspires	___
___	In a neutral, quiet or peaceful place within	___

1. Take turns to share with each other your responses: yourself and partner observations.

2. As the Listener, notice *HOW* you are listening *right now*. Take note according to the above.

3. What awareness or insights do you have about *HOW* you listen and your tendencies together to help with your connection or disconnection?

One of the biggest impediments to connection is that many partners make quick leaps and interpretations based on assumptions of what they thought they heard in their communications. A link is made with some non-verbal and without checking the data; a conclusion is made as 'truth'. Without fully listening to what they each are saying and checking the non-verbal data, misunderstandings can happen.

Here is an example of checking the data from Joyce and Joe:

> **Joyce:** (using her auditory channel as she observed Joe's voice increase in sharpness of tone), "When I hear your tone (mirroring to Joe whose channel is visual) as you are saying 'It does not help to feel sorry for yourself', I just feel shut down. Was your intent to shut me down?" (healthy projecting connection style checking for connection by being a mirror reflecting in behavior how Joe looks when using a sharp tone that she hears)

> **Joe:** (connecting with Joyce's auditory channel and shifting his tone) "I hear you saying that my voice tone with my statement shuts you down. My intention was to ease myself, because I feel helpless (connection with his inner experience and sharing) on how to make it better for you when I see you in so much pain. I wonder how to be helpful when I see you in pain."

Because most of the above is going on simultaneously in couple's communication, it is imperative that partners learn to slow down to notice: how they are listening and what they are hearing. Couples need to share how they are listening and feedback what they got to check assumptions, hunches and interpretations and be open to clarifications. It is valuable to use active listening skills of reflecting back exactly what is heard in a neutral way and bracket one's own reactions or additions in order that both can have room to check whether that was conveyed was received. Through the practice of listening process skills, couples experience their connection in seeing and hearing each other.

Practice Skill of Slowing Down Communication

Sometimes when partners are very upset, it is hard to find a common focus or topic to communicate about. As the communication speeds up, the couple competes for 'air time' further losing their common focus and their connection. Their senses narrow, their breathing stops or becomes shallow, their bodies tense and brace and their language become filled with 'you' sentences in reaction to each other. It seems that while both want to be 'right,' neither one wants to be blamed, made at fault, lose, nor be wrong.

Think of a metaphor to describe your couple/partnership system. We will present a metaphor that many couples have used in order to illustrate this process of *slowing down:* the couples' car. As they name the components of the car, couples describe slowing down with the shifting of gears, releasing the gas pedal and applying brakes to slow down.

Let us go back to the couple, Jason and Marcia presented earlier in Pathway C as they describe their use of *slowing down process* skills to aid in their connection.

- **Jason:** "When I notice myself or Marcia speeding up either one of us will shift to a slower gear. I say, '*I want to slow down to make sure that I heard you.*' And I really slow myself down, like putting on the brake by breathing."

- **Marcia:** "I am more *aware* that together we can talk past each other. I slow down when I ask Jason, 'Please *tell me what you heard me say so I have clarity as to what I gave, as my intention is to connect.*' Then I stop and listen and breathe."

- **Jason:** "I learned to *simply stop talking for a while and breathe.*"

- **Marcia:** "I *notice our energy shifts* when we simply stop talking for a while and *breathe in each other's presence.* Sometime *I will affirm that I am breathing and slowing down.* And I like it when you affirm that you are too."

- **Marcia:** "Instead of using work as my escape when I get defensive, I notice that I can hang in *slowing down* and simply keep on *mirroring back* to Jason what I hear him saying, 'This is what I am hearing you say…. I appreciate your telling me'".

- **Jason:** "I notice when I talk faster or louder, especially when I am upset, that I *play a role* in Marcia's style of retreat to her work. I am *consciously slowing my mind down* in all the scenarios I make of her rejection. It does not help me when I speed up and assume…because we end up disconnecting. To slow down, I do *breathing exercises or go for a walk.*"

  "Then my *energy is better and I can initiate* connection in a clearer way. Marcia and I have *collaborated in giving each other our car metaphor signals*, like our oil gage is down or our system battery needs recharging. It lightens us up and we literally can take care of our couple car system for our time together."

- **Marcia:** "I have learned to *listen to my dissatisfaction or disconnection as a signal*, like when I am running on empty and need refueling that we are repeating our old pattern and I appreciate that I am able *to shift internally* and connect with myself: like noticing my attention slipping away. I appreciate that when I verbalized it, our response together felt present and healthy. I like that we can *slow down by stating the obvious.* That was such a neat tool that we learned in our couples coaching session. I feel so empowered saying the obvious. 'Uh oh, I can feel us disconnecting right now. Can we take a breather and pick it up later after dinner. It feels so clean, present and healthy."

- **Marcia:** "We appreciate that when our communication simply gets too charged and it is really difficult to listen and slow down, that we agreed to go for couples coaching. It helps me slow down and be able to listen better when I am not the focus and Jason is relating what is going on with him. It is much easier to vent to a neutral person who has a systems perspective of us both and does not take sides. I notice that because we feel listened to equally without judgment and are in a safe space, we can listen better to each other and feel connected."

- **Jason:** "This slowing down does not feel spontaneous or real to me. I am glad that we are giving ourselves *permission not to be spontaneous but to be conscious.* Our old pattern that gets us bogged down is spontaneous because it is so automatic. Sometimes I feel weird and I *resist* this slowing down or listening because what I really want to do sometimes is the old way. This time I can do the old way with choice but in a different way. It is funny how I just made all kinds of sounds and you let me...and you chimed in and made sounds too. We ended up laughing our hearts out."

- **Jason:** "I am learning to *listen more fully* rather than listen to my own thoughts and assumptions only. What an amazing awareness that is for me! Slowing down has put me in charge of the gears when I am in the driver's seat. And we now can take turns driving and being the passenger. In *becoming more aware of breathing and slowing down*, I can *connect better with the essence* of what I want to share and what Marcia is communicating. I feel so good within as we are connecting better."

We coach couples so they can learn how to connect through different modes of communication and help to validate their experiences. The beautiful thing is many times what is deep can be accessed and expressed non-verbally and sometimes it is more effective as it transcends the spoken language.

> *"The unique personality, which is the real life in me, I cannot gain unless I search for the real life, the spiritual quality, in others. I am myself spiritually dead unless I reach out to the fine quality dormant in others. For it is only with the God enthroned in the innermost shrine of the other, that the God hidden in me, will consent to appear."*
> *~Felix Adler, An Ethical Philosophy of Life*

Handling Differing Connection Styles as a Couple

> *"Love is strengthened by working through conflicts together."*
> *~Anonymous*

When challenges of crisis and stress surface in relationships, earlier survival connection styles of members of the couple surface and engage. Old trauma patterns and losses each resurface and play out in the present dynamics, which makes the connection even more difficult. There begins to be a time warp and couples act as though the past conflict is the current one.

Because difference is the normal order of life, normal conflict is inevitable in significant relationships and is a part of the life journey of couples. *Conflict is the spark, the charge or the 'electricity'* when difference in styles, perspectives, beliefs, needs, values and wants bump, push and pull against each other. When managed in the present moment, in both a clear and clean way by how couples perceive their differences and deal with them, conflicts can deepen, expand and enrich their relationship and be a healing experience for both of them.

When conflicts are approached as *critical learning opportunities in Pathway C of Connection,* couples:

- Deepen their appreciation of their diversities
- Create mutual respect for the contribution of their unique and different styles in their growth
- Explore creative ways of joining through their differences
- Discover the miracle(s) of Spirit imbedded within the Conflict

We invite you and your partner to take the following exercise, **Reflection on Connecting**. This exercise is a good benchmark for you and your partner to see how you are connecting through your differences.

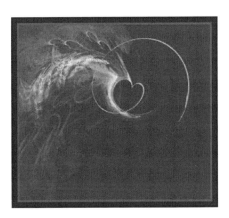

Exercise: Reflection on Connecting

Let us start with rating on a 5-point scale (5-Strongly Agree to 1-Strongly Disagree) your responses to the following reflection questions. First, each one complete alone, and then share with each other. What are you learning about how you connect or disconnect when you have a conflict around your differences?

I/Me   **Partner**

____ I, my partner, we avoid conflict at all cost, because_____. _____

____ We take turns accommodating each other's wishes____. _____

____ When things do not go my/our way, ___ gets mad and ____ gets sad. _____

____ In my family, conflicts were never resolved in a healthy way. _____

____ I/you/we work with our differences and can influence each other to see things from different perspectives. _____

____ When we differ in ___, I smooth things out and look for where we agree. _____

____ I/we are competitive and do not want to lose. We argue and debate a lot. _____

____ I/we work to find win-win resolutions that honor us both. _____

____ I/we work to find growth-growth resolutions to our conflicts. _____

____ We are able to handle our differences better, when we share, listen and treat ourselves and each other with respect. _____

____ We both attend to look and work for the best for both of us the more polarized our differences are. _____

____ I/we trust that when one of us chooses to forgo their want for the other, that we attend to the other as well. _____

____ When we are caught in a win-lose struggle, we stop and slow down, or take time out to cool down, so we can listen and go deeper into what is for us to learn from our struggle. _____

Examples of Connection: Working the Difference

The Rational/Emotional, Masculine/Feminine Dynamics

If a rational person marries their emotional counterpart, they feel 'complete' and so it is the other way around. They connected and 'fell in love' with their other half.

Sue explains her attraction to Ken. "Ken had that special way of knowing how to calm me with his thoughtful way of seeing things logically". Ken appreciates that his life had more meaning with Sue's affectionate and caring ways. They complemented each other.

When Sue's emotional needs for empathy and emotional intimacy would come across as demands for Ken to meet her emotionally, Ken would try even harder to get her to think about their issues rationally.

Ken, now frustrated, "I cannot understand how something so simple cannot be fixed. I need to figure out Sue. I am here to fix our relationship because when she's more rational, we are better."

Underneath, Ken is saying, "I do not want to lose my wife. Emotions need to be controlled as it makes us weak and vulnerable. I am uncomfortable with it."

Though couples want change for connective communication, they also have a part of themselves that resist the change they want. We work slowly and gently as we believe that the part that resist change needs to be valued and honored for the couple to embrace the change they choose. That is for the person who prefers logic and rationality to connect with their emotional/feminine parts and the person who prefers emotional expressions to connect with their rational/masculine part, both without giving up the strengths and qualities they already have.

Couples learn to appreciate how they chose each other on a soul level in order to connect with their own underdeveloped part. Sometimes when couples refer to finding their 'Soulmate', they realize the deeper soul agreement to be in each other's lives in order to become more their whole self together.

Creating a Container: Climate of Safety in the Field of Relational Connecting

As couples are willing to connect as a team, through a team spirit, they move from an 'either-or' way of thinking of themselves to a **'both-and'** incorporation of themselves in a healing love process of relating. We support them to talk with each other about co-creating a climate of safety so that they could negotiate their Pathway of connection in a healing partnership.

They tell us, "We don't have problems with communication. We can talk really well, but nothing happens. We still are unhappy." Often they find that while they can talk, they are not allowing themselves to connect intimately for reasons linked to their fears.

They wonder why they are stuck when they are having two monologues going on concurrently, vying for which one of them has the real 'truth'. They soon realize that no one listening and they are in a struggle.

As they attend together to creating their container to foster their climate of safety, each member of the couple learns how to express themselves in ways so that their partner can hear and listen to them. We have the couples become clear so that the partner knows what is needed at the time.

Some people may need to talk. Others want to vent in a safe way and don't want their partner to respond because they are so filled up that they simply need to express themselves. Others may say, "I am expressing, and I just want to express my thoughts and feelings. I don't know how I am going to say it, but I need to hear myself talking out loud to get some clarity. I need you to be a mirror, just to be there so I can hear myself talking."

Another way people may express is to talk about the emotions they are experiencing, such as feelings of sadness, grief, hurt, anger, fear, doubt, guilt, etc. They simply want a space to be able to express these feelings in a safe place for them both.

Generally, we find that women will many times want to express themselves without telling their partner what they want or the intention of their self expressions. The man will then jump in to try to fix the situation. Depending upon the intensity of the emotional expression, the listener will need to have the skill to attune to the present moment, whether to be an attending listener and witness to hear what his partner is expressing or whether to respond to what they want. During this time it is important for the partnership to create a safe climate for one to detach, be a witness, or the holder of a safe space and the other to vent their emotional 'stress' into a safe container, as an imaginary 'toilet'. It takes practice to learn this relational discipline for their partnership to maintain their container of safety for themselves, and have a way for the stress of 'energetic manure and the slime' of emotionally charged 'negative materials' to release safely. It is through the couples' relational skill to have the intention to hold the container for safety in their relational field together so that it can hold the safe space for each partner to express what they are experiencing, feeling, thinking, and sensing.

The Skill of Listening

The listener needs to have certain skills to know how to listen. Many times couples confuse listening with agreement. There is a difference. <u>Listening does not</u> mean you agree with your partner. Listening means that you hear what they are sharing in the context of where they are coming from and that you are being and attending in the present to them because they matter to you.

Levels of Expression

These are various levels of expression where our inner experience is expressed outwardly. These include:

- our thoughts, our feelings, our experiences, and how we express ourselves physically
- being playful, sharing leisure, joyful, and relaxing connections
- another facet of expression is we make room to express our dreams, our wishes, our thoughts, our plans, our goals, and our ideas of problem solving, using each other as a sounding board
- we need to be able to express with each other how we might manage the details and routines of our home

Sometimes when couples are talking, one puts out an idea and one of the partners switches to an emotional place without letting the partner know they have switched. Now they are on different pages. Or somebody ends up switching to expressing an emotion. They go to a different page or level of communication and the partner just doesn't understand what has happened. There is an important skill in saying "I just switched pages here."

It is important for couples to know how to stay on the same page. We know this is not easy.

Example

For example, if we are talking about our political orientations, someone may say, "I am a conservative," while the other partner is a liberal. Maybe the female has a particular affiliation because she is a feminist. The husband then says, "Why do you become so emotional about this?" He is just expressing a thought.

Then, the woman becomes emotional and goes to a different page. She says "This is what is wrong with you, you are so sexist." They have now switched pages and they are now exchanging on a very emotional plane. They have left the discussion of the original topic and may feel they are attacking each other. This leaves them wondering what happened.

When couples can determine what page they are on now, what they have begun to focus on, this helps the couple be able to stay connected, attending to one page at a time.

> *"Only through our connectedness to others can we really know and*
> *enhance the self. And only through working on the self can we*
> *begin to enhance our connectedness to others."*
> *~Harriet Goldhor Lerner*

Dealing with Emotional Allergies

When certain topics, issues, situations come up, and our reactions are larger than what the present situation calls for, we have an **'emotional allergic reaction'** (Lori H. Gordon). Old baggage is triggered – either by the content of the conversation or by the way the content was discussed. Emotionally allergic reactions are complex, because we often think our partner is doing this to us. Emotional allergies are past in origin, reactions that do not have to do with the present situation but are activated when underlying ingredients trigger its cellular memory Pathways.

When partners are feeling stuck with their emotional allergies, there are healing partnership skills they can learn. They can benefit with the support and facilitation of a coach or counselor *when working with emotional allergies to allow for their re-invention* of themselves. Healing partnerships become willing to:

- Learn to recognize that sometimes you or your partner may be unwittingly triggering emotional allergic reactions from something in the past, though it may feel like it is a present issue in the process
- Learn to slow down and to look at what each partner is bringing to the particular issue
- Understand that sometimes the issue is not the issue at all, but the issue becomes the trigger, as if a landmine is hidden there
- Create a safe container where they can talk about their individual baggage, versus making the partner an issue
- Working through the reaction in a slowed down way so you and your partner can breathe, be heard safely, gain clarity or have access toward the healing process of the unfinished or painful issue
- Understand that if one partner does not clarify what they may be bringing to a particular issue then they can blame the partner, so the issue becomes focused on the person rather than what is being triggered from the past

Helping a Couple Distinguish the Past, Present and Future

For example a couple, Paul and Maureen, are talking in the present tense with each other about politics. Paul makes a generalized comment in the present about what he is thinking about; however, he is not aware of the history of his comments. He says to his wife, "Why are all women so emotional?" There is an emotional allergy between him and his wife because he is the thinking one and she is the emotional one. Somehow they have decided that he is the thinker and she is the emotional one. His statement, "Why are you women so emotional?" is loaded for the both of them and possibly out of their awareness.

Although Paul is having a conversation in the present about politics, he unconsciously has shifted gears to a past issue that he is bringing into the present. When we asked him to explain where the statement comes from, Paul revealed, "This was the same thing with my mom and it is the same thing with all the women I've dated. Women manipulate with their tears like my mother manipulates my dad. I hate it when my wife gets emotional on me." He is no longer in the present. He went to the past and generalized, experiencing the reaction he had as a child. As a boy he was not allowed to have emotions and has disconnected internally to how he felt and is now much more comfortable with thinking. When he experiences any feelings from his wife, he is uncomfortable. His way of managing this is to make the emotions of his wife a problem.

In the original interaction, the page shifted between the couple when Maureen expressed her feelings. Internally she felt that she was "being attacked or degraded. I was seen as weak; I am not good enough. I am less than him." She felt she had two options - to become numb, frozen and not to speak or to go on the attack, blame him and run away. Any of these reactions simply replicate a past pattern of unfinished modes of expressing.

As Maureen, became more aware of her emotional allergic reactions, she paid attention to be in the present moment and distinguish what is in her past story She practiced being in a present connecting way, "You are telling me at this moment, that you are saying in your experience women get emotional, is that what I am hearing?" Instead of attacking or shutting down, she simply reflected what he had just said and added, "Tell me more, what does that mean or how is that important to you? What brought that thought to you when we were discussing this topic?"

> **This next section requires couples to be able to stay present to their inner responses and to be willing to slow down, breathe, and ask 'checking in' questions.**

Ways to Maintain Connections When You Are <u>Emotionally Charged</u>

These are several simple ways for couple's to maintain their connection when discussing emotionally charged issues. This creates a safe container and helps people feel heard. If you are charged and you charge it some more, we could have an explosion. When someone is discharging a 'stress' reaction, you let it happen, and become a witness at a safe enough agreed upon distance so as not to be a receptacle of the discharge.

By creating this, the partners can feel that, "It matters to us that we are in a healing relationship. We are doing our part to allow the discharge to happen, while respecting our healing partnership." How this is done varies with each couple. The following are some suggestions:

1. Make open-ended requests or statements to your partner instead of questions where they can respond with yes or no. Close-ended questions create more conflict that does not get resolved because the yes or no responses can have emotional allergy issues related to them.

   Suppose someone is feeling angry or charged about something. To give an opinion or explanation will charge them more. For example, your partner might say, "You did this and you did that." You could respond, "Tell me more about how I did that" versus "No, I didn't do that, you are wrong." To do this, you have to ground yourself and let your partner know that you are on their page and want to know where they are coming from, "I want to understand where you are coming from to feel angry about that."

2. Reflect what the other person is saying to check that you are hearing them. For example, you may say, "I am going out with our friends to the theater since I am sure you are not interested in the film." You partner responds by saying, "What I am hearing you say is that you are going to the theater with our friends since you are not sure that I am interested in the film."

3. Ask curious and neutral question: "What just happened?" or statements like "Tell me more ..." or "I am interested in your experience. Tell me more..."

4. Check in with your partner in the present moment to gauge each other's responses. You can ask questions like - "How are we doing? How are you being right now with that? Did I hear you correctly? Do you feel heard by me? Are we still connecting? I would like to check in with us about our present perceptions about what just happened."

5. Affirm your presence. Use phrases such as: "This is hard and I am hanging in here with you right now" or "I am present here now" or "I hear and see you now."

6. Affirm their presence. Use phrases such as: "This is hard and I appreciate you hanging in here with me", "I feel your presence" or "I feel seen and heard right now."

The Four Connection Skills: Creating a Safe Learning Atmosphere to Support

1. Learn how to co-create **safe trust** to be self-expressive and to learn how to listen to the expression by the partner with mutual respect, consideration, sensitivity, confidence and a willingness to learn.

2. Learn to identify what the issue is in focus; be specific with each other rather than making broad, general or nebulous statements. This provides clarity.

3. Learn to be responsibly honest with oneself, with one another and to be able to safely hold and hear their multiple 'truths' realities.

4. Learn to be embodied in heartfelt connection to convey your message in a way that supports your relational growth and does not deliberately hurt or harm the other. When we intentionally express things to harm the other, even though we think we are being honest, we lose the connection and can damage a fragile relationship.

Five-Element Connection Practice Process

I. Earth: Create a Climate of Safety

When people feel unsafe, they don't want to talk or reveal themselves. To create a climate of safety, partners will mutually discover what their needs are for support and safety in the present right now. Couples then practice safety with laying foundational supports to strengthen their connections in their communications and conflicts.

II. Air: Focus and Time Frame: Past, Present or Future Time

Ask questions to find out – "Are we on the same page? Are we both in the present moment or are you talking about a past situation?" It is important to know where you are focusing together and to take one page at a time.

III. Space: Align Intention and Impact

Share your Intention and check for Impact. Check with your partner to find out how your statement impacts them. "I intend to do this today. Is that okay with you?" As you work together to have your intentions become congruent with the impact, your connection will be more satisfying.

IV. Water: Nurturing the Heart-Spirit of Connection

This connection occurs in Five Different Levels of communication. It is valuable for couples to get *on the same page* in these five different areas that can save them
some confusion in what they are discussing or sharing. Approaching these areas with sensitivity, empathy, compassion, attention and presence helps in nurturing satisfying communication. You'll want to find out:

1. Are we discussing housekeeping and maintenance, (i.e. scheduling, chores, maintaining the household together)? These are usually "To Do's".
2. Are we problem solving (i.e. about an issue, situation, dilemma that arose)?
3. Are we having intimate talk to create a connection? (sharing feelings, experiences, dreams, etc., this is often with no goal in mind...just being together)
4. Are we creating a joyful experience together? (playful, leisure, memory making, celebrating, etc.)
5. Are we envisioning our futures, goal-setting, action planning, praying and using each other as a sounding board?

V. Fire: Authentic Expression

Expressing authentically with awareness our preferred energy channels of seeing, hearing, sensing, or figuring and meeting your partner in their channel, opens possibilities for connecting energetically with your mind, heart, and being.

Notice what level or page you are each investing a lot of energy, where you have ease in connection, and where attending connects you energetically, you will find that you become present to the emergence of your <u>energized joining</u> in decisions and actions.

SUMMARY HIGHLIGHTS OF PATHWAY "C": CONNECTION AND COMMUNICATION

1. Pathway C is about the balance between connection and conflict. Human beings desire the depth of connection, the joining together so that we can discover ourselves as individuals and who we are as a couple.

2. While connection is **core to our survival**; it is also through our deepening connection that well-being, growth, and understanding are enhanced through how we practice skills of conscious communication and the processes for transformative conflict.

3. As connection awareness and skills are learned and practiced, they become the vehicles by which to negotiate through the rest of the other Pathways.

4. Understanding your style and your couple style can help you understand your strengths, challenges and process skills needed to manage conflict and enhance connection.

5. Pathway C's Connection practice of process skills involves the **Five-Element Connection Practice Process:**

    1. Earth: Create a Climate of Safety
    2. Air: Focus and Time Frame: Past, Present or Future Time
    3. Space: Align Intention and Impact
    4. Water: Nurturing the Heart-Spirit of Connection
    5. Fire: Authentic Expression

PATHWAY D: PATHWAY OF DEVELOPMENT AND DISCOVERY

"The only journey is the journey within."
~Rainer Maria Rilke

The Dance of Stability and Change

Relational and individual unfolding continues into the Pathway D of Development and Discovery, which builds upon the Pathways of Affirmation and Awakening, Being and Balance, and Connection and Communication.

The Pathway of Development and Discovery reinforces the evolution of the couples' soul; both individually and collaboratively. As they draw closer, committed to their development and evolution, they together awaken to a higher level of awareness. This new awareness engages a completely new order of human relationship that heals and co-creates our possible future.

Many couples come to us for help because they are experiencing either an internal crisis and/or an external event that has caused them to reexamine their relationship. Often, the intensity of these crises upsets any stability they may have. Most people wonder if they are 'crazy or doing something wrong' to be experiencing these challenges. As part of the couple's life journey and their process of development, such "crisis" is an opportunity for exploration into the heart and soul of their relationship and an invitation to grow individually and together.

As couples proceed beyond their crisis and seize the opportunity to walk the Pathway of Development, they discover that the Pathway is multi-dimensional, complex and interconnected to their life relationships in many layers. They discover this to be a challenging Pathway of their couple's relationship journey, as it can take them to the depths and heights of their relationship as they face various aspects of themselves and overcome their limitations.

They begin to recognize that in its soul, significant relationships, such as couples, marriages and life-long partners, is the 'university of life' that brings them their soul's 'hardest lessons'. Whether they are aware or not, their significant relationship holds the gift of their soul's transformation in awakening consciousness of Spirit in their lives. More than dealing with challenges posed by circumstances, it is their inner transformations where they learn the healing power of loving genuinely, generously, and with wisdom that is an inspiration to others.

Whether we choose to or not, just being born on this earth and being in a relationship presupposes development. It is as though the entire universe moves synchronistically for our development to evolve our consciousness. Humanity is the only species that has the capacity to be aware and conscious of its development and in so doing, have impact or influence over its developmental evolution.

Pathway D in the couple's journey can be initiated in 'normal' stages or critical incidents as the phases of development or seven-year cycles shifts and changes in their relationship journey.

Let us look at the Four Stages of Development of a couple's relational journey and the thematic issues that emerge at each phase (we will discuss these stages in more detail later in this chapter):

Initial Stage 1: Dependence - Fusion Cycles: 0 - 6th year cycle
- **Beginning Phase**: Courtship: Similarities & Complementing Differences
- **Middle Phase**: Romance vs. Marriage/Partnership & the Inevitable Disillusionment
- **Ending Phase**: Authenticity vs. Illusion/Disillusion

Stage 2: Independence - Differentiation Cycles: 7th- 14th; 15th- 21st year cycles
- **Beginning Phase**: Differentiation & Diversity
- **Middle Phase**: Autonomy vs. Intimacy: Power & Influence
- **Ending Phase**: Self Identity & Intimacy

Stage 3: Mutuality - Interdependence Cycles: 22nd - 28th; 29th- 35th; 36th - 42nd year cycles
- **Beginning Phase**: Recognition, Co-creative Authentic Identity & Connections
- **Middle Phase**: Collaborative Contributions
- **Ending Phase**: Integrative Intimacy

Stage 4: Termination (can happen in Stages 1, 2, or 3) or
Resolution - Integrative Cycles: 36th – 50th + 7 year cycles
- **Beginning Phase**: Life – Relationships Review – Forgiving & Healing
- **Middle Phase**: Making the Best of Life, Legacy & Passing Forward, Deepening Acceptance & Respect
- **Ending Phase**: Endings, Completion(s), & Death

We notice couples seeking counseling around these cycles when their relationship is undergoing these 'predictable' changes, either marked by internal or external crisis.

An inner crisis can occur at any time. They may ask such questions as: "Who am I now?" "What is the meaning of my life?" or "Why am I in this difficult relationship?" - Questions such as these spark their soul's development as reflected in their couples' challenges of the stage or phase of a cycle.

The couple's journey is also marked by critical external events that impact upon the relationship such as: a health crisis, an accident, a job change, a loss, trauma or tragedy. Together, with the normal developmental phases, these critical events can add to the magnitude of the stress on their relationship, particularly when several occur within a short span of time and couples are not prepared to face these challenges.

In growing and developing, couples experience the tension between forces for change and stability. In reaction to the crisis, couples may speed up to a quick fix or resolution, which often adds to the crisis. The challenge is to know how to slow down their inner reactivity to the fast moving "upheaval" that external crisis brings.

However, as they commit to their development and growth, the couple opens themselves to discovery, co-creating, and transformation.

Couples' growth are initiated by collisions that bring their illusions and beliefs of existing paradigms into examination and by a confrontation of habits and repeating patterns that are not working. Taking the conscious Pathway of Development and Discovery requires great courage and commitment supported by inner and outer resources.

"I do not accept any absolute formulas for living. No preconceived code can see ahead
to everything that can happen in a man's life. As we live, we grow and our beliefs
change. They must change. So I think we should live with this
constant discovery. We should be open to this adventure in heightened
awareness of living. We should stake our whole existence on our willingness to explore
and experience."
~Martin Buber

The Landscape of the Journey in the Pathway of Development

Have you wondered about the underlying wisdom of the traditional marriage vows that have been passed on through the generations in so many cultures? Though these vows have gone through many variations, the essence of the vow, promises oneself to commit to life's evolving journey together. Take a moment and truly wonder about this commitment. Ponder on the statement below by saying each word and syllable s...l...o...w...l...y... and pay attention to your inner experience. Breathe and be in quiet reflection. Observe and notice what is happening within you. Consider the inner development a couple's journey brings to their being, their soul, and their spirit:

I, (name), take you (name), to be my (wife/husband), to have and to hold from
this day forward, for better or for worse, for richer, for poorer, in sickness and in
health, to love and to cherish; from this day forward until death do us part.

The journey of the Pathway of Development and Discovery is predicted here. Many stumble through these vows following the minister's lead seemingly in some kind of self- hypnotic trance. As we prepare couples for their life's journey in marriage, many of them have pondered their vows, and designed them in ways that have personal meaning. Whatever the vows are and no matter how well planned they are when they embark on life's journey together, they will be molded unconsciously in the passing on of generational patterns or transformed in their evolving, deepening, conscious, and healing love through the Pathways.

Couples, particularly in the Western world, are mesmerized by the romance of courtship and marriage, and the desire for the true and perfect relationship: to live happily together through life thereafter. This longing for romance is our human quest for that perfect Divine love, and when we 'fall in love', we project our own true inner beauty, inner goodness, and divine qualities on to this 'special someone'. When the stresses and challenges of the 'better and worse, richer and poorer, sickness and health' bring shifts and changes, and the enchantment wears off, couples find themselves in this Pathway where they are now 'facing' themselves and each other with the 'luggage' they bring to their partnership.

In each of their 'luggage' are their unexamined maps, rule books, and prescriptions for happiness. Tucked away in the secret compartments of their luggage are their yearnings, hurts, and unfinished business.

In the wake of negotiating their challenges, obstacles, and opportunities that are all part of the 'tapestry' of their evolving consciousness, some couples stay stuck in this Pathway and after many trials, come to us in search for 'answers' to 'fix' their pain.

It is those couples who face their developmental challenges by taking the inner Pathway of Development, that discover and grow their authentic relationship with themselves and with

98

each other and in the process, evolve to embrace 'Being' with Divine Love. They had a glimpse of this Divine Love, of its stirring presence, heard its melodious voice in the calling of their name, and held in the space of awe and wonder the miraculous moments of union with their partner. Ultimately it is their soul's yearning to recover those 'Divine moments' with their 'Beloved', and of the Love lost in the midst of the weight of 'doing-ness', life stresses, adversities, disappointments, and hurts in their developmental couple's journey.

Hidden in the recesses of consciousness is the wonder of whether theirs will ever be, the Divine experience of connection with the Presence of inner peace and the relaxed joyfulness of giving and receiving love unconditionally and feeling fully Real and Whole.

Through education, coaching, support groups, counseling, and spiritual guidance, couples have found their way to become unstuck in the development of their relationship. Some couples have felt touched by *grace*, a turning point that had "reset" them to come into alignment with their soul's higher purpose; both individually and together, which shifts them into the present phase of their developmental journey.

First, we invite you to **examine and reflect on the development landscape** of the couples' life journey. Imagine yourself in a time machine or helicopter as you do this exercise. The explanations for each exercise are noted in each box.

REFLECTION EXERCISE
THE DEVELOPMENT LANDSCAPE: A HOLOGRAPHIC VIEW

You can do this alone or together.
1. Take a large sheet of paper or a flip chart.
2. In the center of the sheet of paper write your name or initials.

    At the bottom of your sheet draw a line across the sheet to signify "**Cultural, Familial, & Social Structures** that impact your belief, guiding mythologies, cultural roles, and practices." Include such beliefs in the areas around love, sex, relationship, romance, and marriage.

    Below this line, write as fast as you can without really thinking what comes up for you for the following:

    "If my culture/ my religion/ my father/ my mother/ my relatives/ my friend(s)/ my teacher(s)/ my co-workers/ my boss, etc. were here now they would say:

    "Love is_____"
    "Marriage or long term relationships are _____"
    "To make your relationship work, you should_____"
    "We believe that _____"
    "Above_____"
    "My advice to you is_____"

3. Now draw another line across your sheet to be your <u>Development Lifeline</u> while leaving space so you can graph above and below the line. Separate the line by marking decades in <u>your life span</u>.

            10

             5
    your age ....10..........20..........30..........40..........50..........60..........70..........80
            -5

           -10

4. Graph significant events and relationships that have had an impact in your life; putting <u>Above</u> the line <u>Positive</u> experiences and relationships and <u>Below </u>the line, the <u>Difficult</u>, <u>Critical</u> or <u>Negative</u> experiences and relationships. **Note** what you did to survive and what you learned or the values that evolved for you. Doing this will give you a pictorial graph of your lifeline.

5. Take a colored pencil and draw another line across your sheet to represent your Current Significant Relationship (CSR) Line. You can write or symbolize as you chart your processes with your current significant relationship and where you are in your inner/outer developmental journey.

[continued on next page]

[REFLECTION EXERCISE continued]

Mark the beginning date of your relationship and chart it in segments of 7 years (a couple's journey goes through predictable phases and shifts in 7 year cycles).

6. Now take your own colored pencil and chart how you are as a couple developing these processes indicated in the statements below. Name the process skill and move it <u>Above</u> the line to indicate <u>positive development or satisfaction</u> and <u>Below</u> the line to indicate <u>negative development or dissatisfaction</u>. Place a check or star (*), where you feel satisfaction or completion and an (x) to indicate your dissatisfaction. You can also note it in terms of B (body), En (energy), En (emotion), H (heart) M (mind), S (soul), S (system), S (spirit).

7. Now check your developmental process skills involved and highlight each phase of development as a couple. First select from below which applies to you now. Then circle to select which B En Em H M S S S™ applies.

( ) **B En Em H M S S S** How we are orienting and focusing.............................

( ) **B En Em H M S S S** How we are dealing with our differences ....

( ) **B En Em H M S S S** How we discover and create common ground ....

( ) **B En Em H M S S S** How we manage our diversity of inner realities................

( ) **B En Em H M S S S** How we nurture, empower ourselves and each other........

( ) **B En Em H M S S S** How we are collaborating and co-creating......................

( ) **B En Em H M S S S** How we are interdependently growing and connecting within ourselves and with each other............................

( ) **B En Em H M S S S** How we are dealing with separations and re-entry, endings and beginnings, death and rebirth... ....

8. Which growth dilemma of your soul and spiritual development has been, significant for you individually and as a couple? Indicate where you have repetitive struggle and investment of energy. Describe.

Money and value...

Sex and love...

Children and creativity..

Parents and in-laws..

Siblings, relatives, friends ....

Job, careers and calling..

Health, illness and wellness..

Overall overcoming and transforming adversities..........................

To recap, the Pathway of Development and Discovery in the couple's journey includes both the background and foreground of the developmental landscape; including the complexities of the following:

- Cultural, familial, social structures that impact belief, guiding mythologies, cultural roles and practices

- Survival functions involved in the life stages of the couple's journey together with their evolving value systems

- Behavioral oscillations within and between the couple regarding processes of their individual life cycles and their couple's life cycle of:

  - Identity: "who am I, who are you, and who are we?"
  - Influence: "can we influence and be influenced?"
  - Intimacy: "how are we intimate: physically, emotionally, mentally, soulfully, and spiritually?"
  - Completion: "How are we finishing, completing or keeping things unfinished?"

- Developmental process skills highlighted at each phase of development of the couple come from observation and reflective sharing on the following questions:

  - "How are we orienting and focusing?"
  - "How are we dealing with our difference, our diversity?"
  - "How are we collaborating, competing and teaming?"
  - "How are we dealing with separations and re-entry? Endings and beginnings, death and rebirth?"

- Growth dilemmas of soul and spiritual development are noticed in the couple's repetitive struggles through life's phases and cycles.

- Individuals and couples can get stuck in any phase or stage of development. Overwhelmed, couples can become entrenched in the crisis evoked in the stage/phase, and may fare better to learn the skills and tasks to become unstuck and grow in their process with support.

- The challenge is: Can they lift themselves above the chaos to see, as if from a helicopter, to begin to appreciate "the landscape of Pathway D" for their heart, soul, and spiritual development through time and space? If so, they can begin to affirm their conscious awareness of their evolving process of their soul and spiritual path. They unfold and allow their sense of wonder to open doors to the discovery and the experience of the radiant presence within themselves, and the embodied image and likeness of Divine Healing Love.

We love coaching those who are called to gain a *'helicopter view'* of their developmental journey and who are opening to evolve into embodying healing love within!

The Evolutionary Process of Development

> *"The purpose of learning is growth, and our minds, unlike our bodies,*
> *can continue growing as we continue to live."*
> *~ Mortimer Adler*

We are always developing. It is the law of human growth - babies become infants and then children. Children grow into adolescents and eventually become adults. As individuals, we are always in the process of development in our life cycle.

Much research has been done about individual development but there is little work examining the *holographic aspect* of the developmental journey of a couple. Once you begin to look at how two people interact, its' profound complexity, and depth of ground in soul and spirit, spans time and space in the life of generations.

It is usual for couples to subjectively perceive and experience their 'trouble' in a phase of development differently. Their mentally embedded automatic replays cast each other as 'players' in their entwined life movie stories. While they are hoping for a positive outcome, their re-playing of prior experiences in their current exchanges, produce the same familiar experience of dissatisfaction. They feel stuck in feelings of anxiety, anger, fear, guilt, shame, sadness, and pain.

As the couple gains an appreciation of the stories that have been passed on through generations and that these stories unconsciously impact their current interactions, the couple gains a present awareness of the roots of their soul pain and yearning. They choose to shift their "inner gears" to behave consciously and differently, other than the automatic reactions of survival they 'inherited'. They opt to choose the Pathway of developing consciousness, BE-coming and BE-ing in the present awareness of wonder through the developmental phases of their journey as a couple. They become open to the unfolding of the Healing Love Presence within themselves and each other.

Four Stages of Development

The Lifespan of a Couple: Your Developmental Journey of Discovery and Transformation

Let us talk first about the developmental journey of a couple. Generally, couples relationships move through four major stages of development with the beginning, the middle, and the end phases. We see these stages and/or phases as more circular, as spirals of evolution rather than linear.

Stage 1: Dependence – Fusion Cycle: 0 - 6ᵗʰ - year cycle

- Beginning Phase: Courtship: Similarities & Complementing Differences
- Middle Phase: Romance vs. Marriage/Partnership & the Inevitable Disillusionment
- Ending Phase: Authenticity vs. Illusion/Disillusion

The romance phase of this dependence – fusion stage involves couples creating relationship foundations where they orient and depend on their couple's relationship as a stable place of love, focusing on their similarities and creating their identity of 'we-ness'. Differences are seen as complementary, tolerated or overlooked, as the couple bonds to complete themselves in each other. They are building the parameters and distinctions of their bond. Their fusion highlights their sense of togetherness as they mutually give and take. They accommodate in making decisions, attend to their connecting and nurturing of positive feelings, and about building a positive foundation from which to continue building their life together.

In these early years, the couple forms their identity as a couple. They begin establishing patterns of depending on each other through the process of jointly setting routine tasks for housekeeping, maintenance, establishing a home, and managing work/life roles, dealing with parents and in-laws, dealing with money, and managing their time together, and choosing when or whether or not to have children. Whether conscious or not, their ways of relating are impacted by their individual levels of development and how their couple's development is influenced by external factors.

The challenge in this Dependence and Fusion cycle of development and its beginning, middle and end phases, involves the interplay of each of their own life's journey and development. Couples make a shift into their conscious partnership with awareness and owning the fantasies or projections placed on each other, and of expectations of their relationship such as: 'fixing' their life, 'making them happy', being 'the perfect partner', 'fulfilling their husband or wife roles', 'bringing security', and 'knowing what I want without my telling it', etc.

Moving Through the Disillusionment Phase

The inevitable disillusionment happens as the 'realities' of their life set in and the romantic phase fades into the 'unspoken' expectations of their relationship. Although this can occur anywhere after the marriage, this phase of their developmental journey is seen more in the second to the sixth year. The couple begins to discover their illusions of each other, and notice that their disappointments, annoyances, and irritations are surfacing more. This is the *disillusionment* middle phase.

The couple is challenged in this phase to face their disappointments and expectations of themselves and each other as well as their disillusionments about what they expected their marriage to fulfill. They are faced with understanding who they are as individuals and who their partner really is; as well as recognizing and negotiating their differences. When the couple cannot come to terms with their disillusionment and face the reality of themselves, they struggle to recapture the feelings of their earlier romance or project blame on them self or the other for their disillusionment. Unable to face their disappointments together, some have disembarked from their couples' journey in search for another romantic relationship, only to find themselves in this same place again a few years later.

It is here, in the middle phase, that the couple notices that the very aspect of the other that was seemingly so attractive in the beginning becomes the very aspect that is challenging and at times irritating to their comfort zones. Confusion and feelings of rejection and hurt come in as the couple confronts their disillusionment. With acknowledgement and ownership of the projections they placed on each other, they face themselves and each other with authenticity.

As couples work through this part of their intimate journey, they find themselves becoming more real with each other. They also learn how to balance meeting each other's needs, their own needs, and their needs as a partnership. We have seen couples who work through this phase of their developmental journey together to experience a resurgence of their feelings in the romantic phase. As they consciously revisit their 'glow' experience, their awareness brings authentic appreciation to the soulful process of their creation.

Stage 2: Independence – Differentiation Cycle(s): 7th to 21st year cycle

- Beginning Phase: Differentiation & Diversity
- Middle Phases: Autonomy vs. Intimacy: Power & Influence
- Ending Phase: Self Identity & Intimacy

Couples moves into this stage in their developmental journey when the need for more autonomy and independence emerges. In the beginning phase of the Independence - Differentiation Cycle, the couples' differences become more pronounced. They have conflict about their differing opinions, perspectives, styles, and ways of doing things. Their polarities play in almost every area of their interaction and particularly where there is unfinished business of earlier relationships being triggered.

Some couples are more overt in their need for differentiation and whereas others are more covert. Either way, there is tension and conflict. Earlier, automatic survival reactions such as fight, flee, freeze, or fawn, emerge and interplay with each other as this stage initiates around the 4th year, and becomes more visible around the 7th year. Unfinished issues can re-emerge around the seven year cycles of the 14th, 21st, 28th, and 35th years.

In this middle phase, couples' are faced with their struggles for power and influence. Issues related to power, control, and influence come into play with conflicts around:

- Keeping things the same versus the need for change
- Determining who influences and controls decisions

- Understanding what are the needs of the individuals versus the needs of the couple
- Determining how they view and value their diverse perspectives and experiences

This Pathway D journey cycles into their Differentiation-Independence phases, as couples struggle to incorporate these processes in their development:

- Managing their areas of similarity or togetherness and areas of differentiation
- Heightening their awareness and *capacity to hold as valid* the diversity of their inner and subjective realities and values
- Resolving unfinished business that impacts their being present
- Empowering the self and each other to influence and be influenced to deepen and grow their self identity and their intimacy
- Re-discovering both old and new parts of themselves

Many couples in this middle phase may find external events triggering mid-life transitions that impact them on a soul purpose level, such as:

- This is my last chance to…..before I get too old, die, etc.
- Are we a couple that can, together, transform our generation's 'karma'?
- Can our relationship sustain the call of my/our soul's destiny?
- How can we strengthen ourselves in the face of impending 'urgencies' to fulfill unmet needs?
- How can we live, enjoy, be in the present, and celebrate the moment?

Often the inner issues above emerge when life events present karmic reminders of how family members' dealt with critical situations, and how their impact, positively or negatively, is felt in the lives of the succeeding generations.

For example, Justin and Lucy discussed their difficulties with trust and fears that affairs 'might be in their genes'. They wondered about how they could have a stable home and family and stay faithful while growing their professional identities. They spoke about the fact that "No one in our families and relatives on either side has marriages that endured". They empathized and resonated in their common sad plight.   While they joke about it, they played the jealousy-mistrust fight, especially when either one advocates for their need for autonomy to pursue furthering their careers, to be their own person, or to have their own friends.   Whether consciously or not, seven years into their marriage, they feel particularly vulnerable, and their radar for the cues that threaten the stability of their home and marriage, have become even more sensitized. By their 14th year of marriage, these issues have come to a prominent force, when Lucy's much awaited huge promotion threatened the continuance of their couple relationship.

Furthermore, as mentioned earlier, members of the couple bring their developmental life issues to their intimate partnership. Justin and Lucy acknowledged their willingness to be in wonder for how the impact of Lucy's career promotion on their marriage can bring their 'trust' baggage to a healing love level. Their couple's journey brought them to uncharted territory in where they explored BEEHMSSS™ skills, tools, and processes through the Pathways A to E of Healing Love as a couple system.

In reflecting together on their parents' styles that led to their affairs, Justin came to appreciate that his parents avoided intimacy by having intense fights of blame and criticism, whether loud or silent, but rarely shared true feelings with each other. Lucy, on the other hand, became clear about how her parents avoided any conflict and left each other with the silent treatment. "I wished sometimes that they would just let it out. Then my father had an affair and my mother never forgave him."

Justin and Lucy chose to commit to develop conscious 'trust-worthy-ness' collaboratively. Through the process of dialogue, they made a BEEHMSSS™ shift of their survival mistrust to a 'well-being trust signal' for attending to their inner child's bidding and to nurture their safety with presence, dialogue, and connection with their Inner Self and each other. They sealed off any survival repetitions of 'leakages', for reactive avoidance of conflict, or reactive avoidance of closeness from their family cultures. Instead they co-created a way to utilize their survival radar as their signal for safety, and a conscious process for attending, nurturing, and developing their healing love marriage. With growing and strengthening their inner safety and the core of their love, they were able to welcome opening the doors to their independence differentiation processes, which brought vitality and richness to their intimacy. They joined in conscious affirmation of their 'couple-ness' and for their practice of 'full' presence of faith to embrace their flourishing selves with Healing Love.

It is also in the Stage 2 Cycles and phases, where couples' diversities and the differences in men and women's developmental journeys bring challenges to the intimate partnership.

Couple's relationships reflect a microcosm of the reiterations of cultural, generational and familial processes of dealing with diversity and how human conflicts around differences are resolved. In western society, divorce has become an easier option for irresolvable conflicts due to differences. Rather than engage in the conscious awakening of their soulful spirit to their embedded cultural and familial scripts, assumptions and beliefs that underlie the conflicts in dealing with differences, couples may prefer to stay in unawareness and engage in the survival mechanisms that emerge in a couple's relationship.

We acknowledge that in certain circumstances it may be the best choice. However, with many couples worldwide, we see the impact of such decisions in the pain of unfinished business that is passed on from generation upon generation in families and communities. In these current times, more people are searching to fulfill their secret yearnings for Divine Healing Love.

We have observed that generally couples 'marry' an average of three times; whether that is with the same partner/spouse or with different partners. Their marriage reflects their developmental phases in the stages of their lives. To illustrate further:

In the beginning or romantic stage and phases, women marry first so they can nurture and create a family. In the middle phase of the couple's relationship, women negotiate for more autonomy whether for personal development, exploration, and self-discovery, particularly if they married too early in their life. If they divorce, their second marriage may be to a desired sexual and emotionally intimate partner. If they stay married, they negotiate for greater movement between differentiation and intimacy, balancing for self-nurturing versus being available to take care of others. In the later years of the couple's relationship, women move into cycles of this later stage and phases seeing their marriage as one of companionship.

Men generally marry in the beginning or romantic phase for the stability of sex and to establish their autonomy with the support of their marriage for success in their jobs or careers. In the middle phases and as critical incidents occur, their awareness as to what is their purpose for life is heightened and they move to stay in their marriages with a changing focus for family and nurturing. If they divorce, we have found them to be marrying the second time for family; often being nurturing to their second wife's family or having children and becoming more involved. As men progress to the later stage and phases of their marriage, both husband and wife renegotiate to become intimate companions with greater acceptance of each other. If they divorce or experience a loss of their wife, their next marriage or partnership in this phase of their life is one of companionship.

> *"Over time, we have realized that change is inevitable and there is no such thing as security. We have learned that our security is not dependent on the responses and choices of another person. And that money is not our source of security. Our foundation is based on choosing to focus on our growth and development. When we made this decision, we became more flexible and could deal more fluidly with the changes that happened. We learned to see them as a part of our human journey and as an opportunity to know more of ourselves."*
> ~ A Couple's Journey in Pathway D

Stage 3: Mutuality - Interdependence Cycles: 22st- 28th; 29th- 35th; 36th- 42nd year cycle(s)

- **Beginning Phase**: Recognition, Co-creative Authentic Identity & Connections
- **Middle Phase**: Collaborative Contributions
- **Ending Phase**: Integrative Intimacy

Interdependency comes into the couples' development as they have increasing ease in their appreciations and understanding of changes. Their struggles in the earlier stage have transformed into recognition and acceptance of themselves and each other. Having had many reiterations of earlier cycles and seeing their transformations individually and together, they realized their interdependence. What used to be a struggle has shifted to a found co-creative authentic couples' identity, which includes their strengths and imperfections. Those who have succeeded to this stage in their development connect around their collaborative contributions to the world, their community, and their family, with a sense of common purpose. Integrating their many levels of being, their intimacy has deepened. They feel connections from the mundane routines of daily living, to inner and soulful dialogues, to community activities, to moments of silence, and presence. Couples who vibrate in this stage of Interdependence make amazing contributions to a better world.

In this stage, couples' can evoke their creative juices as these phases ignite excitement to rediscover each other anew.

We know of a couple, Ann and Jack, who in their later years, came in to talk about preparing for their 'fabulous' retirement, while they still could, to have no regrets about their life, personally and together, as they grow older. They had secret wishes that they wanted to fulfill but did not want to hurt each other with their revelations. They were a much too caring couple and wanted to be more daring in their lives. Their imaginations were 'titillating' them with giddy nervous laughter, like two teens. The laughter was infectious and they wanted a referee, because they were taking a risk in sharing their secrets for wanting to be able to live a joyous life. They felt passionate together about going out on a limb, now, no matter what and without 'hurting' any of their loved ones. In taking the risk in a safe way, they wanted a discerning dialogue, to really discover each other again, and remembered how they were a "daring" couple who have become 'good and ideal' models in their families, and they wanted to look at the other side of the 'road not taken'. You can imagine how much laughter they generated when they released their fantasies to and with each other. They found themselves joining in a common goal of 'daring' to live joyously.

On the serious side, they explored what could be road blocks such as financial issues. "Do we have enough money to enjoy daring to live joyously in retirement?" They explored their feelings around having their children all grown and on their own, their perspectives on being back with each other after 28 years for longer periods of time together, and their desire to take charge of their own health issues, and to enjoy their interdependence. Ann and Jack's discerning approach to "daring to live joyously" exudes their deepened and "tested by life" real love. They affirmed the trust that they earned, as their shared story of their long relationship journey of *becoming all the possibilities of themselves as possible as can be...and how, NOW, they can* truly appreciate the part they each played from a core and centered place within themselves.

Stage 4: Termination (can happen in Stage 1, 2, or 3**) or**
       Resolution Cycle(s): 36th – 50th year cycle; 50th + 7 year cycles

- **Beginning Phase**: Life – Relationships Review – Forgiving and Healing

- **Middle Phase**: Making the Best of Life, Legacy & Passing Forward, Deepening Acceptance & Respect
- **Ending Phase**: Endings, Completion(s) & Death

If we were to look at the progression of their long-term relationship, the Resolution Cycle(s) of the couples' journey generally occurs in the later years of their life. It is possible that the resolution cycle can occur sooner for some couples, particularly at the onset of terminal illness, where the couple is facing their ending through the death of their partner.

The beginning phase, the couple's sharing involves precious moments of recalling and reviewing their life journey together. Moments of sharing are filled with emotions, pregnant silences, cherished memories, and caring conversations about their transition through impending loss of each other. Forgiving and healing their hearts is their "soul's spiritual" process. As they move into the middle phase, the couple makes the best of the life they have left together, perhaps doing what they had put off and having the conversations they held back. Their hearts are eased with expressions of tender Gratitude, sorrow for life's misgivings and hurts, forgiveness, and release to the Source. Insights of the role they each had in their soul journey together bring their Love to a transcending level of accepting and respectful Love.

Since then, Ann and Jack, returned many years later to help at their resolution cycle because Jack was dying of pancreatic cancer, which he had battled for the last year and felt he was near the end with just a few months to live. This time they wanted to honor their relationship journey and prepare together for: "Jack's going ahead of me to eternity. He says that I must be strong and go on. I know I will, but I find that I cannot stop weeping, every time", Ann tearfully spoke. Jack, holding his wife's hand, said "I am grateful that we had those many years of enjoying our lives, fulfilling our "bucket lists", and living those meaningful and rewarding later years. My life has gone full circle and I would not have been able to do it all without Ann. My heart is full and I have no regrets except that I will be leaving without her. (Now bursting into laughter) God knows how I really do not enjoy travelling alone! So, yes, I am afraid but need to have courage. And to you both (Drs. Phil and Lalei), I hope you continue with my family, because you have been a blessing to me and my wife. I hope I am leaving a legacy to my children of the Power of Love. I am putting my affairs in order not only on this earth, but also with God...that is why we are here."

We felt profoundly touched by Ann and Jack's relationship journey to the ending phase of their resolution cycle and of the full circle of their Healing Love journey of their relationship.

Couples can also go through the resolution cycle of evolving their Healing Love transformation, even after the termination of their relationship through divorce. Such was a situation of Marty and Noreen, who after years of working separately in their Independence-Differentiation cycle that ultimately ended in divorce, decided to come together and meet initially to deal with their son's issues at college. Their meeting went so well, with both of them recognizing how they each had changed and grown. They decided to schedule another session for themselves to have their dialogue in a safe environment with a focus on resolution and closure. They expressed appreciation for their difficult but collaborative divorce, and how they consciously co-parented in a respectful way of each other. They did in divorce, their differentiation, what they could not do being married. They expressed Gratitude to having a son, who with his presence in their lives helped them grow. They recognized what each of them contributed, and to see him now in college doing well and pray that they will continue to be part of their son's life, now in an extended way. They acknowledged the chapter in their lives of their "trial and error" relationship in those previous unconscious years. They regretted the hurt that they each have caused the other and the trauma that it may have given their son. They made amends and forgave themselves and each other. Both expressed acceptance of moving on with their new spouses, with whom they promised to do better, and hope that they could build an extended family system for their son.

Their resolution cycle was an evolutionary gift to themselves and to each other. They felt in the years to come, the positive impact of the resolution in their lives, and in their current marriage relationship.

We also witnessed Phil's parents' resolution cycle. This gave us an embodied experience of their soulful journey as a couple and the gift of presence to their deep love at the ending of their lives.

There are times when the resolution cycle cannot happen and is left unfinished particularly in relationship journeys that end, albeit suddenly, in pain and trauma. Members of that relationship find themselves having to work through the cycles of resolution on their own, within themselves and with other supports. Many times, the unfinished business has new partners with faces of earlier relationships with whom attempts of resolution are being made. We thank those conscious partnerships who are willing to step into the place vacated in our hearts, to be partners in the evolving process of Healing Love.

> "In learning to know other things, and other minds, we become more
> intimately acquainted with ourselves, and are to ourselves better worth
> knowing."
> ~Philip Gilbert Hamilton

Consider the impact of different members at different stages of relationship development: because individual members of a couple are frequently at different stages of development, couples find that when they gain awareness of their individual relationship development cycles, they are challenged to learn how to honor their processes in their differing levels of development. This is particularly difficult since frequently there is unfinished business from previous relationships.

Evolution of Development

Life is not as simple as it used to be, when we could follow the prescribed traditional male-female roles. In those times, it was rare to have conscious individuals following their intuitive guidance to evolve in meaningful relationships. They simply lived with the pre-defined roles and procedures of conduct in relating.

Our lives are changing rapidly. Many people feel called to have more meaningful lives. They are not willing to stay with the status quo and struggle. Nowadays more couples want to fulfill their soul's deepest longings for intimacy, balanced with empowerment and wisdom. This is a new form of consciousness that is so compelling, that is driving us to evolve and go beyond traditional and cultural models and roles... to go beyond our fixed ways and judgments that separate us for survival. As couples are growing in awareness, they are learning to differentiate between their survival brain that is geared to meet their survival and safety needs and their evolutionary mind that is shifting in paradigm to see with evolutionary eyes, that their struggling is an opening to what can unfold for them.

Research studies on the brain show the role of the *'amygdala'* or reptilian brain for automatic, survival responses. So in relationships, people are governed by "standards and belief systems" that reinforce the preservation of survival and safety in their unconscious relationships. While western medicine provides prescriptive medications to manage intense emotions and reactions to survival and safety issues, such as anger/rage, anxiety, guilt, grief, and depression. Conscious, holistic, transforming, alternative, complementary, collaborative, integrative and evolving paradigms and modalities offer couples options beyond survival and safety needs. With more options, couples have greater possibilities to co-create their shifting paradigms for growing and thriving in their love.

As healing partners, couples intentionally co-create their container of safety and survival to ease their 'amygdala' reactivity and support each other to have the resources to enhance their inner safety and strength, and thrive beyond, to experience the depth and breadth of their emotional, physical, mental and spiritual growth and development, as part of their soul journey of evolution.

We notice that when partners show a willingness to discover and appreciate how these differing phases influence their couples' journey, they open themselves to explore ways to navigate the terrain of these developmental stages. Thus, they are less likely to consider divorce as their only solution to difference and conflict, particularly in Stage 2, where safety and survival issues are triggered and when needs for differentiation, independence, autonomy, empowerment, and influence come into intense focus.

With a paradigm shift for Pathway D, critical external events and their critical internal changes become seen as the calling of their spirit for development and discovery of Divine Love.

Couples' relationships are challenged to separate from long held beliefs about oneself and the significant other and to move toward Truth and Divine Love with propelling force. Internally, the compelling feeling is NOW. The time to fulfill a long held desire has no more time for waiting. This shake up in the couples' journey can turn their world upside down and if upside down, the miracle side is up.

Do you now see how complex Pathway D, the Pathway of Development and Discovery, can be? That is why having a perspective of the different stages and phases, as cycles of interconnecting layers rather than as linear stages lets us appreciate how the couple's journey is truly an evolutionary soulful journey.

> *"A calling is asking you to separate from something. The deeper the crisis,*
> *the clearer the choice. Immediate participants in the life of the calling often pay the*
> *price of the calling, such as spouses, children, family and friends...often the demands*
> *of the calling ruthlessly wreak havoc on the decencies of a well-lived life."*
> *~James Hillman, The Soul's Code*

<u>**Process Question**</u>: **Are You Willing to Discover and Develop Your Couple's Dance Between Sameness and Change?**

Have you noticed that most people are scared to change and will do all kinds of things to resist it? Some of the biggest challenges that arise for couples are when partners resist change and also resist sameness. How is this a challenge for your relationship?

> - Change is the only sameness there is.
> - Sameness is the only change there is.
> - Sameness and change happens to us all --- whether we like it or not.

In couples, one partner upholds the want for sameness, consistency, routine and to maintain some sense of order and resist whatever seems to be a change. This gives them a sense that there is some structure, a foundation – something they can count on. The other partner wants variation, change, movement forward. This gives them a sense of accomplishment, growth and purpose.

When you are in the Pathway of Development, there is a *constant dance* between change and routine. In this day and age, *our primary stability is to understand and having the inner ability to move with the change that is occurring.* When we know how to manage change, allowing ourselves to grow and develop, we can make new, conscious choices and shift our old, habitual patterns. We begin to discover ourselves and develop new parts of ourselves through the dance of stability and change.

"Change and growth take place when a person has risked himself and dares to become involved with experimenting with his own life."
~Herbert Otto

Process Awareness of Negotiating the Dance of Stability and Change: Heighten your couple's awareness on what behaviors you are observing that supports your dance of stability and change. Share your observations.

When challenges occur, any stability that a couple may have is challenged. It is helpful during these times if at least one of the partners can see that they have stability as a couple. This creates a sense of togetherness in managing the change. When couples can do this, they seem to be able to weather the changes and challenges of life.

We had the opportunity to work with an amazing couple that learned how to weather the storms of life. The husband lost his job and began to deeply feel the crisis involved in this change. His wife provided a place of stability for them, by encouraging her husband to deeply examine his life and choices. Over time he began to feel that losing his job was actually a blessing. When he was busy being a provider, he did not have the time to examine what he wanted. In this 'container of support', he chose to return to school and there he discovered what he loved to do and changed careers. For many couples, this level of crisis has led to the demise of the relationship. Instead, he discovered and developed new parts of himself. As a couple, they supported this change.

Process of Evolutionary Development of Healing Couples: Share your observations of evolutionary behaviors you and your partner are doing to evolve. Notice how you feel to affirm your evolutionary behaviors.

There is a new kind of couple relationship that we are seeing. These couples, who we would call as Healing Partners, are proactive about enhancing and enriching their relationship. They view their challenges as opportunities for them to grow. They desire deep intimacy. They want to develop their emotional intelligence, understand and appreciate their differences, communicate deeply to increase their intimacy, gain insight and enlightenment as to their soul purposes for their relationship. These couples read and research accessing tools for enlightenment and awareness and are able to take responsibility for their choices. They have the ability for self-awareness and can reflect as a way of stepping back and regrouping to learn from their experiences. They have learned to listen within and are interested in each other's subjective experiences. They value that when one feels something is missing and want to explore it deeply from a mind body spirit perspective. They allocate resources making their growth and development a priority. They have a sense of humor and are able to laugh at themselves. When they know they need balance, they can go into an inner space to quiet themselves, breathe to connect with an inner sensate sense of knowing and self-reflection. They are able to see themselves as a system comprised of them together, and of themselves individually, and can appreciate the tasks and complexity of both, as they consider their needs and their action. They seek consulting and coaching to get unstuck, grow, and transform themselves. They welcome feedback, attend to developing their art of giving and receiving, and make room for their collaborative choices.

Their willingness to learn the skills of relating and be a THOU to themselves and each other is such a heartwarming experience that we know we are moving to a whole new level of consciousness, enlightenment, and feel. We are touched with Gratitude and appreciation to see these individuals and couples and love that we can support them in their community to co-create our world of Healing Love. Their growth and transformation impacts their families, their neighborhood, and their communities. They become transformers of karma by their decisions to change themselves.

Some of them have referred their parents and siblings for couples work and have participated in family sessions. They are talking about spirituality and are open and interested in learning. They have a remarkable ability to view issues from a variety of viewpoints. Their stability and security are not rigid - they are able to shift and view the change as an opportunity to develop themselves. The impact on their parents has been positive and vice versa... there is a mutually supportive environment for growth for all involved.

So why do we see them in counseling? They are involved in raising their consciousness not only for their personal development but also to impact change from within. They are evolutionary transformers - taking their current life journeys and challenging society's prescriptions and limits. Examining their beliefs and breaking through past traumas, hurts, illusions, they are reclaiming respect, decency, and the divine in their love.

These couples are willing to go deeper into developing their inner selves. Because of their willingness and ability to change - they heal each other and profoundly impact others. It is astounding what these couples are able to achieve in the midst of crisis. They make conscious and aware choices. Going for a life of meaning, they choose the sameness and the changes, and paradoxically this is what creates a sense of inner stability in their relationship and their life.

Process of How to Create a Container of Safety and Support: Share together how you notice yourselves co-creating your container of safety and support. Notice how you experience your container of safety and support as you affirm.

To assist couples in making a shift or a change, we teach them how to create a container of safety support so they can feel a sense of stability and embrace the change while various circumstances and awareness' unfold.

A couple needs five primary skills to create a container:

1. Building common ground, a foundation, and a container of safety for their diversity as members of their couple relationship together.

2. Learn the skill of positively affirming differences and offering five (5) "positive", concrete observations for each (1) 'negative' observation regarding a difficult difference. (We call this the 5 to 1.)

3. Slowing down, listening, and observing their own reactions so they can really connect with each other.

4. Checking assumptions and perceptions by asking questions of wonder with your partner and not jumping to conclusions or offering solutions without permission.

5. Maintaining an attitude of honor and respect, fostering a 'field' environment for growing, and deepening our development and discovery of Healing Love within.

The Developmental Journey of the Couples' Soul

Often couples come to us who are experiencing anxiety, restlessness, and depression. Instead of looking at what is wrong with them by examining traditional family dynamics, we help them look at what is at the heart of their anxiety or depression, to wonder how the dissatisfaction can guide them to discover what they really want. We encourage couples to breathe and listen within, and go inward together – to meditate together and to pray together. We ask them to return to what drew them together and to <u>why they fell in love.</u>

When we are feeling attached to old paradigms and traditional roles, we may feel this restless, uncomfortable inner battle about following the call of our soul self and seek what we really are and want to do. When the inner battle is externalized in their couples' relationship, their discomfort is developmentally the call of their soul-being to evolve from doing the same thing over and over again. This is the new level of consciousness that we are seeing in people everywhere. This new level of consciousness is asking us to stretch our notions and ideas of love; asking us to go into the space of healing universal love.

It is in our intimate relationship that we are *stretched,* in the multidimensionality of love. Can you go beyond what you've been taught or what feels familiar? Can you acknowledge what beliefs you have that are holding you back?

Often we give up love or happiness to do the 'right thing,' which is different for different people. For example, when husbands and wives lose connection to their inner self when they give up or give in for each other 'all the time', they end up resentful, bitter, angry and ultimately divorced. For example, Linda could not contain her anger, not only to her husband, but more so to herself, for how she had suppressed her desire to follow her singing career. She felt her anger overshadowed any other emotion. She became even more enraged at her husband's Gratitude for her being his soul mate and amazing wife, feeling that she had betrayed herself at being a fake to be loved and appreciated. Her husband could not understand why she was pushing for a divorce as the solution so that she could follow a singing career.

To ease into meeting the challenge is to *allow love from a heart-centered place of alignment with the flow of Divine Love to oneself*. The easy access is **here and now**, in breathing. It is our **Breath** of life and spirit. Pause for a moment and bring your awareness to your breathing.

Jim felt even more powerless over his wife's intense anger and firm decision to divorce. Linda packed up her things to audition in the next state. Jim blamed himself for holding Linda back from her singing career and decided to slow down his reactions for the future. "Breathing is what is saving me from drowning." Jim further went on to say: "I go to the recreation center daily and swim. My work as a graphic artist has consumed me. In between, I do breathing meditation exercises. I joined a Chi Kung meditation class and I am really slowing myself within. My friends are getting me to go out with other women. But I cannot do that. I love Linda so deeply. I think it is my time to give to her the way she has given to me. It is OK for me to sacrifice a bit I tell them...perhaps even though there is the possibility that she is too angry to even come back." Jim continued with his personal counseling and felt this 'inner sensation of reassurance and trust'. Jim asked his meditation group to help his heart be at peace and aligned with the flow of Divine Love to himself and to his wife. It was six months later that Jim received notice of Linda's return. He felt fear for her and him. Did she give up her singing? Or is she coming to tell me it is definitely over? His thoughts were running through him...then he called for a session to prepare himself to stay aligned in the heart-centered place of Divine Love and Truth, no matter what the outcome is of Linda's return.

We were surprised to see both Linda and Jim walk in for Jim's scheduled appointment. Linda expressed her appreciation for herself, in that she took her biggest step which was to face her fear that she was any good at singing. And, she found that she is. She wanted to affirm herself, boldly to Jim. She is definitely following her call and pursuing a singing career. She was accepted and the demands for the production are great. She knows she must do this. She also was appreciative that Jim did not 'crowd' her and that she really had the space to think. She knew it was very difficult because it is not like her to be so focused on herself and behave in an 'uncaring' way towards Jim. "I did not think that Jim would even last with me. Maybe we have a chance. For me to be in our marriage, I now know that I MUST sing...not just for you Jim, but for the world."

Jim shared that he picked up a book, by Nancy Zi, about the *Art of Breathing*. "I got involved in Chi-kung while you were gone and came to appreciate that singing for you is like breathing." Linda smiled, her energy picked up in resonance...as she shared that in the program she is in, one of her instructors does Chi Kung to help singers with their singing. Jim affirmed his thought to himself..."perhaps this is really what it means to **discover** heart and soul in our marriage."

117

With the Chi Kung practice, I am learning to *allow love from my heart-centered place to align with the breathing flow of Divine Love.* I know that you are the soul mate that God gave to me. And I know you must sing with your heart and soul because that is God's gift to you. I have hope and faith that we will find our art of breathing and singing." Both Jim and Linda paused, their eyes connecting. Jim extended his hand and Linda met his with her hand, "Thank you Jim".

The following is a Reflection Process Exercise on Your Soulful Journey. Please give yourself time to do it first alone then share it with each other. It may spark your further self-discovery in your soulful development.

Processes Exercise - Your Soulful Journey

Introduction to Exercise: Our developmental processes and shifts are embedded in the unconscious and collective consciousness of the <u>Field – Ground of the All</u> comprising of:

- Sequences and patterns that repeat over historical and generational time
- Planetary Time: beginnings, middle, and endings, as well as Solar and Lunar calendars
- Belief Systems: family/group, culture, religions, etc.
- Developmental stages, phases, and cycles of life
- Evolutions of global and universal shifts

The interplay of the above as the "ground and field" of our own developmental processes provide a colorful complexity in our own spiritual and transformational journey. This makes the uniqueness and commonality of our human experience as Spiritual Beings.

While there are many different ways by which to organize and make meaning of your soul's spiritual developmental journey, we invite you to come up with your own way by which to illustrate (Mandela, graphs, spirals, etc.) your own journey.

We shall give brief examples to make concrete the processes of spiritual development utilizing the Ground Sequence model (Belzunce/Gutierrez 1992), with symbols for Body, Energy, Emotion, Heart, Mind, Soul/Shadow, System, and Spirit (BEEHMSSS™).

You may play your own music and bring yourself to a space of quiet reflection. You will need a large flip chart, and crayons or magic markers. You will begin by making a large box for Area 1. Write your reflections in each Area (box) starting at the bottom of the page and moving upward (by putting a large box for Area 2 on top of Area 1, another large box on top of Area 2 as Area 3 and so on). See Area / Box example on next page.

You may reflect on the quotes in each area to assist you in surfacing your feelings, thoughts, and beliefs.

Feel free to do this exercise individually and as a couple.

Area / Box Example
On Large Sheet of Paper or on a Flip Chart

Area #7
Area #6
Area #5
Area #4
Area #3
Area #2
Area #1

Area #1: The Ground of My Beginning

"No one begins life as a conscious "individual" with conscious will power.
We all begin as part of a culture, connected with "tribal consciousness and
Collective will power by absorbing its strengths, weakness, beliefs,
Superstitions and fears…share a moral ethical code handed down from
Generation to generation and codes of behavior, which guide children
Through their developmental years, providing a sense
of belonging and dignity."
~Caroline Myss

- **Think of the culture, society, religion, and community wherein you were born and raised.**

- **List what beliefs, practices were emphasized and how they impacted you.**

- **Write or draw your reflections in Area #1 at the <u>bottom</u> of your chart.**

Area #1: The Ground of My Beginning

Area #2: Power and Influence of My Relationships

> *"The sacred truth inherent here is How we Honor One Another… and all forms of life…from most causal to most intimate. In becoming consciously aware (polarities, dualities, energetic patterns) we see our relationships as spiritual messengers of self-revelation."*
> *~Author Unknown*

- **Who were the significant relationships in your early environment?**

- **How did these significant relationships influence and impact you?**

- **Write or draw your reflections in Area #2. (box <u>above</u> area box #1)**

Area #2: Power and Influence of My Relationships

Area #3: My First Awakening: Trauma of Loss of Safety, Control, and Disillusionment

"How can this happen! This is a dream!
"This is not supposed to be happening to me, to us, to my family!"

- **What was the significant event(s)?**
- **Write the event as you remember it now**
- **Draw/illustrate the trauma, loss and disillusionment**
- **Write or draw your reflections in Area #3. (box <u>above</u> area box #2)**

Area #3: My First Awakening: Trauma of Loss of Safety, Control, and Disillusionment

---

Area #4: My Power of UnConscious Choice…or My Reaction

"The choices made contain the energy either of faith or fear,
And the outcome of every decision reflects that faith or fear."
~Phil Belzunce

- How did you react to the trauma, loss or disillusionment?

- What Body (B) mode (physical activity or actions, habits) did you use to cope?

- What Energy (En) mode did you use to cope (fight, flight, freeze, fawn)?

- What Emotional (Em) mode did you use to cope (anxiety, anger, withdrawal, depression etc)?

- What Heart (H) mode did you use to cope (singing, listening to music, poetry, communing with nature, having a pet, helping others)?

- What Mind (M) mode did you use to cope (writing, reading, talking, thinking, studying)?

- What Soul (S) mode did you use to cope (confession, seeking a counselor or therapist)?

- What System (S) mode did you use to cope (hanging out with friends, drinking in bad company, joining a support group)?

- What Spiritual (S) mode did you use to cope (reading the bible, praying, meditating, gong on a retreat)?

- What supports were there or not there for your choice or reaction?

- How did your "choices" help you survive then?

- Write or draw your reflections in Area #4. (box <u>above</u> area box #3)

Area #4: My Power of UnConscious Choice…or My Reaction

Area #5: The YEARNING of Your Soul

"The yearning of one's soul is born out of unmet needs.
The yearning goes into hiding if threatened.
The yearning's power waits for its moment, yet
Kept alive creatively with many masks
To protect Yearning's vulnerability
And searching, seeking for that special place....
the Divine."
~Lalei Gutierrez

What is the YEARNING of your Soul?

How, where, with whom and what were the journeys that your Yearning took you through? Journal or Draw.

- **Relationships (marriage) and friends**
- **Education**
- **Career and Job**
- **Home, community and locations to live**
- **Write or draw your reflections in Area #5. (box <u>above</u> area box #4)**

Area #5: The YEARNING of Your Soul

Area #6: The Calling(s) To Consciousness

"A calling is asking you to separate from something
The deeper the crisis, the clearer the choice.
Immediate participants such as spouses, children, family and friends
in the life of the calling often pay the price of the calling,
Often the demands of the calling, ruthlessly wreak havoc on the
decencies of a well-lived life."
~James Hillman, The Soul's Code

What were your wake-up calls?

- **Physical wake-up call – an illness or accident?**

- **Emotional wake-up call - loss of relationship?**

- **Mind-Intuitive wake-up call - did you have an experience of truth, vision, or insight?**

- **Soul wake-up call – did you have a dark night of the soul experience?**

- **Spiritual wake-up call – did you experience grace, healing or a sense of purpose?**

- **Write or draw your reflections in Area #6. (box <u>above</u> area box #5)**

Area #6: The Calling(s) To Consciousness

Area #7: ANOTHER CALLING: Doorway into the Realm of the Non-Rational, Energetic or Spiritual

This calling may be without words. That is OK. Let yourself journal or draw what emerges as you wait in your place of Silence.

- How did your Calling transpire?

- What is awakening within you?

- What are you called to let go of? (ego, yearning, perfection etc.)

- Write or draw your reflections in Area #7. (box <u>above</u> area box #6)

Area #7: Another Calling: Doorway into the Realm of the Non-Rational, Energetic or Spiritual

Practice and Processes in Development and Dialogue

Couples want to know how to communicate more effectively. Dialogue is different from debating and discussing. Dialogue is a mutually reciprocal, special kind of conversation that is relational in the exchange of perspectives, feelings, and experiences. Once you learn the skills of dialoguing from this section, you can dialogue about the previous processes that you completed as individuals by coming together as a couple and dialogue about what you realized or experienced.

Practice "I-Thou" Dialogue

"What is common to every person is lived speech-with-meaning, through which we become human with other humans by building with others, a common world of "speech with meaning." 'The life of dialogue' is the ever-renewing presence of the continuous interplay between two primal 'attitudes' or 'ways of speaking' – 'I-It' and 'I-Thou', with all that they involve. They are complementary opposites in continuous interchange with one another. In 'I-It' relations, the other (whether a person, text, nature, or spirit) is objectified and reduced to the content of the observer's own experience. In 'I-Thou' relationships, the other (spouse, family, friend, stranger) is invited to meet me where I stand, in open, mutual reciprocity."

"While our lives in the world benefit in practical ways because of 'I-It relations, developing personal and unique wholeness requires 'I-Thou relationships. 'I-Thou' interactions are direct, open moments of mutual presence between persons and are necessary for become whole human beings, in the timeless space of inter-human in-between-ness."
~Kenneth Paul Kramer, Martin Buber's I and Thou: Practicing Living Dialogue

Seeing a couple in a heart-felt dialogue is a moving experience. The magnetic radiance of their presence with each other includes, confirms, and affirms their Being, their Soul, and their Spirit. Their dialogical connection is open to the unfolding of grace in the Present moment. So how does this happen between couples? And why is the dialogical process a valuable practice in a couple's transformational journey through the Pathways of Development and Discovery?

The way we see it, is that in our yearning for that loving connection with the Divine within ourselves and with a significant other, we partner up with the beautiful, the true and the good in each other and we bring our beautiful, our true and our good to this loving connection. In a perfect present moment, we can feel the Divine connection of our higher selves and we call it our Perfect Love. It is as Martin Buber refers to "the timeless space of inter-human in-between-ness". In that glimpse of the pregnant moment of our wholeness, our human imperfections meld in the light and love of our divine and projected higher selves.

The truth of the matter is that we carry our hidden and blind selves, our lower selves, our hurt and injured selves along as well. We carry our *'luggage'* of unconscious and packaged beliefs, biases and prejudices couched as standards for living and rewarded as survival skills in a material, objective, and 'I-It' world. We invest our energy and our identity with our beliefs and get into debated discussions with each other in order to convince and influence the other in whichever which way for the other to see, do, be, and believe in our way.

And there is our shadow self, which is the denied or disowned parts of ourselves that follows us in the background, often unconscious to ourselves and the other. And interwoven in all that, is our culture, our lineage, and our history that is always present in the background and which frames our worldview, life experiences, and the meaning of our exchanges with people and things. In this objective world, fear and anger are the emotions that make sure we survive, overcome and thrive. In an 'I-It' world, fear and anger protects these parts of ourselves from being seen, lest we feel ashamed, unworthy, judged, criticized, and vulnerable.

In general, couples utilize 'I-It' communications of many forms as necessary communications based on an attitude in an objectified world that requires practical solutions to day-to-day living, problems, and challenges. Couples relate to each other as resources by which to get needs met, goals accomplished, and things done.

And, it is with a significant other, our partner, our spouse, a treasured loved one, where we can feel safe enough to unpack our luggage. In fact, we tend to assume that our significant other will stand under with us to understand and help or assist in carrying or in moving the weight of our luggage. With safety and trust co-created, there is a process for unpacking individually and together which we call, dialogue.

Dialogue is an inner commitment to an inner discipline that involves inner practice of the inner interactive experience with a significant *human* other. As an inner and interactive discipline and practice in their partnership, couples who are able to share their present and conscious phenomenological awareness of their experience of Self with the Other, with authenticity and responsibility, experience their way of contact with each other as:

- straightforward
- caring
- warmth
- responsiveness
- attending
- wonderment
- empathic
- clean
- without hidden agendas of control or manipulation

Their relationship with each other as well as with themselves grows and deepens. The Presence of Spirit becomes palpable and felt in their Love.

Many individuals seek this way of human exchange in order to come to a place of feeling "whole" in their journey in the Pathway of Development. We facilitate couples who want to learn the healing interactive practice discipline of dialogue with each other.

For couples to practice the discipline of dialogue together, the **process** involves:

- Attending to *include each other with empathy* by
  - putting oneself in the experience of the other
  - withholding quick fixes, judgments, and analysis
- Being an attending embodied presence to themselves and each other, with a willingness to know, witness and share how one is presently affected
- Being open to trusting the in-between process where they connect as to what arises from their interaction
  - participating in co-creating and allowing
- Committing to dialogue and having a willingness to on-going dialogue
  - co-creating a container for Spirit to be in the center of commitment that risks can be taken

Below is an example of a couple facing their inner crisis that opened them to attend and develop their emotional connection to themselves and each other.

Matt and Pam, a dual-career couple in their early mid-40's, both value their independence and self-sufficiency. They felt pride over their accomplishments and how they are a well-functioning 'organization'. And yet they came because they felt an inner void, an emptiness, which they could not quite understand. They were wondering about their feelings of unhappiness when there was really nothing to complain about each other. In fact they expressed their appreciations for each other being just perfect, a wonderful partnership, that has been the 'envy' of many of their friends and colleagues.

As we listened to them we heard flatness in their voices, as they expressed that they are able to work out all their disagreements and rarely have unproductive fights. They keep emotions in check specially if there is nothing that can be done about it. Both being logical, they deal with situations reasonably and look at the facts, which have helped them get through life well. They pride themselves with having an efficient household where their teens are pretty responsible for teens. Their children work well with the reward system, are self-motivated, and are really good kids. They talked about how they are goal oriented and accomplish pretty much what they put their minds to. They express confidence that they could do anything they want with the resources they have. They referred to their roles in the community and their standing in society, as to how they have as a couple, and as a family have done so much good for others.

While they continued talking, we noticed how they gave each other space and took turns talking. They did not look into each other's eyes but spoke to us about each other and themselves.

When asked what they wanted, they matter-of-factly said, that they want to determine whether they should stay together, since their emptiness and feelings of loneliness is more than they could handle. They can act and be a 'wonderful' couple to others, but they are unhappy, empty and lonely. There is a discrepancy between how they are perceived by others and their own inner experience. It would be ironic if on their 20th anniversary year they would be ending their marriage. The issue came to a head when Pam returned from a spiritual retreat where she faced the loneliness she felt and the unhappiness that she thinks her husband has but they were both avoiding. Besides where do you begin to talk about your feelings? Their priest referred them to come and see us.

What stood out to us about this couple, Matt and Pam, is they would be a couple that are so well respected and so loved by others. They focused outside of themselves to others and looked to each other to carry their own load. They were great problem solvers and fixers for others and they admired this quality in each other.

In the next session, when they sat facing us, we asked them whether they would be willing to sit facing each other and just notice in the present moment what it is to breathe within and experience what is present with them to be face to face. Matt stated that this reminds him of being in board meetings but awkward since there is no table between them. He is remembering when he proposed holding his wife's hand and "I know we make a good team, so how about getting married?" Pam became misty eyed and shares how she is struck at how they have grown so much older as she is face to face with Matt right now and seeing the features in his face and in his eyes, and in which she had fallen in love with years ago. They turned away and said, "We have not done this in a long time...now it feels really awkward."

Encouraged to stay with each other and continue sharing what their experience is in the moment of being in each other's presence, they spontaneously shared their memories, their thoughts, and their concerns, taking turns as they spoke with each other. They shared how feelings were what they put aside and wondered whether they had become so busy being goal oriented in order to avoid uncomfortable feelings. They became almost muted in their exchange when referring to their daughter who had disclosed her sexual orientation to them and which they had not talked about with each other. They just acted with reason to be loving parents and kept their feelings hidden.

Their time in counseling focused on facilitating their interactive process of dialogue, which they as a couple uncovered so much 'richness' in their emotional and inner world, which they did not know, was there. The process of dialogue brought them to be mutually reflective about their inner experience in multi-dimensional levels...where they talked about their feelings and being parents, the up and coming empty nest, their children being so easy and wondering about the difference with other teens, their feelings, thoughts, and worries about their daughter's sexual preference, their shame and self-blame for her choice, their loss of dreams they had for her and possibly the grandchildren they will not have, Pam's family history of cancer and their fears of their future health. They were surprised that their pursuit of 'happiness' through their work in the world left them paradoxically tired, lonely, unhappy, and empty and not having much emotional energy for each other. They were amazed that they lived with their belief and fear of weighing each other down with their emotions. They believed that how they care for each other was by 'not bothering each other' with feelings that cannot be fixed, that if they faced the many emotions, that they would overwhelm themselves with the weight of it.

The grip of loneliness and emptiness felt as an inner crisis for which they could not find any external cause. They went to their priest for spiritual direction as their thoughts of separation and divorce had become prominent. Framing their crisis as a spiritual one in their marriage gave them a handle in seeing their journey taking them to the Pathway of Development and to re-discover their emotional selves.

Matt stated, "Well dear, I will not assume anymore that you are perfectly capable of handling all things. Being mostly reasonable and believing that we each carry our own weight was good. We did ourselves a disservice, but I do not think I know how to be with emotions or what to do about them. I am not sure that 'dialogue' solves anything. But I am sorry that I waited too long for us to learn how to 'dialogue' (turning to us). I ignored all the signs of pain thinking that it will go away. When you said you were going on empty and lonely, you shook my concept of you. I felt responsible for being unhappy and saw no point of bothering you with that. Then, I remembered your family's history of cancer and for the first time I really got concerned...scared to be honest. Last night I prayed so hard hoping that our anniversary will be a new beginning for our life together."

When they came back from their anniversary vacation a few months later, Pam began by sharing how they each proposed to each other in the new phase of their life journey together. They renewed their vows on a promontory overlooking the Pacific Ocean as they visited places of their first honeymoon. This journey evoked their early dreams together and brought back memories of how some of their dreams had to be laid aside in the pursuit of more responsible goals. Much of the time spent had been on dreaming together about their possible future and savoring the present. They are basking on the continuing effects of the joy they had in their anniversary vacation and are concerned how 'reality' is setting in and that that their old ways of busy-ness could take over and their attention to dialogue would go to the background.

Matt talked about Pam's recent medical checkup and the scare they had with regards her biopsy. He was holding back his tears, "This is such a wakeup call for what really matters. So many realizations...our life...and all that we went through. Thinking alone what does all this really mean? Our time to talk puts so much into perspective. This is so new to me. I used to see it as a waste of valuable time. I have been a success in coming up with solutions to almost anything."

"Now, lonely and empty (swallowing), I feel I failed in my marriage. But facing it and talking with Pam…I am so grateful. This health crisis made me realize how important you are to me in my life. Talking together, I am finding us, you and me again."

Pam responded, "I was surprised at how much you were so very present and how you insisted on going with me to the doctors. As usual I would have done it alone so as not to bother you. To tell you the truth, it was hard for me to take in that you would come with me. I figured it is just my body, my family's genetics. I have to take care of it alone. But having you there for me felt so supportive. I did not have to be scared and strong alone."

As Matt and Pam continued with their process of being in dialogue, they began to co-create a present experience of mutual, open, and heartfelt connections. This overwhelmed them. Their discovery was of a new kind. It took them to the inner development of their soulful connection through the dialogue of their heart. With awareness of their over-emphasis on being "human doings", they shifted to attend to Being in the "Here and Now", to be Present with the care and wonder of one another. They experienced their mutual respect in being present to their felt inner experiences. They enlivened their center of Spirit where the Heart and Soul of their relationship is, and realized that in their growing years that emotion (*energy in motion*) is *how* Spirit moves within and between them.

Process for Conscious Practice Tips for Dialogue

- Make an appointment for dialogue on a daily or weekly and monthly basis. Schedule yourselves into your calendar.
- Make it a sacred time with minimal distraction – 15-20 minutes, at the very least, for face to face presence, whether at home together or in a place of nature. When away on a business trip, make a phone or Skype Internet appointment, be embodied in presence.
- Make a conscious intention and decision to dialogue regularly, as dialogue is of great value in the Pathway of Development and Discovery (Having a relationship coach or facilitator when you become stuck).
- Begin by centering and grounding yourselves: breathe, sharing your positive intention.
- Check in with your BEEHMSSS™ temperature of each other and your relationship:
  - "How are you Being at this moment? Today?
  - "How are you feeling right now as you look back to today?
  - "What is great and wonderful? What do you appreciate?
  - "What feelings, sensations and thoughts are present right now?
  - "What has your wonder, curiosity, interest, and puzzle?
  - "What was challenging or difficult today?
  - "What are your highlights of the day?
  - "What insights, awareness or discoveries?
  - "What are you grateful for today?

- When things are difficult between the both of you, keep in mind the positive and keep your dialogued focus on the positive aspects of your relationship while acknowledging what is difficult or challenging. Put yourself in an inclusive and positive frame to understand where the other is coming from, in a detached, caring, open, curious, non-judgmental, and spiritually centered way.
- Dialogue has **no goal** to accomplish. It is a gift to your relationship and to one another without a hidden agenda. Its *purpose* is to co-create mutual embodied presence, empathy for how you both feel, and appreciate the context of your feelings – your subjective inner reality.
- Stay within your present felt sense experience and present intention, even as the past or future may be talked about. Some examples are:

> "Right now, I notice a feeling of tightness in my chest with you. I wonder what you might want to get off your chest. I am here present to listen."

> "I want to tell you how I got upset, so I can let it go and be present to enjoy our time together."

Practice together and individually holding a *both-and* multiple realities perspective and approach versus an either-or one reality perspective and approach.

The general tendency of people is to have a favored perspective, whether that is a belief, an opinion, assumption, purpose or meaning for an issue. It is important to know your own perspective or from what vantage point you are looking at a situation individually.

And be aware that when we are locked into our own way of seeing reality, we close or stand in the way of ourselves for the opportunities of our development and discovery.

Early in our relationship, we discovered that we each had a favored way of organizing our lives as we were looking at the daunting task of creating our home together. We argued about what was aesthetic and what was practical and useful and did not like the choices of the other for ourselves. We got locked into the belief that the other did not care for our comfort, not by their words, but by how they organized their reality, which excluded the other. It was an either-or struggle, each one advocating for their own reality as their way of being is the only 'right' reality.

So this Pathway of Development and Discovery involves**…the practice of the *both-and* perspective which evolves to *both-and-together* for the '*whole-of-us-is-larger-than-the-Sum-of-our-Parts'.***

Process of Conscious Development of Holding Multiple Realities and Working to Harness Our Differences for the Enrichment of the Whole of Us

Join us in this process by first responding to these questions. Then share with your partner. Continue to read to the end of this section and go back to what you have written to see if you want to add or make changes. Continue to dialogue with each other.

- **What is your 'both-and-whole' vision?**

  _____

  _____

  _____

  Phil: "I see our home comfortably practical."
  Lalei: "I see our home comfortably aesthetic and spacious."
  Both of us: "We see ourselves living in a spacious and comfortable home of aesthetic beauty and practicality."

- **Why does it matter?** (purpose or mission)

  _____

  _____

  _____

  Both of us: "It matters that we both feel at home in love, peace, joy, growth, creativity, and prosperity with Spirit at the center of our lives."

- **How are we to co-create our vision and live our mission** in this present situation or in this moment?

  _____

  _____

  _____

- What **strategy** can we experiment with right now? _____

  _____

  _____

- How will we each **contribute** to co-create together? _____

  _____

  _____

You may choose to review with your partner, what you have written for answers to the above questions. Reflect and dialogue about how and where Pathway D is taking each of you both, individually, and as couple. Below are some suggestions to consider.

The "How" involves ways to experiment with holding a _both-and_ perspective. Here are some HOW approaches we took with our vision and mission in mind. We took an experimental and experiential attitude to see what works best in the present moment. With practice these options became easier and available. Together with the practice and process of dialogue, these strategies helped us 'negotiate' the Pathway of Development in our couple's journey of healing love.

1. Accommodation of each other's knowledge, resources, and preferences.
2. Compromise by looking where we can come together, when the either does not work for the other. We find a middle ground that is acceptable to both.
3. Making an appointment for each of our presentations of thoughts and feelings around the topic and a timed discussion in a neutral place to advocate for our position.
4. Taking turns in being in charge of a way of going about doing things and the other being willing to follow the lead of the other, with feedback from the follower's experience of keeping abreast or up with the one leading.
5. Being in the negotiating process until we are in a *grow-grow* place.
6. Staying with valuing of our multiple perspectives and approaches by exploring *one focus at a time* with an attention to the others, and to get together at an agreed later time.
7. Attending to the *Whole is Greater than the Sum of the Parts* by looking for how each part (of us) contributes to the whole (of us) and vice versa.
8. Living with our difference and diversity in its contribution to our individual and couples growth and transformation as a Whole.
9. Practicing tolerance and acceptance of *What Is* with Love and Peace.
10. Be open to the miracle of the evolving In-Between.

Integration

We want to close this chapter on Pathway D: Development and Discovery, by inviting you to quietly meditate on the quote on the next page.

"Yet constant struggle leaves us tired and empty. Our struggle for reform needs to be tempered and balanced with a capacity for celebration. When we lose sight of beauty our struggle becomes tired and functional. When we expect and engage the Beautiful, a new fluency is set free within us and between us. The heart becomes rekindled and our lives brighten with unexpected courage. It is a courage that restores hope to the heart. In our day-to-day lives, we show courage without realizing it. However, it is only when we are afraid that courage becomes a question. Courage is amazing because it can tap into the heart of fear, taking that frightened energy and turning towards initiative, creativity, action and hope. When courage comes alive, imprisoning walls become frontiers of new possibility, difficulty becomes invitation and the heart comes into a new rhythm of trust and sureness. There are secret sources of courage inside every human heart; yet courage needs to be awakened in us. The encounter with the Beautiful can bring such awakening. Courage is a spark that can become the flame of hope, lighting new and exciting pathways in what seemed to be dead, dark landscapes."

~John O'Donohue, Beauty: The Invisible Embrace

SUMMARY HIGHLIGHTS OF PATHWAY "D": DEVELOPMENT AND DISCOVERY

1. The life journey of a couple's relationship brings with it opportunities for soul development of the individual and the couple.

2. Crisis such as adversities, challenges, and struggles, present learning and spiritual growth for the couple who seizes this opportunity for exploration into the heart and soul of their purposeful partnership.

3. Life on earth is the stage where the interplay of events and repetitions of patterns of interactions in different life phases can bring for a couple the healing opportunities to participate in each other's development, transformation and evolution.

4. Our developmental processes and shifts are embedded in the unconscious and collective consciousness of the Field –Ground of the All.

5. It is helpful to view Pathway D holistically, as this gives couples a multi-dimensional perspective to ease them from blaming themselves or each other and to see their journey through the cycles of stages and phases, individually and together, as the interweaving of interacting processes wherein they are an important part of the evolution of humanity.

6. Generally, couples relationships move through these <u>four major stages</u> of cycles of development in evolving a circular beginning, middle and end phases rather than linear steps in growth.

   Initial Stage 1: Dependence - Fusion Cycles: 0 - 6th year cycle
   - **Beginning Phase**: Courtship: Similarities & Complementing Differences
   - **Middle Phase**: Romance vs. Marriage/Partnership & the Inevitable Disillusionment
   - **Ending Phase**: Authenticity vs. Illusion/Disillusion

   Stage 2: Independence - Differentiation Cycles: 7th- 14th; 15th- 21st year cycles
   - **Beginning Phase**: Differentiation & Diversity
   - **Middle Phase**: Autonomy vs. Intimacy: Power & Influence
   - **Ending Phase**: Self Identity & Intimacy

   Stage 3: Mutuality - Interdependence Cycles: 22nd - 28th; 29th- 35th; 36th - 42nd year cycles
   - **Beginning Phase**: Recognition, Co-creative Authentic Identity & Connections
   - **Middle Phase**: Collaborative Contributions
   - **Ending Phase**: Integrative Intimacy

Stage 4: Termination (can happen in Stages 1, 2, or 3) or
Resolution - Integrative Cycles: $36^{th} - 50^{th}$ + 7 year cycles
- **Beginning Phase:** Life – Relationships Review – Forgiving & Healing
- **Middle Phase:** Making the Best of Life, Legacy & Passing Forward, Deepening Acceptance & Respect
- **Ending Phase:** Endings, Completion(s), & Death

7. Dialogue as a process practice skill in Pathway D is an inner commitment to an inner discipline that involves inner practice of the inner interactive experience with the significant *human* other. As an inner and interactive discipline and practice in their partnership, couples who are able to share their present and conscious phenomenological awareness of their experience of Self with the Other with authenticity and responsibility, experience their way of contact with each other through their journey in Pathway D of Development and Discovery.

PATHWAY E: PATHWAY OF EVOLVING
LEARNING HOW TO LEARN FROM EXPERIENCE

"There are really no mistakes in life...only learning experiences. All experience is for learning. The real wealth is if you know how to learn from experience."
~Don Pepe Valero

Introduction

The Pathway of Evolving is vital to the development of individuals and a couple. We all know, we can either learn from our experiences or we keep repeating them. When you learn from experiences you understand that there are no mistakes as everything is simply a part of our evolving soul journey.

For many humans, the challenge of learning from experience is to be able to learn to BE in the PRESENT, seize the moment with present awareness of self and other in the WHOLE present, in the HERE and NOW. This involves allowing yourself to be fully embodied in being, sensing, feeling, attending to What IS within self in the moment as you are attending to your partner. This involves being in the FLOW and movement of Energy. This involves reflecting on your experiencing and the unfolding moment to moment shiftings.

So breathe, stop and BE for a moment. Experience this moment. What are you noticing in your body sensations...your feelings...your thinking...your images and so on? What are you noticing around you? Notice what begins to stand out and how you are impacted in the present NOW?

In Pathway E, the couple, with intention, co-creates safe space to learn from their relating experience in a fuller way. Though this Pathway can be challenging, the benefits of learning from experience are vast. When we can learn from our experiences, we can have rich, deeply meaningful exchanges and feel connected to ourselves and to each other. We do not have to push others away, but can be with each other, with all our imperfections, flaws and challenges. In their willingness to learn from experience, both partners individually and jointly consciously co-create their container of safety.

And it is in co-creating their container of safety that both partners expand in their learning from experience that unfolds and brings them to all their growth adventure and possibilities. They are aware of the intention and impact of their interactions. They attend to the aesthetic sense of how they are being with each other and practice their interactive skills to develop their inner art. They allow themselves the space to experiment with co-creating, to notice what is working, what is helpful and not helpful, what supports and inspires and what and how they are transforming within themselves. They tap into realms of experience of body-energy-emotion-heart-mind-soul-system-spirit (BEEHMSSS™) as in meditation, prayer and their dreams. They access dimensions that expand them to perceive and think outside of the box as well as nourish their inner well-being. They connect with all possible experiences of themselves; consciously deepen in their soul growth to 'witness' self and each other in the image and likeness of the Divine Love Presence in their living experiences.

How The Prior Pathways Help You Learn From Experience

When you are experiencing Pathway "D" (Development) you become conscious of how your histories and programming from your culture and family formed your perceptions and shaped your experiences. When you deepen into Pathway D you study, research and become curious about the impact of how you developed in the journey of your relationship. You use the tool of *Dialogue to* help you share in ways that brings you into the present and to appreciate where you have both come from.

These skills are pivotal to help you move into Pathway E. In your relational journey together, you appreciate the impact of your earlier life experiences on your present experience individually and together. Through dialogue with each other you activate the co-creative process of your evolution in learning how to <u>learn from experience</u>.

Let's start with a story from our lives so you can understand how the Pathway of Experience can play out in a couple's life. As you read, please allow any reflections of how you have learned from experience to come into your awareness.

Lalei:

"My first conscious introduction to Pathway E happened when I was a teenager. I was in a major car accident. The head-on collision totaled our family car, almost severed my brother's arm, and left me seriously injured, my spine immobile and in total traction for three months."

"Family and friends were so glad we were alive. They nurtured us back to health and supported our rehabilitation while we re-learned the basics of eating, moving, standing and walking."

'Traumatized, I vowed to never drive again. The consequences of the accident left me feeling fully responsible for the domino effect that occurred, causing significant financial and emotional setbacks for our whole family."

"My grandfather noticed that I had grown fearful of going out or taking any action. Six months later he came to our house in his new "Cadillac", he insisted that I get into the driver's seat and drive and he would be there with me in the passenger's seat encouraging me on. Thus began my driving lessons with him."

"He told me words that would profoundly change my life and carry me through hard times to come."

"He said, 'Get in the driver's seat of your own experience. Breathe and go slow. Watch your experience and be in your body, in the present. See what is behind you in the rear view mirror. Let your senses tune into what's around you, so you are conscious of the other drivers and where you are. Just relax and breathe. This is NOT the time to pull back and withdraw into your fear. Learn from this and I guarantee you will be an even better driver."

"I did not want to displease my grandfather so I tried it. I felt the tremors of fear transform as his tangible support, gentle encouragement along with consistent practice linked me to experiencing conscious courage. And... more than anything...this poignant experience served as a metaphor, a cellular memory, and an imprint of the value of learning how to learn in life's journey!"

"This gift from my grandfather during a time of great adversity was a spiritual opportunity for my inner development. His loving presence created the SPACE for me to learn and experience in a non-violent, strong, focused, kind and memorable way. This approach has been one of my primary grounding tools to support being present to learn from experience."

"I remember on those drives he told me, "Even when you touch one life, that one life will touch others. Let your presence be one that lets God's love flow through you in your intimate relationship with God (the universal energetic field) and with those that you love."

"This was a primary experiential link for me that taught me how to learn from experience."

"Many months later after the accident and the death of my beloved mentor and teacher, I heard while dreaming, 'Life relationships are not always easy. Even as you grieve for your loss, it is because you felt loved. This is about learning in the real "school" of living and love. Learn to seize this difficult moment. Experience the spiritual opportunity to awaken the power of love. It is here for you in your heart Now. Your mentor is within your heart.'

"I can now see throughout my life, both in my intimate relationship with Phil and with the many people I have worked with, the ripple effects of my grandfather's intuitive guidance that came from a universal reservoir of grace."

"The riches of what he taught me, I have found confirmed over and over again in research studies and by many master teachers we've met throughout our lives."

"Together as a couple, we have learned from experience that our life is an adventure and intimate relationships provide us room for personal discovery and growth from a place of Love. When one learns from experience, they have choices and the relationship has more room to have lasting impact to positively transform generations to come."

EXPERIENCE IS THE TEACHER AND RELATIONSHIPS ARE THE "SCHOOL" OF LIFE

"In life, you think that you have set your mark or your direction. Then you discover you are lost. Getting lost can be a blessing. You learn to orient and be present with your senses. Notice nuances. Be open to listen to the spaces. Each step unfolds another step. And you find a different way. When you practice this art of getting lost, you discover new Pathways."
~Papa Joe

Along your relational journey, you will find that Pathway "E" is **not** a linear process.

'How to' or 'should do' prescriptions provided by moral, religious, societal and cultural standards do not guarantee us happiness or fulfillment. Often we hear from individuals and couples that inner work has been necessary in order for them to learn *how to learn* from experience and see profound transformation.

- Have you wondered how to allow experience to be an adventure in self-discovery so you can learn about yourself and each other during your life journey together as a couple?
- Are you willing to see yourselves as learning partners and choose to learn *HOW* to learn from experience?
- Do you wonder how you can co-creatively grow and evolve to become more authentic and whole individually and as a couple?

Experience: Your Relationship 'DANCE'

As soon as we come into this world we are quickly introduced to the environment of our family, community, and culture. We learn to play our part in the interactive *'dance'* of our family, community, and culture in order to survive and get our needs met.

Interestingly, you find that survival methods do not meet deeper, human and soul needs.

Then you experience this inner hunger, this restlessness, this boredom, this anxiety, this anger, this sadness, this ache, this hurt, this elation, this relief, this joy, this peace....You ask yourself...what does this experience mean?

You say, "why is it that even though I/we may know better, I/we tend to slip into our habits and react automatically even though we each know we could do better?"

You may stop and wonder..."there must be a different way, a better way than this..."

So, would you be willing to reflect on the following questions as a segue to examining your experience in your significant relationship?

- Are you willing to recognize your *'dance'* or pattern in your relationship?
- Are you honest and trusting enough to face your experience of satisfaction or dissatisfaction?
- As you *'dance'*, what is the 'stumbling block' that your relationships fall into and gets stuck in?
- What is your experience of your being stuck?
- Where did your stumbling blocks originate?
- What are you <u>each and both</u> trying to achieve with your relationship *'dance'*?
- What have you tried individually and/or together to shift your *'dance'*?

> *"Trust allows you to laugh. You can just as easily laugh and play while you grow and become serious and overwhelmed. Spiritual partners can laugh at the richness, beauty and the playfulness of the Universe. They enjoy each other. They see the frustrations of the wants of the personality for what they are, learning sometimes great learnings for the soul."*
> *~Gary Zukav*

Reflection Exercise

The following short story is your Exercise, wherein you fill in the chapters. You can adjust the chapters to fit your own experience. Before we go about learning how to learn from experience, we would like you to script your own experience(s).

Fill it in with your own version. Add a chapter, if you may. Share with your partner your short story version. Notice where your stories interconnect and the *'dance'* or patterns that emerges.

Then reflect on your experience of doing this exercise as a couple, of sharing your short stories, seeing where your versions interconnect, the similarities and differences. Notice what you are learning from your experience of sharing your experience of your Seven Chapters: A Short Story of Experience.

As you read the following short story, pay attention to what it evokes in you. Reflect on your own intimate experience and what has happened for you as a couple during each cycle.

The Seven Chapters: A Short Story of Experience

Chapter 1: The Meeting. Two people walk down the road. They meet each other and fall in love. They find things in common and dance. One falls into the hole in the road and then the other falls in, too. They are happy to be in this hole together.

At this experience phase, when a couple meet they like to spend time together and talk about the things they have in common. There is a sense of inclusion and joining. Even if there is a problem, they still enjoy themselves.

Chapter 2: The Bump. The couple walks down their common road hand in hand. One falls into a hole and then the other falls into the hole, too, but this time their heads knock. They are dazed by the hole they fell into.

At this experience phase, their baggage begins to fall out. As they spend time together, feel safer, do more and become familiar or at ease, they also begin to knock heads. Disagreements, disappointments, unmet expectations, and reactions start. People would like to go back to the first chapter, but this chapter is where the electricity resides, the sparks that lead to growth and development. These first bumps aren't easy.

How they maneuver this time is based on how they've worked through earlier past experiences. If their pattern is to fight, they fight; if their pattern is to flee, they flee, if it is to freeze, then they freeze; and if it is to fawn, then they fawn. If the pattern is to work through things – then possibly the couple may be able to go onto

Chapter 3. It takes willingness on both sides to be there and work through the challenges.

Chapter 3: Meeting with Others. This couple walks down the road to meet each other and is aware of the holes that they fell into in the past. But they trip again and fall into a hole that feels like the previous hole too. But they find out this hole is crowded with others in the same hole. The hole pulls them into their reactions and they feel powerless.

In this experience phase, the couple realizes that they aren't the only ones struggling, that others experience similar challenges, but nobody around them is working through this in positive ways. In this stage, everyone they meet up with is commiserating or trying to fix each other.

Chapter 4: The Struggle. This couple walks down the road to meet each other. They realize there are holes along the way and alert each other. "Oh, there's the hole, watch out"...but they fall in anyway. "I don't like being in this hole," they say to each other and struggle to get out of the hole.

During this stage, the couple may struggle for a long time trying to fix each other. They do the same thing over and over again and it seems to go on endlessly. During this phase, they could bail out from the relationship or if married, divorce.

Chapter 5: The Hope. The couple walks down the road together with a wheelbarrow full of dirt. They meet at the hole in the middle of the road and slow down. Then they help each other fill the hole with rich earth which they have gathered together. They continue breathing and sharing together. They walk back and forth with the wheelbarrow until the hole is filled with their special mixture. Then, they can plant their own flower garden, full of rich soil as a foundation.

For those that have stayed together and come to this stage, they have said to themselves, "There are more chapters for us. There must be something more to our relationship" and wonder why they are going through this experience. This is where they begin to slow down and discover things they didn't know before. They begin to fill in the hole with their discoveries and learning as they dialogue, connect, and communicate. They do something different than what they have done before, maybe like going to a workshop or get coaching. There are glimmers of hope.

Chapter 6: Savoring and Cherishing. Now the couple walks down the road to their garden of flowers. They tend to their garden and watch it bloom and grow through the seasons of empowerment, compassion, and wisdom.

During this experience phase, the couple has begun to learn together from their experiences of attending and cultivating their garden. They can begin to catch their patterns and they feel more successful because they practice what they learned in chapter 5. They take time to savor their learning through the seasons, and cherish the challenges that their relationship is now overcoming.

"I am cherishing how we stayed, learned and grew together to see our love bloom to a stronger and deeper place."

"Me too, and I am savoring as I breathe into my cells so we remember this together, as it takes a lot of conscious muscle to do this."

Chapter 7: Resting in the Space. This couple sits in the garden divine. They rest together and are replenished as they feel a deep sense of Gratitude.

During this experience phase, the couple can be in the fertile space of possibilities. There is a sense of going back into the self. The couple integrates what they have learned. And life is quieter. They can enjoy the simple things together. They rest doing, they are being.

Now...pause and take a moment to notice your reflections together. Notice your learning from your experience of doing this exercise together and sharing. Notice the entire relational context of your relationship.

It is possible that you may get more insights as you go along and your short stories become richer through learning from experiences.

When individuals and couples learn how to learn from experience they can build and deepen their intimacy. In the West we are very individual within our relationships and tend to work out our problems individually and solely without an appreciation of the contextual or relational field of the relationship. This makes coming to resolution very difficult. Often the solution, created by the individual has an impact on the system of the couple. And the couple is at it again in a similar dance wherein contact is broken off – as in the 'me or you', or "If you win, I lose and if I lose, you win." So the process of learning how to learn from experience involves the interactive process of the couple's present experience in the relational field of their past and current relational 'luggage'.

Learning How to Learn from Experience

Have you noticed that you seem to re-experience the same feelings and thoughts in your relationships, even when you want something different? Does it leave you bewildered? Are you ready for something very different?

This bewilderment can be the great beginning for you and your partner to begin to awaken and learn from experience. But this only happens when you are ready to respect experience as your teacher and to allow your significant and intimate relationship(s) to be your 'school'.

From this stance, you can learn to respond more deeply to what you are already experiencing in your inner senses and to appreciate who you already are in your essence.

> *"You are my likeness, for we are prisoners of two bodies formed of one clay. You are my companion on the road of life and my helper in the understanding of a truth concealed beyond the clouds."*
> *~Kahlil Gibran*

It is amazing to behold the couples who 'get it', who learn from their experiences together. They are willing to humble themselves in order to learn *how to learn* from their experiences *with* each other.

They understand that a significant relationship can help you face yourself and inspire you to deeply discover your SELF (Soul Essence Life Force) and to see more clearly your core goodness and beauty.

> *"The POWER of NOW, is in the PRESENT experience."*
> *~Eckhart Tolle*

How you relate to your loved one is a clear mirror of how you relate to yourself. However, we often carry into our significant relationships distorted reflections of encoded experiences from our earlier relationships.

In John Welwood's book, <u>Love and Awakening,</u> he discusses how significant and intimate relationship is the vehicle for us to discover how we can awaken lost dimensions of the sacred within us. Here we discover our essential self in the *present* relationship to our Divine connection within.

"Do you know how to learn from experience?
Or is your relational life a repetition of more of the same experiences?"

Awakening Into Learning from Experience

> *"We like to think that we are finally evolved creatures, in suit-and-tie or pantyhose-and-chemise, who live many millennia, and mental detours away from the cave, but that's not something our bodies are convinced of. We may have the luxury of being at the top of the food chain, but our adrenaline still rushes when we encounter real or imaginary predators. We still create works of art to enhance our senses and add sensations to the brimming world, so that we*

can luxuriate in the spectacles of life. We still ache fiercely with love, lust, loyalty and passion. We still perceive the world, in all its gushing beauty and terror, right in our pulses. There is no other way to begin to understand the gorgeous fever that is consciousness. We must try to understand the senses — how they evolved, how they can be extended, what their limits are, to which ones we have attached taboos, and what they can teach us.
To understand, we have to "use our head", meaning our minds. Most people think of the mind as being located in the head, but the latest findings --- suggest that the MIND does not dwell in the brain but travels the whole body on caravans of hormones and enzymes, busily making sense of the compound wonders we catalogue as touch taste, smell, hearing and vision."
~Diane Ackerman, A Natural History of the Senses

For this level of learning to occur, an individual or couple often experiences a significant crisis. This may be external, such as a significant change in environment, a job loss, a divorce, death or accident, or an internal challenge, impacting one's health, a loss of meaning or a spiritual crisis, like a dark night of the soul.

Often, a triggering event can be the tipping factor that activates other unfinished business or unresolved crisis in one's life, such as the death of a beloved pet brings up unresolved grief stored in cellular memory over losses in life and relationships. These critical incidents then impact the relationship and other dimensions of the significant relationship and can come into play as unintended consequences...often with a huge domino effect. A crisis, whether it be big or small becomes the opportunity for the couple to *learn how to learn from experience* and bring closure to unfinished business.

Meg and Brian's journey in Pathway E was heightened when they noticed their son's aggressive behavior toward his sister and his refusal to go to school due to fears of bullying. They sought help which brought them to look at the devastating impact to their individual and couples' soul of their own early life experiences of being bullied. Their intense and polarized approach to their son's aggressiveness brought them to confront and learn from their own experiences. Their couple's healing work empowered them to their higher goal. They incorporated both their heart wisdoms and their team approach for safety and appropriate empowering behaviors, wherein they mutually checked in, examined and affirmed their learning experience.

As their journey of learning from experience and healing continued, they prepared for another learning experience wherein Brian's upcoming class reunion, which they avoided for many years would bring him to meet his childhood tormentors. It was important for Brian to bring closure in a healing way for his inner peace. Their healing journey and experience as a couple together allowed him to meet face to face with the childhood bully from 30 years ago. They shared their touching surprise when the bully ex-classmate approached them to make amends, as he was not sure whether his asking for forgiveness would be received. While he shared that he is leading a sober life and making amends to the many people he had hurt, Brian extended his forgiveness, releasing himself furthermore and coming to deep peace within. Meg and Brian noticed how "every ounce of fear has left our couple's soul". Brian felt the presence of inner courage and peace as he calmly and confidently relayed the impact his bully friend made on his arduous life journey to recover his sacred essence and turn it into a learning experience that has made him and his marriage strong.

Brain and Meg's journey through Pathway E had many cycle processes of learning from experience.

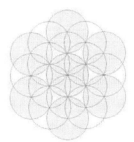

In this following section, we are presenting the Pathway E Process of Learning from Experience Cycle. This template is a process guide for your awareness and practice of learning how to learn from experience.

The Experience Cycle Processes: An Interactive Experiential Learning Practice

This process guide is adapted from the Cycle of Experience that we teach at the Gestalt Institute of Cleveland. Some process innovations of our own have been drawn from our own experience as a couple and in our work with couples in their learning from the experience process.

- Experience Cycle with and through your Inner and Outer Senses
- Experience Cycle of your Awareness and Intention
- Experience Cycle of your Activating and Joining Energy
- Experience Cycle of your Inspired and Energized Action for Experiment
- Experience Cycle of your 'Contactful' Connection
- Experience Cycle of Assimilation of your Learning
- Experience Cycle of your Solitude, the Space of the Fertile Divine

1. **EXPERIENCE CYCLE WITH AND THROUGH YOUR INNER AND OUTER SENSES. Notice and identify the LOCATION of what and where in your physical self you are experiencing.**

   We all take in the world and experience relationships with our senses of seeing, hearing, feeling, smelling and tasting as well as our Inner senses of intuition and felt or gut sense. Your body is the home/temple of your Soul/Spirit. You are an 'En-souled body' interacting and relating with your Self, with Others and with God (Spirit, Nature, Universe). You are 'Thou' experiencing life.

> *"Our body is a multilingual being. It speaks through its color and its*
> *temperature, the flush of recognition, the glow of love, the ash of pain, the heat*
> *of arousal, the coldness of non-conviction...it speaks through the leaping of the*
> *heart, the falling of the spirits, the pit at the center, and rising hope."*
> *~Clarissa Pinkola Estes*

Our physical body is created from the breath of Spirit and the elements of Nature: Earth our grounding and support, Water our blood, flow and nourishment, Fire our current of life and passion, Air our breath of living spirit, and Space our oneness.

For many of us humans, we have learned to be disembodied in our culture and disconnected from our senses in order to survive. We tune out, desensitize and treat ourselves as objects, things and machines, to get jobs done, handle responsibilities, and achieve goals and dreams. Even when our bodies call our attention through pain sensations, we ignored the signals of sensation, medicated our sensate feelings with pills, alcohol, food, or sex. We lose touch with ourselves. In treating our physical experience as separate from Self, we split from our Wholeness. To heal is to come home into our 'Wholeness', our 'Self in Body'.

> *"My belief is in the blood and flesh as being wiser than the intellect. The body*
> *unconscious is where life bubbles up to us. It is how we know that we are alive,*
> *alive to the depths of our souls, and in touch somewhere with the vivid reaches*
> *of the cosmos."*
> *~D.H. Lawrence*

Particularly in the last fifty years, human consciousness is evolving to reclaim our energetic body Self, our wholeness, our spirit, and our emotions. Candace Pert, in her book, Molecules of Emotion, discusses how our body-mind-spirit Self carried in its tissues, muscles, peptides and DNA, our life journey experiences as memory patterns, genetics, habits, culture, race, sexuality from our pre-conception, conception, birth experience, body life history and how we interactively experience our inner-outer environment.

As we integrate our sensate experiences and body impulses, we regain our natural intelligence, grace and our kindness in love. We appreciate ourselves as Spirit beings having a human sense experience of grounding, centering, wisdom, compassion, empowerment, vitality, connection, creativity, authenticity, diversity, and unity.

As a WHOLE person, I am/We are Body, Energy, Emotions, Heart, Mind, Soul, Systems of relations and Spirit (BEEHMSSS™).

> I am/We are a Body with Energy, Emotions, Heart, Mind, Soul, Systems of Relations, and Spirit.
>
> I am/We are Energy in motion with Body, Heart, Mind, Soul, Systems of Relations, and Spirit
>
> I am/We are Emotions in a Body with Energy, Heart, Mind, Soul, Systems of Relations, and Spirit.
>
> I am/We are Heart in a Body with Energy, Emotions, Mind, Soul, Systems of Relations, and Spirit.
>
> I am/We are Mind emBodied presence with Energy, Emotions, Heart, Soul, Systems of Relations, and Spirit.
>
> I am/We are a Soul emBodied with Energy, Emotions, Heart, Mind, Systems of Relations, and Spirit.
>
> I am/We are Systems of Relations energetically linked with Emotions, in Energy, Heart, Mind, Soul, and Spirit.
>
> I am/We are Spirit energetically emBodied in Energy, Emotions, Mind, Heart, Soul, and Systems of Relations.
>
> *I AM/ We are One Whole Universe.*

Sensory Exercise

To become conscious of your sense experience is the ground for learning from experience:

A. Notice your senses, what you see, hear, smell, taste, feel.

B. Notice your present sensate body experience.

   Take a moment to check in with your body self right now? What is your felt sense? Notice where are you alive in your body? Notice where you are tight, tense, compressed, numb, cut off? Notice where are you pulsing, vibrating, tingling, burning, itching, prickly, aching, paining? Notice where you are breathing or not breathing? As you are noticing, where are you sensing yourself expand, stretch, shake, release and/or relax?

C. What is/are the **observable fact(s)** or data of your present _sense awareness experience?_

   Practice being concrete and hold off interpretation. Play with it and notice your experience. Identify what you see, hear, feel, touch, taste. Take turns with each other.

D. When you name or identify the concrete observable fact of your sense experience, you each know what and where the location is of your experience is.

A Couple's Example

Mark:	I look out our window and see the sun out.
Marie:	Oh yes, I see so many flowers in bloom. I hear birds singing and I am hearing a song in my head.
Mark:	I smell the lilacs. Is that your fragrance or the lilacs out our window?
Marie:	I feel myself smiling and notice how alive I feel when I see sunlight.
Mark:	I am opening the windows. I love breathing the fresh air.
Marie:	I feel the warm breeze on my skin and I see you kick off your shoes.
Mark:	I can feel my feet on the wet grass. I am itching in my feet to go outside and feel the earth.

People tend to go right into interpretation and they do not hear where each one is coming from. Staying with your sense experience allows you and your partner to know where and what you are attending.

As you experience your senses and share what is observable, you bring **awareness to where you are focusing** and observe the meaning or interpretation you have attached to it.

2. EXPERIENCE CYCLE OF YOUR AWARENESS AND INTENTION

Let us continue with the example of Mark and Marie.

- ***Being aware*** involves *observing* and *noticing what **begins to stand out for you** (awareness of focus) from your awareness of* your physical sensation, emotion, thought, behavior, an exchange or interaction.

Marie: I am aware that you noticed me see you kick off your shoes to walk barefoot on the grass. I noticed myself go "Ewww" inside of me when you said how you love the wet grass on your feet. We are so different, because I like shoes on my feet and the further from the ground I am the more I like it (ownership of own subjective experience).

- Being in **awareness of experience** is noticing and **owning your interpretation** (the meaning you are making of your experience with your feeling sensation in the present moment. Your story may involve a memory, an imagination, an assumption, a hunch, theory, and hypothesis or guess (interpretations), a belief, and/or a feeling emotion. Be aware of your interpretation of your '*FACT*' concrete sensate experience. Your interpretations are neither 'right' nor 'wrong'. They contribute to your own **SUBJECTIVE EXPERIENCES** *(feelings and thoughts and the meaning you make).*

Marie: Being barefoot makes me think of the 'yuk' that I could be stepping on (her subjective experience). I remember stepping on a nail as a child and being brought to the hospital for a tetanus shot (story with an unpleasant memory).

For this matter: we would say that all experience is SUBJECTIVE.

Mark: I appreciate hearing you tell me of your experience. That way, I now know what your 'yuk' means for you because my experience with the ground and the earth brings so much happy playful memories.

Marie: I love nature and its beauty and to me it is like seeing God's amazing art on the huge space of the universal canvas, like from our window.

Mark: Indeed we are different in our appreciation of nature, because for me, my appreciation comes with me wanting to play in God's amazing playground.

- **It helps to take ownership of your experience rather than put it on the other.** It is cleaner when you can identify what your learned experience is and the belief that you draw out of your own your sense experiential story. Notice how Mark and Marie are sharing their own meaning (subjective experience of bare feet on the ground), without interpreting the other's experience. Their use of "I" helps in this situation.

Let us follow Mark and Marie again as they move through the Pathway E – The Pathway of Evolving and Learning from their Interactive process of Experience.

- **Stance of Exploring subjective experiences.** This aspect of learning from experience can enhance their appreciation of experience by bringing each other to the other's subjective experience to get a FULL awareness of the interactive **'dance'** of both their subjective experiences. It is important and valuable that the couple be open and interested to have a FULL awareness of the **'both-and'** of their experiences versus staying in the **'either-or'** experience, **to move to Learning from Experience.**

Marie: "I see your clothes on the floor (*observable sense experience*). I sense myself tensing my shoulders *(location of inner sense experience)*. I am thinking (*thought*) you don't care about me (*interpretation*). When we were little, mom would scream at dad and all of us when we leave our clothes scattered on the floor 'I am not your maid' (*intense associative memory*). When I think that you are treating me like a maid (*association to mother's story*), I feel resentful and angry (*feeling emotion*). I want to be excited to see you come home (*desire*). But when I see clothes on the floor (*fact/trigger*), I feel a loss of energy and I turn off inside of me (*energy experience from visual cues*). Then you are affectionate and I am so turned off that I do not want to get near you (*reaction subjective experience*)."

Mark: "Seeing my clothes on the floor (*location of concrete sense experience*) feels like home (*association cue to sensation experience*). I let my guard down and relax the moment I come into my garage (*kinesthetic subjective response to garage*) and like a snake I shed off my work clothes (*kinesthetic metaphor*). I feel cool and my skin breathes (*kinesthetic sensate feeling*). Home (*context*) is where I relax (*kinesthetic belief experience*). It makes me angry (*emotional reaction*) to think (*thought*) that you do not want me to relax in my own home (*interpretation possibly connected to belief with associative memory.*) I cannot believe that we are making such a big deal (*reactive thought*) about "clothes on the floor" where our fights would become so intense it is so ridiculous (*reactive judgment*), that we make each other miserable (*co-created experience*)."

Marie: "I know I am not an obsessive cleaner. It is important for me to feel relaxed in our own home (*joining value of relaxation*) as well. When I see your clothes on the floor from the garage to the bathroom and bits and pieces of clothes as you pass by each room, I experience myself nagging (*observation of behavior pattern that stands out as noticed*). I tense up and bite my tongue and my head is exploding with lots of angry thoughts (*inner subjective experience*) and really do not feel relaxed in my own home. I have tried strategies to keep me from getting more frustrated. Sometime, I disappear and go for a walk, or play music, or exercise, or meditate because I keep feeling that only if I shut up and just pick up after you it will become quiet and relaxing for you at home (*subjective experiences of coping*). Then I worry that I will turn up to be like my mother, feeling used and alone (*future concern of individual adjustment*). The worse part for me is becoming really angry with myself and resentful towards you for putting me in this position (*repetition of learned helpless victim story*) repeating the experience as though I inherited it and it is just the way it is.

Mark: "Well... I tell you to relax and just sit, and watch TV, kick off your shoes and not to cook. I can take care of myself. I will eat when I am hungry and I will pick up all the clothes in the weekend. Saturday can be my cleaning day (*problem solution strategy offered*). I know that I have really helped out on Saturdays and made it a thorough cleaning day. I feel I have done my share so you can relax on Saturdays (*individual strategy response*)."

Marie: "That strategy works for you but not for me because there are actually five days that I am so tensed up running around to keep an orderly house with you and our little children that it is really difficult to enjoy relaxing on Saturday. You want me to relax with you and I really would love to collaborate and find an experience that works for us together. Right now, it feels like either you or I and that does not feel good to me."

- **Taking an experimental stance to gain fuller couple awareness of their interactive subjective experiences.** This aspect allows the couple to enhance their repertoire. They try out new experiences by experimenting with different ways to see how it works and then making adjustments.

- **The Experimental Stance** involves an attitude of learning and experimentation. When the couple takes on this attitude, they learn to give themselves room for exploration, to do things imperfectly, to make 'mistakes', to try things on, to open themselves to new ways of looking, doing and being. They expand themselves to the possibilities of their SELF individually and their SELF as a Unit.

This has the possibility of their being teachers to each other about their styles of ways of being without the demand for changing each other.

Our experience is also informed by the *FIELD* (context, environment) of our experience. The *field* provides the background, informs our experience and supports the cues and triggers for the quality of our experience. One way to learn from experience is to learn *How* to learn in the *Present,* here and now.

In what way is your current experience in their present, reflective of and linked to past experiences and/or your apprehensions or plans for the future?

What belief(s) do you hold about yourself, about your relationship, NOW? From where did these beliefs originate? Are they helpful or not helpful, *Now*?

As Marie and Mark's explorations brought them to visit more consciously with their parents, they became aware that they were operating as though they were living in a time warp in the contextual field of their repeated couples' experience.

The present fact (clothes on the floor) is a trigger for Marie to re- experience the past (Marie's association with her mother's and father's repeated 'belittling' of each other story and the circumstance of Mark's living with his father where he felt more relaxed as a teen).

Coaches: "As you try on this experiment of sharing the impact your story of your present experience of talking about your concerns for the future, pay attention right now, as to what you are experiencing in this present moment, as in your breathing or your body sensations."

Marie: "I feel right now a deeper understanding of my mother's frustration (empathy with mother's experience) and I feel a sadness in my heart (*touching chest in the present*). I do not want to have this fight of ours to go on because I am afraid I am turning into my mother and I think Mark is turning into his father (concerns for future). I own my judgment because to me their way of relaxing is tense. However, I think I got attracted to Mark, because I want to learn how to allow myself to just *be* without judging myself as a slob. I believe I judge Mark and have resisted learning what he is trying to teach me without losing my appreciation for the relaxation I feel with order and beauty. I am grateful to have learned that from mother after all those years."

"Now I can really feel appreciation for her artistic sense because that is me too. I enjoy seeing my home orderly, colorful and aesthetic. I enjoy the clean smell of a clean home. Right now, I feel so good just describing my picture of our home. And I am assuming that you love it too, because you tell me, Mark, how you are so lucky that I give you a comfortable, orderly home, that smells so refreshingly clean. So I am assuming that you like that too."

Mark: "Wow! I love your clarity. I understand where my feeling of the threat of divorce comes from. I know it is from my parents, as they were unable to reconcile their different living styles. To come to think of it, this 'small thing' is not worth us getting divorced over…but sometimes, my frustration can be so huge that I want to get out of our beautiful house and have my own sloppy cave. I know I am with you because much as I resist it, I really love that you take care of me when you pick up after me. It is as though I am testing you and believing that you will get frustrated anyway and like my mother who left my father and my father who drove her away. I always yearned for my parents to work things out. My mother would compare me to my father and I resented when she did that."

Coaches: "We notice that as couple, it matters that you both see your home as a place to feel at home and feel relaxed (*reflecting their joint intention*). You both have a FULL awareness of how your relaxation styles mirror ways your parents coped. Your story is now a more conscious story for you in your present dilemma on how to join in co-creating your relaxing home experience that incorporates <u>both and together</u>. By being presently aware and attending to how you are together and co-creatively turning your individual strategies to appreciate both, you find ways to join together in the care of both your relaxation needs."

Mark: "Yes. I get it now. Marie, our challenge together **brings us to this fork in our journey of experience: do we continue doing what we learned from our family, defending and excluding each other, or do we join to experiment with our *both-and*?**"

Marie: "Yes, I am so clear now, too. I really see it."

Coaches: "Yes, you get it and you are clear how you **'both-and'** can support expanding your repertoires of relation and be on the Pathway of Learning how to Learn from life experiences. Your challenge and opportunity is HOW to co-create learning experiences to support you *both-and* find relaxation with beauty, order, ease, playfulness, letting go... As you explore to incorporate both your energies, take an experimental stance. Nothing is cast in stone. You are collaborating in co-creating and innovating new experiences. It is OK to stretch your comfort zones to see and feel relaxation. Takes turns teaching and learning, trying on each other's ways, playing with it. Let this be your opportunity to re-invent your relationship creating it to be uniquely yours. Let yourselves bring your learning experiences to inform and expand your relationship, to see what works. Take it as an adventure to become aware of your **present experience in the NOW,** a step at a time as each step unfolds for you both to another present experience."

3. EXPERIENCE CYCLE OF YOUR ACTIVATING AND JOINING ENERGY

In moving through the ***experience cycle of your joint energy***, notice what awareness has your energy. As you interact with each other, attend to what joining of your couples' awareness has your joint or collaborative energy. As you experience your awareness, perceive how your consciousness heightens together and your joint energy becomes activated.

Clue: **How are you breathing**? Where in your body are you breathing and where not?

Clue: What **intention is energized and/or activated** for you both? What awareness has your ***both-and*** energy? ***How do you know*** it has both your **joint** energy? What is the ***quality*** of your joint energy?

Clue: This ***unique quality of your joint energy*** is your own (which you had a glimpse of when you fell in love). It was the ***SEED*** potency of your combined energy. In the ***SEED*** are all the possibilities of its blossoming through life's experiences.

> **Marie:** "I became clear that my *intention* is not to come across as criticizing or attacking. My intention is to have my *relaxation together with you* when we both are home at the end of a work or stressful day. To do this, I am *experimenting being in the present with my specific request.* "I have a bin in the garage for **our joint relaxation** because I know that you like to shed your work clothes when you come home. The bin *for now* is **my love acknowledgement of** your shedding work clothes **to relax and my self care to be at ease.**"
>
> "I was surprised when I stated my request in the present, Mark's response was so clean and refreshing (*impact matched her intention*). I felt so encouraged and empowered that I could make a difference in our relationship. We had a great relaxing connection (*joint impact)*."

Mark gave an example of how he managed his energy anticipating that Marie will meet him expecting that he was going to 'mess up' and he noticed himself gearing up for his defense coming up for his style of relaxation by ignoring (*self-awareness observing his subjective experience*). ***Appreciating learning*** about Marie's visual energy and his kinesthetic energy, he expressed his ***intention*** as to ***co-create*** relaxing feelings in their home.

> **Mark:** "I stretched myself to verbalize (**tonal channel**) so she could hear that I see and *acknowledge* how she matters a whole lot to me and to *support* myself in taking this conscious effort (**experiment**) Look honey, no mess. I am consciously putting my clothes in the bin because I care that it pleases my honey to have a clean and orderly home. I feel so special that my honey wants me to feel relaxed that she has this special bin for me with a huge smiley face hmm hmm hmm." It took consciousness on my part to be aware to shift my energy. She came over and gave me such a huge hug (**impact matched intention**). That felt so good. (**Joint Quality)**"

Mark and Marie's joint awareness to both support and learn relaxation activated their energy to explore and experiment with their joint goal:

> **To co-create experiences that enhances and supports our relaxed joyfulness together and to learn from our experiences in order to grow and further enhance the relaxed joyfulness in our relationship.**

Their learning from experience involved being PRESENT to:

- *Intention* and *Impact matches their energy.*

- *Energetics* of relating (Clue: what is your and your partner's way of relating).

Learning experientially how your couple energies interact is a continuing process and a mutual learning experience. We each will be our energetic ways of perceiving, organizing and processing information even more so under stress.

Learn the channel where you both can meet. When you commit to the Pathway of learning from experience and taking an experimental stance, you both have taken a huge step to forge a strong path of moving into all the possibilities that your learning will take you both to discover. Find out what your energetic channel is for each and for both.

> *Digital or logical...........................rational ('processes heart through theory')*
> *Visual...seeing; imagining*
> *Auditor ....hearing nuances of tones*
> *Kinesthetic...................................body sense; touch*

Phil's Notes: *Couples' energetic processes use different channels. Generally, women tend to be more tonal and visual. Many clients tell me "I married my husband because he tells me how much he loves me, he says nice and loving words that speaks like poetry to my ears and songs to my heart. When husband stops giving the sweetness of words and speaking acknowledgments and appreciations, she notices the tonal qualities of his speech and closes the channel that speaks to her heart. I believe women need to hear wonderful heartfelt authentic expressions.*

Generally women are tonal and engage in talk and conversations, as they listen to nuances of tone, pitch, volume, loudness and sound. What might sound like 'yelling' for a woman may be a man's rational verbalization or 'grunts' because I think men learn to 'tune out' or become tone deft as survival.

We all have our preferential energy mode, especially under stress. Generally, men will withdraw into their cave and be in their kinesthetic channel (work out, mow lawn, chop wood, dose off in front of the TV, fix something) or digital, logical to problem solve by rationality or figuring out. Generally, men in many cultures lead using the digital/rational and/or the kinesthetic energetic channels. When you look at the careers and jobs and the places where men are rewarded and excel these channels have been the most explicitly accessed.

However, men that can access their feminine are able to be tonal and access intuitive auditory nuances and are able to listen empathically. And women who can access their kinesthetic and rational/digital channels gain a sense of empowerment in body and mind.

If both were the same, there would be no bumping. Relationships that have **harnessed their friction into positive** bumping last longer than those that don't. They have energy, electricity, and more life. There is more passion. As they learn how to harness their friction and *learn how to learn from their co-creative experience,* their unique relational energy creates new learning experiences for themselves and others.

In significant love relationships*, LOVE presents the opportunity to experience the fullness of the ENERGY within one's being, within one's soul and evolve to one's Whole Self by experiential learning through the vehicle of relationship to their couple's soul.*

4. EXPERERIENCE CYCLE OF YOUR INSPIRED AND ENERGIZED ACTION FOR EXPERIMENT

What *Action(s)* is/are energized? How are you joining for inspired or energized action?
Clue: supported by full awareness and appreciation of 1-4.

Review Above:

A. Experiencing of Senses. Identify observable concrete data or fact. Hold off jumping to interpretation.
B. Experience of Conscious Awareness, and Awareness of Intention and Impact of Experience
C. Experience of Energy: individual, interactive and joint
D. Experience of Energized Action as Experiments for co-creative experiential learning: individual and joint.

Marie: "We experimented with a whole lot of different ways. We both went out and shopped for lovely decorative laundry bins for each room, along the "shedding path" of Mark. That was so cool that we did that together. We had so much laughter and fun."

Mark: "We experimented on our own to have alternating days: my days for doing it just as I had been, was Monday, Wednesday and Friday. And on Tuesday, Thursday and Saturday we do it Marie's way for one month. Then we flipped where I had Monday, Wednesday and Friday. Saturday night we date each other taking turns again as to where we go. Sunday we both relax in our own way. Interestingly, on Sunday I noticed that I do not let clothes go on the floor. We both pay attention to having relaxed joyfulness on Sunday."

Marie: "After two months we reflected on our learning experiments personally and together. And looking back, I learned new things about Mark that I did not see before."

Mark: "I really got it in my body, what Marie goes through when we exchanged places and I got to put away a lot of stuff. It is exhausting. I began to understand why my mother left us four boys with my father, because she had no support from my father."

Marie: "It's so interesting what has unfolded because Mark invited me fishing. I mustered courage and joined Mark as he paddled on his boat to be in the middle of such a beautiful pond. He taught me to sit in stillness and wait for fish to bite. Who would believe that I would get my feet in the water and feel the wet mud below and getting myself all wet! That was such an experience! I was surprised at how much I enjoyed myself. At the end of it all, Mark joined me sitting in the balcony of our hotel room, taking in the sunset. It was as though the sky lit up in its splendid glory and smiled. My heart smiled too as we expressed our Gratitude to each other for a wonderful learning experience."

5. EXPERIENCE CYCLE OF YOUR 'CONTACTFUL' CONNECTION

This is the experience of your 'I-Thou' *HEALING* relationship dialogue. (Check Pathway D: Skill of Dialogue). You both deepen your experience as you meet each other, sharing your experiences individually and together allowing yourselves to be seen **intimately** (in-to-me-see) to yourself and to each other. Your experience of authentic contact connects you to learning from your experience that can touch your Souls and Illuminates your journey of transformation through the Pathway E.

The experience cycle of your contact embodies:

A. **BEING Skills:** for authentic contact with I-Thou dialogue that connects authentically. Dialogue is the vehicle to a deeper intimate connection to one's being, soul and spirit. Through dialogue in a healing partnership, the couple experiences the "I Am" presence of Divine Love, beyond the 'it' connections for negotiating tasks and problem solving in their daily life.

B. **VALUES** inherent to a Divine Love connection that fosters the couples and individual well-being. Being in dialogue involves the relational experiences of:

- *Inclusion (listening with empathy without losing own self; co-creating a safe environment that fosters trust, validating, and honoring multiple perspectives of inner experience)*

160

- *Presence* (embodying presence to self, other, and us by attending, witnessing and sharing in the Here and Now)

- *Namaste* (contact in-between and co-creating is more than something two people can do with each other, Power of Spirit in Dialogue)

C. **The Energetic Field of Divine Connection**:

In experiencing your Contact together – body, mind, emotion, energy, soul and spirit meet – you create the space to experience yourselves divinely. Sensing your *Pregnant Present* **moment** together, you pause in awe of Presence.

Mark: (reaching out for Marie's hand) "I love how you take care of me and how you are so real to me. I love experiencing life and growing together with you."

Marie: "It pleases me to hear you tell me that. My heart is warm."

Mark: "I thank you for allowing me to truly see you and for being patient with me."

Marie: "I am so moved by how my world has expanded (tearing). I feel empowered and I deeply appreciate us."

Mark: "You stretched yourself and I know you did it to reach out to me."

Marie: "You noticed that! I am so moved to hear you tell me that…. I had to be honest with myself, and be in my heart as to what truly matters. I stretched myself for me too."

Mark: "I also put an effort on shifting my habit and stretch myself to go out of my box. There is a higher purpose as to why we are together. It is like God answered my prayer and it is up to me to receive the blessing in the present moment."

Marie: "Oh…wow… Mark. I can feel what you just said right here in my heart."

Mark: (taking Marie's hand to his heart). "You are awesome. You make me feel so good about me. We are truly awesome."

Marie: (Staying connected nonverbally placing her hand over Mark's hand). "Yes, we are."

1. EXPERIENCE CYCLE OF YOUR ASSIMILATION OF YOUR LEARNING

This part of learning from experience is especially valuable as it involves Be-ing with assimilating one's experience of learning by savoring, cherishing, celebrating. It is the memory making part, reviewing the process that has past by going through it together affirming success and learning, insights, taking in what worked and also acknowledging what was accomplished. For the couple together, this part of learning deepens the how they learned and encoding it in their memory making "log" in their tissues and cells.

At times, it is their *Pregnant Present Pause.* Energetically, you notice yourself as a couple relaxing, enjoying quietly the closing of experience. You are reviewing, reflecting, appreciating, expressing Gratitude, savoring how good you both feel, and cherishing how satisfied you both feel in the Present. At times, it is the pregnant quiet of taking in, breathing and receiving Spirit within.

> **Mark:** "I remember how we started and here we are now. I cannot begin to tell you how grateful I am that you are my one true love. I have grown so much with you. And I am still me."

> **Marie:** "I am cherishing every moment we have right now. A movie is going on for me in my mind and I feel so very confident that we will be able to work through any difficulty we may encounter. I have deep respect for our struggle because although on the surface it seemed so simple, I am so full with such deep love to see your and my willingness to go deeper into the process of learning from experience together. I might have been able to do it on my own. But this is so much more satisfying that we are able to learn together. I believe we have transformed a dynamic that ended our parents' marriages. I believe we transformed the **karma**."

> **Mark:** "You know, my brother is just so amazed that our marriage is really working. He asked me on the side, "What are we doing?" and I said that you and I partnered to learn from experience together. He said, "Really". And I said, "Really.""

> They both look deeply into each other's eyes.

> **Marie:** "Really." Taking a deep and full breath.

> **Mark:** "Really, learning from experience partners."

Your Savoring stretches deepens in your couples tissue memory cells. And the more you cultivate these memory cells, Love memory cells grow, strengthening love.

Review, reflect, and celebrate your experiential learning(s) together and thus by deepening your sensation with Spirit, you both enrich your relationship with many happy memories to cherish in your ever present moments of your life's journey together.

2. EXPERIENCE CYCLE OF SOLITUDE, THE SPACE OF THE FERTILE DIVINE

Growth and Transformation from Experiential Learning is further deepened as each allows space to experience *REST* into the space of the Fertile Divine. Whether that is in quiet do-nothing moments, prayer and meditation, sleep, reading, journaling, or alone time, the experience cycle of solitude, brings one to *pause, be still and behold the fertile divine void within...*

"Be Still and Behold, The Kingdom of God is Within You."

"Most of the time...we find ourselves striving toward that which always seems to lie just beyond our reach. We are caught up in doing rather than being, in action rather than awareness. It is hard for us to picture a state of complete calmness and repose in which thoughts and feelings cease to dance in perpetual motion. It is through such a state of quietude that we can touch a level of joy and understanding impossible to achieve otherwise."
~Paramahansa Yogananda

163

SUMMARY HIGHLIGHTS OF PATHWAY "E": PATHWAY OF EVOLVING AND EXPERIENCE

1. Pathway E - the Pathway of Evolving: *Learning How to Learn From Experience* is vital to the development of individuals and the couple. Experience is the 'teacher' and relationships are the 'school' of life.

2. For many, the challenge of learning from experience is to be able to learn to BE in the PRESENT with conscious awareness of self and other in the contextual field of relational processes. With awareness of patterns of experiences from your past repeating and impacting your current experiences and ways of relating, you have a present opportunity for learning and growth.

3. In their willingness to learn from experience, partners value co-creating their container of safety and learn how to learn and grow in their learning experiences as partners. They appreciate how their learned survival strategies are actually reactive patterns that contribute to their automatically replicated couple's dance, which often does not meet their deeper human intimacy needs and soul's purpose.

4. Your significant relationship can be your learning, healing and spiritual partnership to help you connect within yourself and your partner and inspire you to deeply discover your SELF personally and as a couple. In Pathway E, Learning from Experience, the evolving soul's journey in this world is to know and reconnect with the Divine within; thus transforming through growing the Healing Presence connection of the Eternal Thou that resides Within.

5. The Experience Cycle Process guides your interactive experiential learning practice to facilitate your couple's journey through the Pathway of Evolving through the:

   - Experience Cycle with and through your Inner and Outer Senses
   - Experience Cycle of your Awareness and Intention
   - Experience Cycle of your Activating and Joining Energy
   - Experience Cycle of your Inspired and Energized Action for Experiment
   - Experience Cycle of your 'Contactful' Connection
   - Experience Cycle of Assimilation of your Learning
   - Experience Cycle of your Solitude, the Space of the Fertile Divine

PATHWAY F: PATHWAY OF FREEDOM AND RESPONSIBILITY

"Freedom leads to freedom. Those are the first words of truth. You do not know what truth is because you do not know what freedom is.
All the 'truth' that you know today is only truth in quotation marks. There is another truth but it is not theoretical; it cannot be expressed in words.
Only those who have realized it in themselves can understand that truth."
~G. I. Gurdjieff

Introduction

Balancing freedom and responsibility for a couple is multi-layered. Both have many nuances and cover a huge ground of possibilities. To clarify your understanding, let us begin by examining the essence of response-ability and freedom as the soulful Pathway of the couple's transformational life journey.

> **Freedom:** God-given within all humans is free will because we are all created in the image and likeness of Divine Love. From within our inner being, we have choices of the heart regardless of our circumstances.

> **Response-ability:** Comes from the root word of *spond* and *spons,* which means to **pledge** and **covenant**; and *ibilit* is the "ability to respond." When there is a sense of balanced response-ability between intimate partners, they can pledge and re-pledge their relationship.

The intimate relationship provides a relational and magnetic field environment for the partners to develop their inner awareness and connection to their embodiment of heart-mind and spirit. As both parties are committed to understanding their relational response-abilities and gain inner awareness of their interactive processes, they are better able to clarify their intent and the impact of their actions and choices on their partnership. As their interactive processes deepen the couple into truth and love, it allows for healing and transformation to be magnetic in their field.

Do you wonder how this would be in practice? What would the process be of our attending to the balance between relational responsibilities, personal responsibilities and our experience of inner freedom and our choice-fullness in love and truth in the balancing?

Relational response-abilities involves how the partners stay in touch with each other by their presence, informing, inviting, sharing, listening, dialoguing, empathizing, and supporting. They engage and connect, check in with each other, as well as, attend to one another as they are interacting.

Personal response-abilities involves how you take care of and love yourself, how you care for your whole being in spirit-soul-mind-emotions-energy-body. It includes your connection with your Higher Power, your living practices that foster health, well-being, growth and enhancement of inner virtues.

Relationships that grow and last have a vital combination of the awareness of one's inner self and personal responsibilities, as well as a collaborative connection to their relational responsibilities. The effects of the energetic resonance that this balance radiates in the couple's heart field, is a palpable and true commitment of loving devotion that gives each other a feeling of freedom to BE Love.

With the spirit of devotion, responsibility takes on a higher purpose. Freedom with the regard of others, its intended and unintended consequences, leads to unfolding possibilities. Your choices impact your experiences and 'your becoming'. You feel empowered as you own your capacity to create and choose how you respond regardless of your circumstances.

Few truly understand this in our world. Most people view things from an external or either-or perspective that they impose on themselves and on each other. Unconscious choices are made in a quest for "freedom" that actually leads to forms of 'slavery'. For example, couples who identify their human worth according to material standards alone battle for 'freedom' by attempting to accumulate more wealth, thinking this will lead to freedom. Thus paradoxical results occur.

Through the morass of worldly demands and stresses, without even realizing it, many find themselves struggling for freedom from earlier unconscious or karmic choices. As one moves to higher levels of consciousness, yearning for truth and authentic freedom, one can appreciate that the illusions of freedom are temporary. Interestingly, as couples become devoted to their Spirit of learning, they develop awareness skills and practice disciplines they can peel away at the 'chains' that keep them from being true and free and respond from within a place of peace, joy, and healing love.

This chapter lets you begin to appreciate the value, richness and depth of Pathway F. You will glean insight into the transformational journey that a couple experiences in regards to balancing feelings of freedom and having responsibility.

The Complexity of Pathway F

As the relational and contextual field shift and change, imbalances between partners can increase to high points of tension. When one partner insists on freedom without boundaries there will be chaos. The one who wants freedom may say:

> "Our relationship isn't alive. I have lost the feeling. I want to be happy and free."

> "I want to be free of all this responsibility. I want to do as I please sometimes I forget to consider the both of us."

> "I lost myself. I need to be free to be me, to say what I think and feel."

> "I need to be free to follow my interests, have my own friends, and listen to my own music. I want to get rid of this feeling of being controlled."

The other partner will insist on responsibility, duty, obligations, consistency, dependability and structure; which leads to feeling as if the relationship is a task, chore or burden. Pathway F guides couples to learn the practices of inner and outer responsibility so they can experience feelings of inner freedom and the fullness of love, even in the midst of stress and outer chaos. The one who pulls for responsibility may say:

> "There are so many things to do and accomplish. We are adults. We have the children to consider and take care of."

"We are responsible for what and how we speak and act. We are not as free as before."

"We need order and predictability in our lives. I cannot stand the chaos."

The challenge of Pathway F is that it is paradoxical in nature. When stuck and perplexed in the pain of their struggle, couples will look for more and more ways to fix each other or oneself according to how they or we 'should be'. In their attempts to **"fix"** the assumed problem by giving advice, suggesting solutions, or taking action without checking or consulting with the other, couples actually polarize and become even more stuck.

The **risk** for couples is to bring conscious awareness to their unconscious reactions. When they do this they become free from their inner muddle of thinking, emotions, and actions that limit them from experiencing the healing power of love.

There is a misconception that responsibility blocks spontaneity, creativity, and freedom. It is with response-ability that meaning can be found and masterpieces of art are created. It is with responsibility, that we are more likely to experience the freedom of unconditional love. With embodying a balance between response-ability and freedom, couples are more likely to experience vitality and growth in their love relationship.

To laugh is to risk appearing the fool.
To weep is to risk appearing sentimental.

To reach out for another is to risk involvement.
To explore feeling is to risk expressing our true self.

To place your ideas, your dreams before the Crowd, Is to risk their loss.
To love is to risk not being loved in return.

To live is to risk dying. To hope is to risk despair.

To try is to risk failure. But, the risk must be taken,
Because the greatest hazard in life is to risk nothing.

The person who risks nothing, does nothing, has nothing, is nothing.

He may avoid suffering and sorrow, but he simply cannot
Learn, feel, change, grow, love or live.

Chained by his certitude, he is a slave, he has forfeited freedom.

*Only a person who risks is – **free**.*

~Author Unknown

The Beauty of Freedom and Responsibility

Freedom and responsibility are not mutually exclusive. For individuals within their couple relationship, it is about how to find **freedom through responsibility and responsibility through freedom**. This polarity is heightened in significant relationships as the intimate relationship triggers deep, unconscious, and unresolved struggles. Embedded in this Pathway is the opportunity for conscious examination, exploration, and connection to each other in deepening levels of healing love as they are stretched and impacted profoundly by their inner freedom to be authentic.

When there is a dynamic balance between freedom and responsibility we have observed partners to be:

- Spiritually and soulfully centered within themselves
- Devoted to each other and able to honor each other's truths
- Full with their essence and spirit
- Free to be authentic with each other
- Response-able, present with one's self and with your partner, with a great range of freedom to be
- Able to connect with each other to check assumptions, attend, share, and live your responsibilities interactively
- Able to live in a **both-and** capacity
- Able to evolve in the presence of each other
- Appreciative of where there is freedom and responsibility in your relationship
- Able to trust that when you go off track, both can seek the necessary supports to get back on track

Dynamics in Couples

People notice the magnetic inner radiance of a couple's love connection when their energy chords of freedom and responsibility are synchronized and harmonious. When there is disharmony, the one who clamors for freedom often feels the chords are too tight and may want more freedom. The one, who pulls for responsibility, often feels the chords are too loose and wants more stability.

As a couple polarizes, each partner holds one end of the pole so their reactions towards each other are disproportionate to their current situation. Therefore it is safe to assume that there are unconscious chords tied to tales unbeknownst to both of them.

When couples can delve into Pathway F, they will become consciously aware that they have the power to see beyond the surface of material, external or political freedom by living more fully in awareness and become more fully *response-able*. Because old patterns are challenged, this

Pathway can be frightening for some couples, even though they say they want to be free or want to be more responsible and have control of their lives.

It is easier to succumb to the belief that one is powerless, deluding oneself that "there is no choice." Paradoxically, making no choice is still a choice. The beginning of the journey of transformation in Pathway F occurs for many couples when they begin to face how their choices of numbing, avoiding, ignoring, depressing, medicating, acting-out or blaming has led to their in-authentic, unconscious, and irresponsible living. Something within them wants to be freed of their inner pain and their unhappiness. So the journey of Pathway F begins.

Two Types of Couples

There are generally two types of couples that struggle in the journey through Pathway F. The first types are couples where one or both parties focus on their freedom and individuality. Unless they learn the couple skills for developing the relational response-abilities (Pathways A to E) of how to connect, dialogue, and co-create, they will end up creating the conditions to divorce. For them, freedom through divorce becomes the solution. While the reasons vary, these couples describe that the emotions connected to the 'pain' of the loss of their own individuality while co-managing their differences is virtually impossible.

The second types are couples who have been married for many years and one or both parties will say, "We are good people. We do all the right things but we are not happy... but... we do not want a divorce." Upon further exploration, one or both may say, "I don't know who I am or what I want. I don't know who he or she is." They have collapsed their individualities and they 'lack' the skills and responsibility to experience the freedom to be individuals in their coupleness. When the priest or minister says the two shall become one, it sounds romantic and sentimental. The question is which one? These couples have conformed to the expectations and values with the promise of happiness, and cannot understand why they feel 'dead' inside.

The question is -- how does one navigate the polarizing terrain of Pathway F in the complexities of current living? Both types of couples that are committed to growth are looking for different paradigms that will bring a sense of balance in dealing with the polarity of freedom and responsibility.

There has never been a time before in the evolution of human consciousness and the re-awakening of intuitive wisdom such as what we are experiencing now. Because of this, we have more opportunities to make amazing shifts and changes in so many levels of our lives. This is such an exciting time to be living where unconscious possibilities are constantly being uncovered and explored.

Evolving couples are listening to their inner restlessness or soul stirrings and are taking the challenge and the risks of partnering to go deeper into the Inner Pathway F of Freedom and Responsibility. When they stop and begin *to wonder* how they could deal with their dilemma of freedom vs. responsibility as a couple, and what appears to be virtually impossible, opens for exploration, that can lead them to body, emotional, energetic, mind, soul, and spiritual realms of freedom and responsibility. What may come into their awareness are deeper levels of ground that have been imbedded in the soulfulness of this dilemma.

Process Tool: My, Your, and Our Window of Freedom and Responsibility

To begin to help you understand the many facets of Pathway F, we offer you an awareness tool that we have used ourselves and with our clients. The purpose of this tool is to provide a present glimpse of your view of the 'reality' of where you and your partner are in Pathway F. As a visual aid to broadening your dialogue process as a couple, you can utilize this awareness tool to see yourself, your relationship, and your couple's relationship window of freedom and responsibility, in a clarifying light.

The objectives of this process tool are to:
- Help you gain awareness of your personal window and your couple's window of Freedom and Responsibility
- Give you a visual aid when you dialogue with each other

Instructions:

- When doing this process , how you complete it will depend on your individual outlook and temperament:

    o Cognitive and visual people will enjoy this process tool.

    o Persons who are tonal (listens to inflection of sounds) may write or tell a story or put it to music.

    o Kinesthetic persons (those who like to move and learn by doing so) may feel what is in those boxes and can doodle or draw it. If you are kinesthetic, place the following diagram on a big chart and place it on the floor. Put things in the environment and put it in the boxes to represent the areas. This allows the cognitive or visual person to see the soul of the other. It will help the kinesthetic or tonal to change the channel to connect with the cognitive person.

Take your time alone, so you can reflect on your own Window of Freedom and Responsibility. Give each other space for each of your alone time.

- After each of you have finished with your own Window of Freedom and Responsibility, take another blank flip chart, which is your Couples Window and plot out your responses in the Quadrants. Please see the example of Al and Bea in the following pages.

171

My Window: Alone Time

F = Freedom   **R** = Responsibility

In each **Quadrant**, list the area(s) that are fulfilling, pleasing, gratifying, satisfying, important, relevant and/or troubling, worrying, upsetting, unsettling, to you **<u>NOW</u>**, such as Family, Children, Parents, Work/Career, Money, Time, Health, Friends, Relationship, Intimacy, etc. or any combination thereof.

Quadrant 1: List the area(s) of your life wherein you have HIGH **F** and HIGH **R**. Give 3 specific examples.

Quadrant 2: List the area(s) of your life wherein you have LOW **F** and HIGH **R**. Give 3 specific examples.

Quadrant 3: List the area(s) of your life wherein you have LOW **R** and HIGH **F**. Give 3 specific examples.

Quadrant 4: List the area(s) of your life wherein you have LOW **F** and LOW **R**. Give 3 specific examples.

A. Take a moment to breathe and connect within. Notice your inner experience of having filled in your Freedom & Responsibility Window (F & R Window).

Next, mark with an (*1), (*2), and (*3) with <u>3 as the most **important**</u> according to their importance for you at this current time.

Next, mark with an (x1), (x2) and (x3) with <u>3 as the most **urgent**</u> according to their urgency for you at this current time.

NOTE: What is the difference between urgent and important? Share with each other the difference in the meanings of urgent and important.

My, Your, and Our Window of Freedom and Responsibility

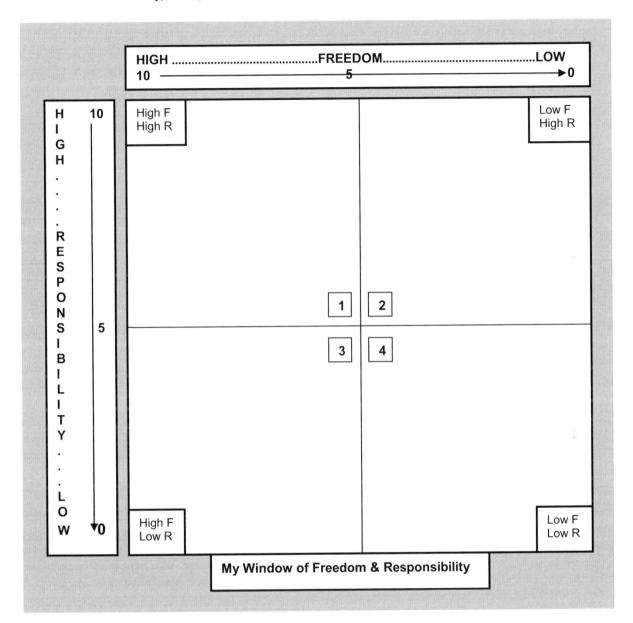

Combined Window: Together with your Partner

A. Breathe, ground and center within. Acknowledge your inner Intention, before taking turns to present to each other your F&R Window. Take turns being the presenter, and the listener. Attend to gain a full awareness and appreciation of your Window and your partner's Window and the component parts of your couple system F&R Window. Practice curiosity, discovery and wonderment. Refrain from judgment either of yourself or of each other.

B. Dialogue with each other; checking, clarifying and sharing to have a sense, picture and appreciation of your couples F&R Window with its component parts. Notice similarities and where there is agreement. Notice differences in your experiences and perspectives.

Our Window: Together

A. Drawing from your dialogue, and incorporating both of you windows, fill in together the component parts of your couple's F&R Window. Notice how you are gaining in your awareness together of your partnership present F&R window as you check in, clarify and share.

B. Slow down within and connect to your inner Window in your heartfelt space. Take a moment and breathe within your heart. You may place your hand over your heart and your High Heart (thymus gland). You may tap your heart space and feel the resonance of tapping. Tapping activates the energetic flow in your heart center. Notice your inner experience of placing your hand over or tapping your heart space. Imagine and affirm the magnetic field of your heart Window that opens, connects, and links you both in the Energetic Field of Divine Love.

C. From within your heart, share your awareness and learning from doing this process together. Affirm, appreciate and/or celebrate your awareness and present learning.

D. Reflect how you are co-creating in this MOMENT now, your Freedom within to Respond and Love within your Being. Energetically feel it in this moment.

A Couple's Example – Al and Bea

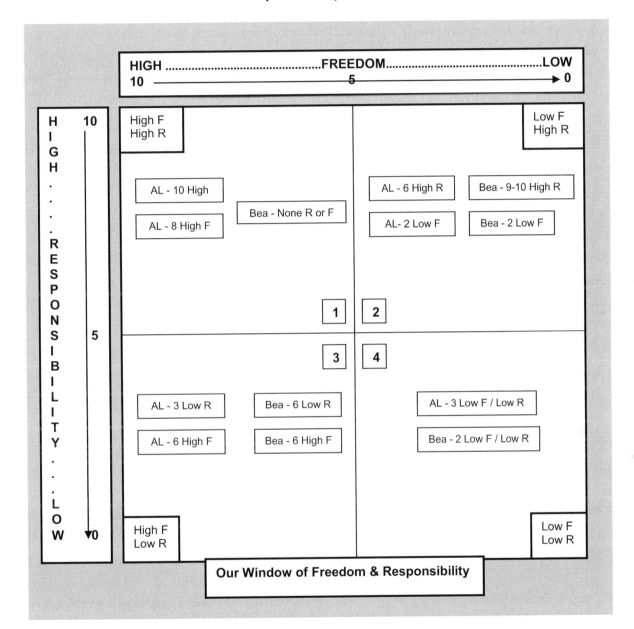

Our Window of Freedom & Responsibility

Al's Window of Freedom and Responsibility

Quadrant 1: Career / Business

High F -- 8 (1) "CEO of an innovative, creative and cutting edge company. I would put this as 10, but my Freedom is tempered by the High Responsibility I have. (2) Freedom to be really productive, I am happy and love what I do. I have a purpose in leading a company that makes a difference in people's lives."

High R -- 10 (3) "Responsible for 15 highly skilled loyal employees-dedicated to the mission of our company. We are like family; not only surviving in this economy but are also providing an important service to the community."

Quadrant 2: Parents and Children

Low F -- 2 (1) "Very concerned for my aging parents as they have serious health issues. I am not able to be with them and my mother especially reminds me that I need to visit more often. (2) Same goes for my children. The only time I get to see them is to tuck them into bed. (3) I am most lacking in time with my wife, Bea. Bea is being very understanding about the stress in our marriage. I need to create free time to be together."

High R -- 6 "I have the power of attorney in my parents' care and I should be more available to my family."

Quadrant 3: Friends and Leisure

Low R - - 3 (1) "Bea takes care of our social life, as she is the more sociable one. She also takes care of our family fun activities. I just show up when I can...which she is not happy about."

High F -- 6 (2) "My free time is spent exercising to release stress in the gym, as my schedule does not allow me an active, physical life."

Quadrant 4: Money

Low F Low R: 3 -- (1) Bea, being an accountant, is better with money than I am. I let go of being responsible for our money and I am relieved. I just turn over all our household finances to her. (2) Sometimes I am irritated that I am not free to spend irresponsibly."

Bea's Window of Freedom and Responsibility

Quadrant 1: Money, Investing Home Business

High F and High R: none right now

Quadrant 2: Children, Household and Finances

High R --10 -- (1) "Since the children are little, I am the one mostly with them, except for when they are asleep or I am able to get my mother to watch them so I could do some errands or go for a run."

9 -- (2) "I am in charge of our finances. It comes easy to me and I have a knack for making good, conservative investments. I am disciplined and we live within our means."

Low F: -- 2--(1) "I do not want to leave the children with a baby sitter as they are little. Al comes home around 7pm when they are ready to go to bed. While he tucks them into bed and has his special time, I am cleaning up the kitchen, etc. At the end of the day, I am exhausted."

Quadrant 3: Friends and Leisure

High F Low R: 6 -- (1) "We have friends who love the both of us. I have a great deal of freedom to be myself. Al likes my friends and lets me interact with them. (2) I am the one who plans our social and leisure events...consults Al's schedule...that is why it is 6."

Quadrant 4: Intimacy, Couple Time, Me Time

Low F Low R--2-- (1) "Our time together is brief, as well as scheduled. (2) End of the day; sharing our exhaustion and debriefing the day. Not much fun...except we try when we can to go out to dinner at least once a month and sometimes that gets changed because of Al's work. (3) I wish I would have some influence on this...but I take it a day at a time and do not focus on it. (4) I need some time away from all this for myself...at least some balance. Looking at all of this, I need more freedom."

After both Al and Bea completed their Quadrants, they shared them. They noticed where there was agreement was in Quadrant 3. Creating dialogue where they listened and were curious about where each was coming from helped to clarify what they each meant. They practiced the discipline of slowing down, which connected them to listen from within their heartfelt place. In so doing, they were able to be open to see what would evolve from their sharing.

They affirmed what is and came up with a feasible experiment to bring some balance. They appreciated that they both were in the process of working on this Pathway together.

Al and Bea: A Couple's Example of the Dance of Response-ability and Freedom

Bea felt safe and free to disclose her feelings of being burdened and seeming powerless. She struggled with her growing resentment of being married and feeling stuck in blaming her husband for her lack of freedom, with all her time taken up with caring for the needs of the children and him.

While she complained, she expressed her appreciation of Al's listening to her experience. Al acknowledge that he has the freedom to make all the decisions regarding his job, his relaxation and felt free to do whatever he wanted.

Bea discovered that she lost connection to her inner self. She became aware that what she chose was the easy way to blame, rather than be response-able to herself. When Al, connected to his heartfelt compassion for his wife's experience and his possible contribution to her experience, he asked, "If you were free, what would you love to do?" Bea breathed deeply, creating space to connect within her heart. "I'd really like to go to the gym and exercise. I'd like to be able to take some yoga classes."

There was a paradox here for when she was asking for freedom, she also had to create some connection to her inner self in order to have the ability to respond to her need for freedom.

As Bea and Al continued to dialogue from the heart, they realized a loving space was opening for negotiating their time collaboratively at their couple level for personal time for Bea and for personal time for Al to freely experience his own father time with their children.

Bea's inner experience mirrored their resonant response-ability in their whole 'system' energy. They felt empowered in their renewing 'dance' of more room to feel loving, caring and connected with each other.

Freedom and Responsibility in These Present Times

In these times of great change we cannot take the freedom that we had for granted. In the West, the changes in the economy are hitting many in ways that are being felt profoundly on an inner, energetic and soul level. These internal changes are very hard to put your hands around. It is like the sensation of trying to squeeze water by grabbing a hold of it. It seems elusive. Yet, holding water within the palm of your open hand can also refresh you with creative possibilities unfolding in the relational field.

Let us consider that by our very human nature, we bond to meet our needs and desires; whether for survival, safety, belonging and/or support, esteem and/or recognition and actualization and/or optimizing our fulfillment. The bonds of love can tighten with the stresses that adversity brings. Couples can experience their bonding as 'bondage' or as a sanctuary of love and support.

Our humans bonds require us to engage in certain responsibilities or behaviors to create connection. Our responsibilities ordain the path so we can gain mastery, character and strength on our quest to free ourselves from personal struggles and to better relate with others as well as to succeed in the world.

Those who are on a path of soul development seek master teachers, elders, mentors, coaches and guides who model response-abilities that have contributed to their freedom and that of others.

The environment of the relationship gives partners opportunities for their soul to deepen into an inner space embodied within the energetic trinity of body, mind and spirit. The relational space in-between are the couples' co-creative process of their intentions and the impact of their interactions. Their interactive university of life experiences can bring to the surface layers of the unconscious body and past life memories and emotional reactions that trigger mental maps so they can be re-examined, released, cleansed, and transformed.

When life's challenges are faced from an embodied stance of response-able presence and connection, couples share how they experience constraints being lifted by their commitment and choices for their growth and healing. Then they experience the sweetness of freedom.

As couples connect with their inner voice - the truth within - their experience of freedom becomes their present experience. It resonates with a vibrancy of honest truth that frees and that can be acknowledged.

Experiencing true freedom entails being able to let go of what doesn't work and to be able to come into the present moment. In the present, true dialogue allows for authenticity of your experience, thus being able to keep what works while releasing what is not working.

Many paradigms and institutions, such as governments, economics, health, and religious organizations may have given people an illusion of a sense of security that has now shaken people's existence by how it was defined and that they depended on to feel safe. This stress is reflected in a certain edginess that people experience and it is often felt even in the most intimate relationships.

In order to become current in their relationship, couples revisit their old agreements and renegotiate their differences, values, and expectations of themselves and each other. It is here where they discover new possibilities, as old structures and processes that no longer works are transformed to meet their current needs and circumstances.

If we look at the context of life – speed is present. It feels like there's no time because everything is in hyper-speed. Over-stimulation and stresses of current daily living create little time for one's intimate and significant relationships. Sadly, affairs and relationship breakups are the stories that sell. Numbing through addictions causes breakdowns in many relationships resulting in disease in mind-body and spirit.

Now, more than ever and since 9/11, relationships and intimate partners are being called to be aware of how they treat themselves and each other. Across the board of human interactions, kindness, support, empathy, and respect are desired response-abilities, while freedom to speak one's truth, to pursue one's goal and to value one's belief or faith will now require partners to cultivate a higher order capacity of authentic Love to hold seemingly conflicting energies in their strengthened spiritual relationships in the unified field of Healing and Divine Love to oneself and to each other.

We believe that a two person system as in significant partnerships, friendships, or couples' relationships *is the seed*...like the mustard seed...that can energetically and exponentially transform humanity's relationship. The couples' relationship is where, when brought to the higher levels of divine love, shifts the tide of karmic debt that over time heals and transforms. Now, the time has come for co-creation in the energetic matrix of our divine connection as the freeing of our response-ability for our inherent human kindness with the couples' relationship as the vehicle to this connection.

Our emotional relationships mirror in field of reality what we choose to co-create in our lives. Gregg Braden describes in his book the **_Divine Matrix_**, how current scientific research is now documenting that the heart is 5,000 times stronger in the magnetic field than the brain, in response to the emotions we create.

Present Challenges Couples Are Facing

1. Many couples are facing the dismantling of institutions that kept in order their daily lives. The **'shoulds'** that have been handed down over the generations are now in question and relationships are challenged to awaken to a level of consciousness that can cause major shifts in relating. Many couples and partners feel an inner-outer conflict as their material-based freedom has become limited and their stability threatened. One way couples are handling this global scale stress is to go deep into the heart and soul of their relationship, to reawaken ancient wisdom that respects the spiritual interconnectedness of humankind.

    For example, a wife may project her inner conflict about being away from the children by expecting her husband to take care of the household and children the way she does. She struggles between resenting being the 'only one' who has work and the 'woman's job is at home'. He feels unappreciated and depressed and that despite all of his efforts, he still cannot find work. He projects his stress on her 'low opinion' of him and he feels that there is nothing that he does that will please her. Their beliefs limit them and bring significant stress to their relationship.

2. Many couples are experiencing a lack of free time -- both in time together and in personal time. And when they do have free time they do not know what to do with themselves or how to be. As they allow themselves to start wherever they are being, even in their not knowing how to be or what to do with this free time, they become consciously free in the moment. In order to ground and reconnect, partners must carve out time for oneself, for each other and for their relationship so they can experience new options, an inner freedom for the healing of their heart and spirit.

3. In the West we value individuality, following our own separate and unique path for growth, development, and success. Freedom tends to be equated to success, being your own person and the discovery of one's own self and expression. Such a quest has led to the conquest of self, and of others, to overcome obstacles, challenges, and adversities.

The challenge for most couples is how to appreciate the empowerment in their connection and collaboration rather than the old paradigm of competition with each other for worthiness. *True freedom lies in the Divine Matrix of our relationship and interconnectedness.* We will expand on this more in Pathway H.

Reflection Exercise: How Intimate Relationships are Being Impacted

During this time of profound change, intimate relationships are being affected on many levels. Take a moment and reflect on your significant relationship.

Instructions: Reflect on the following statements listed below. Check in with yourself to see if you are experiencing any of these changes.

On the lines after each statement, you can write about how you are feeling about these changes. Are you feeling limited? Trapped? Or controlled in any of the following? What would freedom from any of these below look like for you? What response-ability(ies) would be supportive for each of you and for both of you?

We are seeing changes in:

1. Expectations: Many of the roles we have given ourselves may not work any longer (i.e. a husband should; a wife should). You may have brought from those roles expectations for security that is now being challenged.

   _____

   _____

2. Feelings of Isolation, Shame and Embarrassment: Many have had experiences that have caused their freedom to narrow. You may feel isolated, shamed, guilty, angry, hurt, limited, worried, bitter, fearful of failures and mistakes, and that you no longer have your chance to be your very best.

   _____

   _____

3. Physical Health and Sexual Intimacy: Stress levels are profoundly affecting people physically, emotionally and sexually. You wonder what is happening to you, healthwise.

   _____

   _____

4. Emotional Challenges: When people do not feel empowered, they can become controlling. You many feel a loss of confidence or powerless in your circumstances. In your attempts to control the situation, you act in hurtful ways towards yourself and others.

_____

_____

5. Abilities to Connect: Many are feeling disconnected, withdrawn, distant, checked out, and are absent. You may feel stuck in a misunderstanding and find it difficult to get unstuck.

_____

_____

6. Decreased Communication and Expression: Communications are stuck and unfinished. You may find the ability to express yourself is limited and/or you are doing so for self-protection.

_____

_____

7. Difficulty Finding Direction: Many cannot see a direction of where they are and where they are going. You may find yourself feeling downhearted and unclear.

_____

_____

8. Feeling Trapped in a Situation: Some are trapped in their circumstances. Are you struggling to see options for how you can free yourself, how you can succeed, etc?

_____

_____

9. Feeling Disconnected from Spirit of the Source of Divine Love Within: Because of this level of disconnection, many find it difficult to pray, meditate or be spiritual. You feel lost as though you are undeserving or forgotten.

_____

_____

The Energetic Tension of Pathway F

Negotiating Polarities

How does a couple work through and manage the tension between the polarities of freedom and responsibility? How do they negotiate the dance between 'I need to be free to be my own person' and we need to be response-able together? When there is too much focus on either responsibility or freedom, there will be tension instead of balance.

In order to be in balance, couples can engage their tension to go towards the core of their tension. Here, they will discover and gain awareness to leverage and illuminate their **both/and** perspective. Perhaps, the couple braces with care and caution in negotiating the risk of discovering the power of how they affect one another in this polarity. The freedom they uncover in Pathway F brings with it a new sense of responsibility or response-ability that takes them to the center of Love and Truth.

> *"To love one another truly is to walk in the light, to live in truth,*
> *to be truly alive, and perfectly free."*
> *~R.D. Laing*

How Couples Lose Their Relationship to Self and Other

Many couples are relating unconsciously most of the time and cannot figure out why they keep repeating the same patterns over and over again. These relationships are framed by expectations where shoulds, musts, ought to, have to, never, and always, require behaviors that fulfill standards and roles based on familial-cultural-religious contexts. For a while relating within-the-box may provide some sense of external safety or belonging, but does not lead to fulfillment.

However, the very nature of love relationships awakens within the heart, the soul's inherent yearning to be free...to free the spirit of the **'I Am'** Presence of the infinite possibilities that the couple's love can contain and express. Their angst can set them free from the shackles of the inner chatter of their limiting beliefs, from the muddle of stuck emotions and frozen stances, and from the 'drama' of reciprocal hooks and triggers. Thus, couples feel this call of their souls to take them to their spiritually transforming journey into Pathway F, the Pathway of Freedom and Responsibility.

What and How Partners Get Out of Their Emotional Muddle

In order to get unstuck from an emotional muddle, both partners need to be aware of how they co-participate in getting stuck. When you can own your participation in your relational stuckness and accept your own response-ability for each of your parts, a freeing process of facing 'What Is True' in your co-created experience emerges. By realizing your possibilities of how you both co-participate in your freeing process of getting un-stuck are now opening with the awareness of your inner choice-fullness. Together, you both allow yourselves to see, in an evolving way, what each does that is different.

There are many layers of an emotional muddle involving both unconscious and conscious patterns that the couple engages in:

1. Are you aware of what, how, when, and where your patterns together get stuck?
2. How do you know it?
3. What is your experience individually and together of being stuck?
4. Describe your thinking, feeling, and behaving with each other that you experience as stuck without blaming or judging.
5. Are you able to share your perceptions of feeling stuck and own your part as your contribution to how your interactions become stuck?

When couples understand this on the conscious level they wonder why they still feel terrible. This is because old unconscious emotions are still being triggered by each partner. When a couple can learn to relate and talk to each other, they can choose to explore and acknowledge how they each contribute to 'hooking' each other and getting stuck. Slowing down allows them to focus on one part at a time, rather than snowballing. As they now are able to own their participation in the co-creation of their muddle, without blaming, they start to notice that they *can choose* how they can participate with awareness.

Let's say partners are having a discussion which triggers each other and one interprets that what the other is saying 'is making me feel like I am not good enough'. So they may decide to delve further in this belief of 'I'm not good enough' by exploring it more, looking into where it comes from. They explore how that belief got triggered here in this particular moment. That conversation may be along the lines of:

> "My intention was to share my own thoughts and that I am interested in what happened to evoke your feeling of 'not good enough'."

They learn how to talk in such a way so that it is not his fault or her fault to have triggered that theme. This way they can pay attention to the present moment of how the 'old stuff' got re-enacted in their present interaction. If they create a climate of safety, it is possible that the 'old stuff' may reveal an opening for the 'soul wound' to be free to heal.

How do you know when the 'old stuff' surfaces in your interaction? It is when your reaction is larger or more than what is called for in the present moment. It is like a 'tsunami' that just wells up waiting to be released from the 'earthquake' underground.

Over time, the more one practices their freeing of unhealthy beliefs and releasing their stuck emotional energy, the healing partnership reframes the 'inevitable' interactive stimulation of 'old stuff'. Together you view the 'old stuff' as opportunities for helping each other release its grip on

© 2013 Philip Belzunce and Lalei Gutierrez • www.ehealinglove.com

your present life and co-create response-abilities for supports in finishing and healing. As couples practice the tools of freeing themselves from their emotional muddle – the energy shifts, the emotional intensity changes, and the unhealthy cognitive belief patterns subside and transform. Over time, it loses its potency and intensity.

We work with couples on how they can coach each other to help illuminate and leverage the present moment experience so they aren't contaminated by an unconscious emotional reaction from the past.

Over time you begin to feel free.

The Interactive Freeing Process

1. The first thing couples do is co-create their safe container to look at <u>what they are doing to contribute to their experience</u>. A place for looking at how you contribute to the experience can be empowering. For example, look at how your *intention* and *impact* plays out in what you are saying and doing with each other. Practicing this discipline increases awareness so you notice your experience of replaying your muddle of reactive spinning downward or exploding at each other. With awareness, you develop an interactive discipline of realizing and attending to your co-participation in practicing response-ability together. Here is an example:

    > "My intention is to share my thoughts to think out loud instead of letting it spin around inside of my head. My request is that you do not interpret it as blame. I will do my best to share my own experience. If you hear it as blame, I will appreciate you stopping me so that I can practice sharing in a way that I can experience feeling clear. And you can help me by listening and reflecting back to me what you hear me saying so I can clear my head and be present here and now with you. Would you do that with me?"

2. It is important to remember that partners tend to automatically take it personally, because you are personally involved with each other. That is why slowing down, grounding with your feet on the earth, breathing to <u>be in the present moment and with each other is so critical</u>.

    > "OK. So I hear that it's OK, when I say, "We need to slow down and stop for a moment if I am beginning to feel any blame. I will breathe and pace myself and check what you mean. It is important for me that I am able to listen to you in the present. It helps me to hear your intention and manage with you the impact you want to have."

This is the place where the mutual freeing process is happening with their conscious co-creating in the present.

> "OK, I appreciate that we are working together on being non-blaming. I am really open to know when I am triggering your feeling blamed. That way I can work on being clear with my intent matching the impact I want to have. I want to express myself cleanly and clearly. I will appreciate what you see and hear so I can check myself as to how I am coming across to you as blaming when that is not my intent."

3. It is helpful to <u>be specific in the present with concrete data that is observable</u>.

> "When I see your eyes narrow like this and I see your finger point and you say 'you are wrong', I hear it as blame. Rather than tell me 'you are wrong', tell me how you see it differently. It is helpful for me to know that you want me to listen to your experience or perspective."

4. It is here the couple practices their <u>mutual correction or adjustment.</u>

A couple is a relational system that mutually feeds each other's dance. When you consciously begin to look at your parts in your relational dance, you shift your part and choose to experiment in ways that frees you both from your stuckness.

The following is an example of how taking <u>personal response-ability supports relational response-ability.</u>

One member of the couple may take their time to slow down their own internal reaction. This individual might ground by feeling their feet on the ground, go for a walk, or might go into an inner place of prayerfulness. This individual internally dialogues with self, and could if it seemingly suitable, to express their inner process:

> "I am so confused right now. I'm working hard internally to manage my reactivity. I am feeling rather hyper and stressed. I am not in a good space to talk. I need time out so I can decompress. I will go to the gym and work out and clear my head so I will be in a better frame of mind. I would like to continue our dialogue later. Will you be OK?"

Internally, you may individually <u>manage your energy by having an inner connection</u> with yourself by using methods such as grounding, centering, inner prayer, breathing, and meditation or in movement methods such as walking, tai chi, yoga, exercise, and dancing, or with self care methods such as massage, journaling, listening to music, reading drawing etc. When you consciously shift your own energy, be open to notice the shift between yourselves and how your emotional and mental frame shifts impact your exchange with each other.

When you both have taken personal response-ability time and notice your own shift, it may be possible that your partner may not be ready to engage. However making it known to your partnership of one's readiness for connection, allows for movement to re-engage.

5. There are <u>three points of re-entry with each other in the freeing process</u>. It is helpful to know your energetic channels for connection, where you are different and where you meet. It is also helpful to assess which entry channel is most accessible in the present with attention to all parts. For example (refer to Pathway C):

> Points of re-entry in the freeing process:
> **A.** <u>your channel is</u> auditory or tonal

B. your partner is digital or logical

C. and both of you are visual

You are choosing to re-engage with both of you, by inviting your partner to re-engage in a visual way.

> "I notice that we enjoy reading books and seeing movies together. And I love that about us. While I was listening to my meditation tape, I saw a visual of our movie together and I drew it. When you are ready I would like to show you my picture of where we got stuck, I want to see your picture of your intention because when we draw, I am able to follow and listen better."

You partner notices the shift in energy channels and is willing to join.

> "I want to clarify our misunderstanding and see your picture of what happened. I am glad that you are willing to see mine too. I appreciate that we are working together to free ourselves from the old way and find our new way."

6. The Steps in the Freeing Process

- Be aware of each of your parts in the muddle.
- Be aware of what is a 'programmed belief' versus a 'chosen belief'. What are the emotions connected to this belief? If it is not in your awareness, what is the context in the present? Look at the storyline that you put around the belief.
- Be aware of how your individual programmed beliefs trigger each other.
- Attend with an embodied presence to your intention and the impact you intend to have and check with each other for the congruence of intention and impact.
- Join together to experiment with present new ways that offer each other a different way of feeling. ("How would you have preferred to have that said to you?") Find ways to give each other what we would have wanted to have received. Be concrete. Come up with 'do-able' behaviors. When couple's run into trouble they say, "I want respect." Describe how you want respect. When it becomes do-able then couples are more likely to give each other something concrete. What does respect mean for each of you?
- Take a moment to look at what you love about what you did and your partner did, so you begin to co-create more deposits in the bank of positive experiences. Celebrate in the present moment.
- Remember: **Freeing is a process**.

When you find yourself stuck, you help yourself by getting help to gain conscious awareness of how your repeating interactive process gets you both stuck. It is often when you become consciously aware of how and what you are contributing in the present to your experience of stuckness, that you now realize that the 'choice-full' possibilities to co-creating experiences can free both of you. To be true and free in the deepening of your love, will now become your choice for your exploration.

The Artful Skills of Being a Couple

For intimacy to become a true and loving expression of their spirit, couples learn skills and practice with awareness their disciplines of response-ability, (from Pathway A-F) in order to evolve and freely grow beyond surviving. By practicing these skills, they develop, learn, and thrive into the highest possibilities of their partnership.

It is in the skill of learning to dialogue (Pathway D) and having positive tension in the relationship, where both parties can be individuals and at the same time relate as a couple. The more couples learn how to learn from their practicing skills of balancing their individualities and their coupleness; they are also evolving their unique art of freedom and responsibility. As freedom and responsibility integrate in your life experiences as a couple, you gain an interdependence of support, growth, and loving devotion together.

Using a Container of Safety for Personal Freedom

A couple in a coaching session asked this question: "How can we feel a sense of personal freedom in our relationship when our stability and feelings of safety is threatened? We wonder how we can create feelings of safety for ourselves on inner levels as external circumstances change and no longer provide the guarantees of safety and stability they previously provided."

The guidelines below outline the answers to this question:

1. **Response-ability versus Reactivity**
    When our safety feels threatened, our tendency is to be reactive, almost automatically to the perceived danger. Often, when this occurs between the couple, they take out the perceived threat on each other, which then increases the sense of feeling unsafe. For example your ability to react is useful when your house is burning. However, more often you allow for your *ability to respond,* both individually and together, by creating a safe space where you can have a degree of freedom and connection to be able to pay attention to your individual ways of managing your stress levels. With a container of safety, you create the conditions necessary for your response-ability.

2. **Response-ability to Co-create the Space of Mutual Support**
    While most people are racing through life trying to get their needs fulfilled in increasingly diminished spaces of time, you take time to breathe. As a couple you take the time to create space for yourselves together; to stop the chase to accumulate things, while you release and exhale these constraints and create space for mutual support.

3. **Response-ability from Within: Safety from Within**
    As you create safe space for connection and mutual support, you become able to go within for your inner safety and inner grounding. Many people these days are afraid of losing what they have or that it will be taken away from them. When connected to safety within, in your

ability to respond, no matter what the circumstance, difficulty or loss, healthy response-ability provides you the inner freedom to BE and respond appropriately.

4. **Response-ability To and In the Relational Energetic Field**
   There is the 'Relational Field' of the couple in the present and there is the Relational Field of the couple within their family as well as within their community.

> **When we are in a positive community that supports our well-being and evolution personally and together, couples thrive and are sustained in the relational energetic field of connectedness.**

We are all interconnected by an energetic grid or matrix. It's easier to shift one's own energy by one's self. If I have responsibility skills, I can see the impact of my shift in the field.   We tend to take care of our own energy by ourselves or I'm out there taking care of you. Response-ability on a higher level uplifts managing and dealing with oneself and each other to the unit of the both-of-us as a couple and to the **relational energetic field of our relations.** When couples are able to appreciate the impact of their interactive resonance with and on the field, their relational skills, their being, and their presence changes the field.

A Couple's Journey in Pathway F: Working with Freedom and Responsibility

We recently worked with an amazing couple that beautifully exemplifies how they created a sense of safety to work through the tension of freedom and responsibility. They came to us feeling ashamed and immobilized, as they needed to declare bankruptcy. They hadn't been able to tell anyone what they were going through. Feeling isolated from their friends and community, there were also rapidly losing their intimate connection with each other.

We encouraged them to acknowledge the WHAT IS of the situation so it would stop having such a strong hold over them.   They began to dialogue - sharing their fear and shame, their own thoughts and feelings. By slowing down moving into quick fixes, they were able to listen and hear without accusation or blaming themselves and each other. They became aware of their tensions dissipating and their embarrassment easing, as feelings of safety increased.

This created an opening for their 'response-ability' as a couple. As they joined in choosing to mutually support each other through their feelings of fear and shame, they affirmed their strengths of having overcome many other adversities. Options included seeking to connect with others that are going through similar experiences to discover ways to empower themselves. As their session ended, we noticed them walking out the door holding hands.

In practicing the discipline of open dialogue, they gained new learning in developing their response-ability skills other than their survival skills of fight and fawn under stress. They began to appreciate their parts in contributing to **their present situation.** "This is so humbling for us that we became unconscious slaves to our success."

189

Their mutual awareness was an epiphany for them. This **'aha moment'** was especially poignant, since they over-valued their individual freedom and self-sufficiency. They admitted to each other that their current financial loss can be their blessing as they choose to respond by developing their couple's ability to operate from the principle: that the whole of them together is greater than the sum of their individualities.

Encouraged to safely grow together, they began to admit their situation to a support group of strangers. Their 'shame' began to transform as they found out they weren't alone. They noticed that they could laugh at their situation together as they found humor in the cosmic joke of their soul's lesson for true freedom. Their energy freed even more as their intimacy increased. "This is so ridiculous. We are so bankrupt. We can't even buy underwear without our calculator." They laughed themselves to tears as the levity of the present shifted their energy even more.

On their anniversary, they shared going to the park to spend the Sunday praying while communing with nature. During this time, they reflected back to when they were younger and didn't have much money. Back then, they created fun and really enjoyed themselves because they were so in love. Reflecting back to that time in their life helped them discover that the freedom they felt wasn't tied to their external circumstances.

This realization took them into examining what the deeper meaning of this experience was for them. They affirmed the truth of how they took their abundance for granted when their focus was external and how disconnected they had become with busy-ness, with no time for what really matters. Now that they had connected to their own inner spaces and to each other, they became aware of their spiral into imbalance.

Their journey in Pathway F brought them to experience reclaiming their *true* freedom in truth and with love. Their old belief about security which was tied to financial freedom was transformed and evolved into their attending to the Power of the Present in their connection to the Divine within themselves and each other and the energetic grid of their connectedness to Love.

> "This has for us been a meaningful experience. Our TRUE wealth is gaining real inner Freedom in developing our abilities to respond in the adventure of all our self-discoveries together. This one is by far the deepest journey and the most expensive one, but it has opened for us the portal to amazing possibilities."

Using Daily Practice Skills

Gandhi advocated that freedom is acting from non-violence. While many of us are not doing violence externally, we are doing violence internally, mainly to ourselves, when we chase what isn't here. Then suffering happens as we live in the past that was not and in the future that will not.

So how can you as an individual and as a couple co-creatively embody a container of safety in body-mind-spirit in your daily life?

Your daily practice skills strengthen your inner safety for freedom and response-ability. Your aligning internally with NOW ends suffering, big or small. Allow yourselves, both individually and together, the Sacred Space to be self-response-able to develop this inner discipline. To BE with Embodied Presence in the NOW. With practice, you enhance your inner freedom from the sanctuary of safety within your Being. With an embodying presence that radiates a more expanded sense of yourselves in your coupleness, you experience your greater freedom.

Use the metaphor of a car as your embodied whole partnership. As parts, one of you is the engine and the other is the transmission. Individually, you may want the freedom to be your unique selves. With the brake on, the transmission can do its unique shifts and still stay in the garage. The transmission is not the car. When the engine is overemphasized by applying the gas pedal, you can run into a tree. The engine is not the car. All parts together in harmony and balance with the 'car' of your partnership, you contribute to your greater response-ability (brake and transmission) and freedom (gas and engine) to go places.

> *"True freedom and the end of suffering is living in such a way as if you had completely chosen whatever you feel or experience at this moment.*
> *This inner alignment with Now is the end of suffering."*
>
> *"The key is to be in a state of permanent connectedness with your inner body to feel it at all times.*
> *This will rapidly deepen and transform your life.*
> *The more consciousness you direct into the inner body, the higher its vibrational frequency becomes."*
> *~Eckhart Tolle*

For your embodied daily practice we are creating a movement video - **Embodied Dynamic Presence** - that will be made available at www.eightpathways.com.

Daily Practice of Relational Response-Abilities

Developing abilities to respond involves disciplinary practice. Often we can admire couples who have the kind of relationships we wish we have. Upon further examination, you find out about the daily practice they engage in, that enhances the development of their art. Those couples who have developed their discipline of response-ability show great flexibility, empowerment, connectedness, unity in their diversity, and team-spirit, therefore they feel a greater freedom of choice and expression to be their best possibilities. Their presence and energy contributes greatly to a better world.

Daily Process Skills to Co-Create Response-Ability

Reflection: Review the following 11 Daily Process Skills and place an asterisk (*) on those that you are currently practicing, individually and together. Reflect on the impact of these practices your experience of freedom in your healing relationship journey. Place a (**x**) on the practice response-abilities you want to explore and enhance.

1. **Practice Pathway A** - Affirming, acknowledging and appreciating in present awareness.
   "Right now, I am appreciating our struggle."
   "I acknowledge that staying in the present is difficult for us."
   "I affirm our efforts."

2. **Develop a sense of 'We-ness'** - View your team/partnership as a single, larger entity that includes the 'I-ness' of its members and is greater than the sum of all your parts.
   "We allow each other to grow."
   "We bring back to each other what we each learn."
   "Together we help each other become stronger."

3. **Acknowledge Experiences of Emotional Intimacy** - Mutually share inner experiences of feeling connected with each other and with yourself. The paradox is when, as a couple, you can acknowledge feeling disconnected as a way to help you begin to reconnect.
   "I have been feeling disconnected and I'm glad we are having this time to reconnect."
   "I feel deep Gratitude for you in that I can allow myself to be vulnerable and safe with you."

4. **Explore with interest, value, and respect** what you are being called to develop - together as a couple. Express verbally (words) and non-verbally (energy, movement etc) in constructive harmony.
   "I am experimenting with verbally supporting your interest. It is not spontaneous because I tend to think and now I am verbalizing. Do you feel my support?"
   "Thank you for telling me. Now I notice even more of your support."

5. **Foster Goodwill and Faithfulness** - Your partnership attends to the best interest and well-being of the whole, yourself and each other.
   "When I was away at a conference, I kept on thinking of the goodness of us and our relationship so that when one of the participants invited me to have a nightcap; I felt the strength of our devotion and affirmed our marriage."
   "I am so touched that we talked that evening and that you thanked me for allowing you to share."
   "It really matters to me to be faithful to us."

6. **Create a Sense of Connection** - Focus on empathy and resonance acknowledging each other's being, presence, impact, and contribution to you, your partnership, growth, and soul journey from an inner space of presence and being.
   "I am afraid that I might not know how to be of comfort to you when your mom dies."
   "Sharing our feelings right now about her eventual passing is comforting to me."

7. **Resolve differences** with resolutions that respect one another's value and the *'We-ness'* as a whole unit.
   "Even though we disagree on our ideas about what's an enjoyable and relaxing vacation, I value that you listened to my view and I respect that you have a different view."
   "Let's keep exploring this, because the bottom line for me is that we both relax and enjoy our vacation. It matters that we both get what we want."

8. **Value and Recognize Inner Subjective Experience** - Do not require agreement in experience or interpretation of fact for inner, subjective experiences.
   "Tell me more as I want to understand what it means for you to have your own voice."
   "When I share my view with excitement, particularly when there is family or friends around, I notice your eyes roll and I feel a sinking in my chest. I assume while you consciously want me to have a voice, that you are uncomfortable when I speak my views. It matters to me to know what is going on for you when you roll your eyes."

9. **Co-manage Conflict** - Together, manage the frequency, quality and intensity of your conflict so that it is subjectively acceptable to both partners and that you are co-creating the container wherein you can hold your different perspective, energy, and experience.
   "When your tone is loud, it feels harsh and angry to me. I am checking... are you angry?"
   "No, I am very frustrated."
   "I became startled and my heart began pounding. Then, I had difficulty hearing what you are saying."
   "OK, is this tone better? I want you to know why I am so frustrated. My intention is to share my frustration and not startle you. Are you able to hear me now?"

10. **Foster Belief and Mutual Trust** - Use reciprocal statements and actions that communicate Gratitude, truthfulness, devotion, caring, self-awareness and pleasure in each other's presence.
    "I am with you; we are in this situation together."
    "Thank you for watching my back."
    "I believe in you. I believe we have each other's good at heart."

11. **Explore the Deeper Meaning** - Be with openness for the deeper meaning of your lives- both as an individual and as a couple in the unfolding journey of your life together.
    "I wonder what our deeper purpose is together."
    "With our anniversary, I would love to explore what our life journey has meant so far."

"I can share what I learned and the deeper meaning I feel with you, me, and us as we move on to the next phase of our journey."

Connect to your Center of Peace: Daily Centering Practices

We find that connecting with your Center of Peace on a regular or on a daily basis is a meditative, contemplative practice of Centering that helps us to achieve a relaxed, focused state of mind. This can be the first daily practice aside from being the last practice at the end of the day. Centering practices helps us feel peaceful and connected within to the Core Center of Divine Love. As a spiritual and energy practice, it is especially helpful in chaotic or emotionally stressful situations. It is like the calm in the EYE of the hurricane or tornado.

The practice of centering creates a freedom for partners to be who they are; free and peaceful in the external or internal 'chaos' that surrounds them and at the same time, develop inner response-ability so they can uncover the mystery of the 'darkness' or the struggle of themselves. Again, it is another paradox.

Breathe now. B...R...E...A...T...H...E...

- Can you connect or access your Center of Peace? Is it in your heart? Your head? Your belly? Is it a place that you visualize in your mind's eye? Is it a song, poem, prayer or mantra? Is it a physical place of nature; church or in your house? Is it the Higher Power, the All That is, that you call by Name?

- Let yourself embody and feel peace. Feel it move within; from the top of your head, through your being all the way down to your feet. Let yourself step into the EYE; the Center of Peace and let the space around you enfold you in Peace.

- You may tap lightly using the tips of your fingers or place the palms of your hand on the crown of your head, on your mid-eyebrow, on your throat (Adams apple), on your sternum (heart center). On your solar plexus, on your belly (around your navel) affirming within to yourself, "Even though there is anxious chaos around I accept myself completely and profoundly as Universal Divine Love is present within me in every cell of my being." You may let both your hands rest on your heart. "I breathe peace. I am peace. Peace...Peace...Peace...I am Peace..."

Practice of Releasing Breaths

This practice of **'releasing breaths'** is a freeing, clearing practice of moving the energy of thought-emotion, as emotion is *energy-in-motion* (e-motion). Intimate relationships are thinking-emotional relationship. And when the past or the future occupies our thoughts and emotions, we tend to hold our breaths or our breathing becomes shallow. We find we are not living and being in the present experience. Stressed and reactive, our tendency is to fight, flee, freeze, or fawn our e-motions and store them in our bodily organs making tissue memory copies of experiences of e-motion in the Field. This practice of releasing breaths interrupts the recycling of our stressful thought-emotions and lets the natural flow of 'releasing breath' sounds clear our body-mind field. Our spirit then has clear space to become an embodied healing presence to ourselves and each other. It then allows us be in synchrony with the universe by transforming stress into vitality. When practiced on a regular basis, these releasing breaths become our inner supports for our empowered, compassionate and wise response-ability.

In our human interactions, we can be a Divine healing presence to ourselves and to our partner's negative emotions. When we manage our own emotional triggers and allow ourselves to become clear and clean in our emotional response-abilities, we contribute to our relational field's capacity for transformation.

Six Releasing Breaths Practice

These releasing breaths are adapted from the energy practice of Chi Kung, an ancient breathing practice, which we learned from Master Mantak Chia at the Tao Garden in Chiang Mai, Thailand and in which we adapted to support the processes of our response-ability to ourselves and our partner.

1. **Sadness, grief or depression are thought-emotions that tend to get stored in the lungs when stuck.** The releasing breath sound is "Ssssssss". Visualize letting air out of a tire as you place your hands over both your lungs. Together while releasing the breath sound of "Sssssss", slowly press your palms upwards, facing towards the sky, until your breath empties. Then inhale, while visualizing breathing in the clear oxygen and white refreshing light while placing your palms over your lungs. Breathe in *affirming courage* into your lungs. Repeat 3 times.

2. **Anger or frustrations are thought-emotions that tend to get stored in the liver when stuck.** The releasing breath sound is "Shhhhhhh". Visualize wind of nature blowing among the forest green trees as you place your hands over your liver-located on the right side, under your ribs. As you look upward and press your palms toward the sky, exhale the releasing breath sound of "Shhhhhhh" until your breath empties. Then inhale while visualizing the refreshing green light of nature's trees while placing your palms over your liver. Breathe in *affirming kindness and patience* to your liver. Repeat 3 times.

3. **Fear or anxieties are thought-emotions that tend to get stored in the kidneys when stuck.** The releasing breath sound is "Choooooo". Visualize the waters of nature as ocean waves lapping on the beach or waterfalls into a cool pond while placing your hands over your kidneys at the back of your waist. As you exhale, press the palms of your hands downward and back while releasing the breath sound of "Choooooo" until your breath empties. Then inhale while visualizing the purifying blue light of nature's

waters while placing your palms over your kidneys. Breathe in *affirming gentleness and kindness* to your kidneys. Repeat 3 times.

4. **Worry and anxiety are the thought-emotions that when stuck get stored in the spleen and stomach.** The releasing breath sound is "Whooooa". Visualize the yellow golden sunlight abundantly bringing splendor to all of nature while placing your fingers over your left side under your ribs. As you exhale, direct your fingers of both hands towards your spleen while releasing the breath sound of "Whoooooa" until your breath empties. Press in and under gently and imagine the radiant beams of sunlight melting the gray of worry away. Then inhale while visualizing the strengthening, yellow, golden light of the sun while placing your fingers of both hands on your spleen and/or stomach. Breathe in *affirming calmness* to your stomach *and strength* to your spleen. Repeat 3 times.

5. **Hurt, unforgiveness, and bitterness are thought emotions that when stuck, get stored in the heart.** The releasing breath sound is "Haaaaaa". Visualize Universal Divine Love in All Creation while placing your hands over your heart. As you exhale, bring your interlaced palms facing upward over your head and press towards the sky while releasing the breath sound of "Haaaaaa" until your breath empties. Then, inhale while visualizing the loving pink-red light of Universal Divine Love. Breathe in *affirming love, harmony, forgiveness, generosity, beauty and joy* into your heart. Repeat 3 times.

6. **Stress comprises all the thought emotions that gets stuck in our tensing body self.** The releasing breath for is "Heeeeee." Visualize Universal Peace while placing your hands above your head with fingers reaching towards the sky. Then let your palms face down and with the releasing sound of "Heeeeee," slowly pushing your palms downward to the earth emptying stress as you exhale towards the ground. Repeat at least 3 times, releasing the gray of stress. Then, with hands opening upwards towards the sky, visualize a column of radiant light, with you in the center enveloped in Peace. Breathe in *affirming Peace*, while placing your hand over your Heart. Be embodied with the Universal field of All Oneness, and let the Light of Peace and Love radiate from within.

It is best to practice these releasing breaths regularly. Many couples have shared they are sleeping peacefully, feeling relaxed, and free of stress at the end of their day. Repetitions are unique to your needs and you may use a releasing breath sound to move a stuck feeling in any given moment with yourself or to release stress or tension in your relations.

In interactions with your partner, once you have practiced these releasing breaths, inner memory will be with you as you support yourself to be an embodied breathing presence. Let yourself notice the impact on your interactions with each other and how your response-ability supports of your devotion, intimacy, freedom, and faithfulness.

HOW DOES THE RELEASING BREATH PRACTICE CONTRIBUTE TO COUPLES RESPONSE-ABILITY AND FREEDOM?

As intimate partners and couples are in the relational field of each other, a couple's emotional energy impacts each other. More than our words, we are interacting and responding in this field of energy. More recently, scientific research shows the relationship of emotional energy in the field, on our heart body-field response and our on health and well-being.

Below, a couple shares the effect of this releasing breath practice on their capacities for inner and outer response-ability with each other.

> "I noticed that I am better able to listen to my wife's frustrations with inner peace. It's a big change from my automatic impatience and advice giving. I am even able to step back and observe my thoughts. The releasing breath that I mainly practice is "Shhhhhh" as I release my own frustration over my wife's frustrations. It helps me slow down. With regular practice, I am able to become clearer about my frustrations, actually being kind to myself rather than easily letting it get to me. My wife was anticipating my outburst of frustration. I stopped. I placed my hand on my liver and asked her to explain to me while I felt the breathing release internally. It's weird. I saw the whole room in a green light. It became so clear and we were able to resolve the issue. You did not tell me this, but I find myself seeing green light over my co-workers livers. Whether it is true or not, it helps me. There is more a kind of generosity when we are all looking out for the good of the whole. I think a change in my energy has an influence. I did not realize how much impact I had. On the way home, I do releasing breaths in my car. It's amazing, because my wife appreciates that I listen to her and we talk, which she really likes."

> "We have been doing these releasing breaths as meditations before sleeping. It is a great de-stressing meditation. We do not dump on each other as much as we used to. When I feel that I am getting stuck, I do these releasing breaths. I slow down and become present. It helps me by not jumping into my old tendency to fix and problem solve."

Embodying Presence: Connecting Infinity in Your Unified Body-Field

This is a bonus if you get to this part in your daily practice. For us, this is the Freedom practice...as in our belief, the ultimate freedom is *INFINITY*.

This practice of embodying presence involves three parts of the Infinity Loop of your Unified Body-Field:
- Grounding (check Pathway B)
- Centering (check Pathways A and F)
- Aligning in the Embodied Field of the Infinity Loop

Embodied Field of Love Practice

This can be customized according to what works for both of you individually and as a couple. After grounding, centering, see your center(s) heart, third eye, solar plexus, radiant and linking all centers of spine in alignment with the Universe and the Earth. Expand from within and see the Unified Field of Love surrounding you. Expand further and see the radiance of Light toward your partner, embracing you both in this Unified Field together. You can visualize this as the Infinity Loop. We teach this practice in our workshops Being in this Energetic, Embodied Field helps each of us in being with each other and in our connective dialogue.

> *"Verily, all things move within your being in constant half embrace,*
> *the desired and the dreaded, the repugnant and the cherished,*
> *the pursued and that which you escape.*
> *These things move within you as lights and shadows in pairs that cling.*
> *And when the shadow fades and in no more, the light that lingers*
> *becomes a shadow to another light.*
> *And thus your freedom when it loses its fetters*
> *becomes itself the fetter of a greater freedom."*
> *~Kahlil Gibran*

SUMMARY HIGHLIGHTS OF PATHWAY "F": FREEDOM AND RESPONSIBILITY

1. Balancing freedom and responsibility for a couple is multi-layered. Both have many nuances and cover a huge ground of possibilities.

2. The intimate relationship provides a relational and magnetic field environment for the partners to develop their inner awareness and connection to their embodiment of heart-mind and spirit. As both parties are committed to understanding their relational response-abilities and gain inner awareness of their interactive processes, they are better able to clarify their intent and the impact of their actions and choices on their partnership. As their interactive processes deepen the couple into truth and love, it allows for healing and transformation to be magnetic in their field.

3. Relational response-abilities involves how the partners stay in touch with each other by their presence, informing, inviting, sharing, listening, dialoguing, empathizing, and supporting. They engage and connect, check in with each other, as well as, attend to one another as they are interacting.

4. Personal response-abilities involves how you take care of and love yourself, how you care for your whole being in spirit-soul-mind-emotions-energy-body. It includes your connection with your Higher Power, your living practice that fosters health, well-being, growth and enhancement of inner virtues.

5. Freedom and responsibility are not mutually exclusive. For individuals within their couple relationship, it is about how to find **freedom through responsibility and responsibility through freedom**. This polarity is heightened in significant relationships as the intimate relationship triggers deep, unconscious, and unresolved struggles.

6. There are generally two types of couples that struggle in the journey through Pathway F. The first types are couples where one or both parties focus on their freedom and individuality. The second types are couples who have been married for many years. They have collapsed their individualities to fulfill their couple's responsibilities. They 'lack' the skills to experience the freedom to be individuals in their coupleness.

7. To begin to help you understand the many facets of Pathway F, we offer you an awareness tool, *Window of Freedom and Responsibility*, that we have used ourselves and with our clients. The purpose of this tool is to provide a present glimpse of your view of the 'reality' of where you and your partner are in Pathway F.

8. The couples' interactive university of life experiences can bring to the surface layers of the unconscious body and past life memories; previous emotional reactions and trigger mental maps so they can be re-examined, released, cleansed and transformed.

9. Many couples are facing the dismantling of institutions that kept in order their daily lives. The **'shoulds'** that have been handed down over the generations are now in question and relationships are challenged to awaken to a level of consciousness that can cause major shifts in relating.

10. In order to be in balance, couples can engage their tension to go towards the core of their tension. Here, they will discover and gain awareness to manage the **both-and** perspective. Perhaps, the couple braces with care and caution in negotiating the risk of discovering the power of how they affect one another in this polarity. The freedom they uncover in Pathway F brings with it a new sense of responsibility or response-ability that takes them to the center of Love and Truth.

11. In order to get unstuck from an emotional muddle, both partners need to be aware of how they co-participate in getting stuck. When you can own your participation in your relational stuckness and accept your own response-ability for each of your parts, a freeing process of facing 'What Is True' in your co-created experience emerges. Your possibilities of how you both co-participate in your freeing process of getting un-stuck opens with the awareness of your inner choice-fullness in the *Interactive Freeing Process.*

12. Couples Using a Container of Safety for Personal Freedom develop:
*   Response-ability versus Reactivity
*   Response-ability to Co-create the Space of Mutual Support
*   Response-ability from Within: Safety from Within
*   Response-ability To and In the Relational Energetic Field

13. Couples develop abilities and skills to respond through the:
*   11 *Daily Process Skills to Co-Create Response-Abilities*
*   Practice of Releasing Breaths, as a freeing, clearing practice of moving the energy of thought-emotion, as emotion is *energy-in-motion* (e-motion)

14. Couples' practice of Embodying Presence enhances their range of Freedom and Response-ability through grounding, centering and aligning their connection with Infinity of their Unified Body-Field.

PATHWAY G: PATHWAY OF GRATITUDE AND GRACE
GIVING AND RECEIVING

"Gratitude unlocks the fullness of life. It turns what we have into enough, and more. It turns denial into acceptance, chaos to order, and confusion to clarity. It can turn a meal into a feast, a house into a home, a stranger into a friend. Gratitude makes sense of our past, brings peace for today, and creates a vision for tomorrow."
~Melody Beattie

Introduction

The Pathway of Gratitude and Grace, Pathway "G", is particularly dear to our hearts. It touches and opens us to the *Present, Here and Now,* to receiving life's blessings, presented as the Universe's gifts wrapped in a mixture of multi-dimensional human experiences of our soul.

"When the rhythms of our body-mind are in synch with nature's rhythms, when we are living in harmony with life, we are living in the state of grace. To live in grace is to experience that state of consciousness where things flow effortlessly and our desires are easily fulfilled. Grace is magical, synchronistic, coincidental, and joyful. It's that good-luck factor. But to live in grace, we have to allow nature's intelligence to flow through us without interfering."
~Deepak Chopra

Gratitude is simple; yet extremely powerful. We notice this key ingredient of Gratitude as a strong thread in successful couple's relationships. Their emotional vibration of Gratitude and love makes it seem easier to manifest life's blessings. People wonder how to cultivate this key ingredient when they are experiencing challenges, otherwise known as blessings in disguise. Their focus on heartfelt Gratitude to the Divine Presence, though unseen, shows up in every aspect of life.

In this chapter, we present how Pathway G, the Pathway of Gratitude and Grace, is a vital Pathway for sustaining, deepening, and enhancing successful, satisfying, and intimate relationships. Radiating Gratitude within one's heart has a powerful enlivening force that is magnetically infectious. When embraced as an inner, real state of being, Gratitude becomes the center for unity and strength.

Pathway G fosters learning how Gratitude is a potent attitude, e-motion, and an inner state of being within Grace. It emanates a radiance that creates a field for long-lasting, evolving, and an inspiring healing love relationship.

In this Pathway of Gratitude, we open to receive Grace. We become present on how Gratitude connects and aligns us with the flow of the Universe. When couples embrace the Pathway of Gratitude within themselves, they become aligned with the Universe by being with the natural flow of giving and receiving. Like breathing, we inhale to receive and exhale to give. When couples embrace the Pathway of Gratitude within themselves, they open to receive the Grace of the Universe. A couple's ability to give and receive is the core, process skill in their capacity to experience and co-create true love and Gratitude.

Wherever the couple's journey takes them, the healing power of Gratitude can even bring divorced couples to appreciate and respect each other. Being with Gratitude helps them glean forgiveness of themselves and each other. These couples find in their divorce that they have become better friends and co-parent partners for their children. Their children are able to heal through the pain of their parent's separations and become light and healing presences, making a positive difference in the world.

The 'force' and power of Pathway G brings us to receive the flow of blessings and grace in what has always been present for us but may have been lost and buried **in** the layers of convoluted coping strategies that thwart the flow of Gratitude and Grace.

Challenges of Pathway G - How Gratitude Becomes Convoluted in Relationships

When couples are on Pathway G, they can either feel that Gratitude is missing in their lives or feel its overflowing energy. When couples feel Gratitude is missing, it is important to notice how this powerful energy has been thwarted, convoluted or misunderstood.

In our own personal relationship and in our work with couples, we explore the past and present experiences of Gratitude:

- as an emotion
- an attitude
- an energy and vibration
- as reciprocal giving and receiving
- as embodied thought and intention
- as congruent action
- as God's divine grace
- as core in all our wholehearted relations in the Universe

Accessing Gratitude may offer couples the nourishment that refreshes their relationship when confused, stressed or challenged. But first, they must gain awareness of the messages, beliefs, and experiences that both support and hinder their experience of being with Gratitude.

The challenges in Pathway G often originate in past experiences that create a 'block' in the universal flow of and to Gratitude and Grace. Those with such blocks are unable to truly receive the blessings that are in Pathway G. At times making a detour through Pathways A to F helps to savor being in Pathway G. At other times, accessing Pathway G and practicing the processes therein, helps movement through the other Pathways. These Pathways work together in the transformational journey of the couple.

Following are examples presented by couples. Gratitude has become a 'doing' activity disconnected within and resistances are experienced by rushing through thankfulness. They wonder why no matter how many blessings there are, the inner feelings of satisfaction, peace or love is missing.

1. **No Matter What, It's Never Enough**

   "Growing up, I never got thanks for anything I did. My parents never trusted each other or us when we would say thank you. My mother always noticed what was missing. My wife does the same thing. It's always about the next thing. I never am done. It was always, "uh oh, here it comes." All my life, I felt manipulated just to get a 'thank you'. I feel bad with it and without it. I wish I could have the real feeling of Gratitude."

2. **Expectation or Manipulation: To Control or Be Controlled**

   "I find it hard to thank people for doing their job. I do not expect thanks because it is my job. It is my wife's duty is to take care of the children and the house, as it is my job to provide just as it is my children's job to do their chores. Why should I be thankful when they are expected to do their job? It is weakness to want or expect thanks for that and I do not want to have to manipulate anyone by thanking them."

3. Strings Attached

It seems that there is a class system attached to Gratitude. For some, they believe that people who have more privileges, wealth, and status get more Gratitude from those who have less. Those who have less are beholden to those who have more. The more grateful they are they get special favors, "In my family, we learned as children when you get what you ask for, there are strings attached and thank you means you do what the gift giver wants from you. So, I refrain from being grateful to avoid those strings."

4. It's Just Another Ritual

Different cultures have different ways of expressing Gratitude. Often these ways are connected with material things. When someone from one culture does not appreciate the customs by which the other expresses Gratitude, this can lead to misunderstanding and hurt feelings related to not being seen or disrespected. "In our culture, food is a major part of expressing Gratitude. My wife cooks something and sends it to someone and then the receiver cooks something and sends it back. It seems more like obligation than a true connection."

5. It's Another's Chore, Obligation or 'Cliché'

It seems like in my family we have an obligation to be grateful. "Do I have to?" they ask themselves. If someone expresses Gratitude, you are obligated to express Gratitude back to them and it never ends. "I feel I have to be on top of the game all the time. "It's business" my Dad would say. You have to thank as a common courtesy. Or something to just get it over with...so you can get into or out of business." We say 'thank you' simply as a common courtesy. It's a 'cliché'. It's expected, even though we do not feel it in our heart.

6. Feeling Indebted and Guilty

"There seems to be a debt of Gratitude that weighs on my family members to pay but it can never be fulfilled. My family said we are indebted to all the generations to come because my grandfather owed his life to this man and his heirs for saving his life. In my culture and family, children are indebted to their parents for their life. Even though I know this to be the expected custom...somehow I feel my life is not my own. I felt so guilty with my family when I moved away and followed my own career path. Indebted Gratitude is a very heavy weight. I send money and gifts home, because if I do not, I feel guilty. I do not want to pass this feeling of indebtedness on to my children, but I am at a loss on how to impress upon them the value of being grateful. It is painful, as my son is fighting me now, and wants to get away...I am scared that he will go so far away and that I could lose him. My parents say it is karma paying me back for what I did. My parents viewed me as ungrateful."

7. Hurt Disguised

There are those that believe that "I do not trust people who are always thankful or positive. It feels disingenuous because I wonder what they are really thinking. It is better for me to know their negative side. I was deeply hurt by someone I loved and trusted and with whom I felt so grateful. I refrain from feeling grateful to avoid feeling vulnerable and hurt."

So we ask:

- How can we both clean and purge the muddy waters of guilt and shame that have become polluted by our generational and collective misuse of Gratitude and our human abuse of love?

- If you can sift the "gold" from that what would you like to release: What would you like to keep?

- Do you wonder how to realign with the spiritual and universal inherent power of Gratitude and Love for your healing transformation together?

Robert A. Emmons in his book, *Thanks!: How the New Science of Gratitude Can Make You Happier*, (2007) found that people who feel grateful are also more likely to feel loved. Gratitude encourages a positive cycle of reciprocal kindness among people as one act of Gratitude encourages another. Gratitude is the 'magic ingredient' that takes us outside of ourselves to see how we are part of the larger, intricate network of sustaining relationships that are mutually reciprocal.

John Gottman's 1998 study on marriage found that couple's thrive when there is a ratio of 5 positive comments to 1 negative comment. Several studies that explore the importance of Gratitude in creating a healthy relationship found that the more couples practice Gratitude from the heart, the more this powerful emotion helps them through challenging times. Gratitude as an attitude, emotion and a conscious choice in awareness becomes the cornerstone to the couple's connection. Gratitude brings smiles, affirmation, laughter, joy, peace and kindness; all of which helps the couple transcend and transform as they open to embrace the energy of this emotion. There is ample evidence that shows how Gratitude and satisfaction in relationships link Gratitude to heart health, healing, and longevity, as well as relieves stress, depression, boosts the immune system, increases energy and optimism, improves sleep and spiritual awareness, along with overall health.

In his book, *Messages of Water*, Masaru Emoto's intriguing study demonstrated how emotions of Love and Gratitude, when written on a piece of tape and affixed to a glass of water or when people focused these emotional thoughts on the water, he found that when looking at the water under a microscope a beautiful crystalline structure was revealed that was not visible before and that previously was not there. (see picture of water crystal on page 227)

> *"Throughout our lives, we exist mostly as water. This connection to water applies to everyone, all over the world. So how can people live happy and healthy lives? The answer is to purify the water that makes up your body. Water in a river remains pure because it is moving. When water becomes trapped, it dies. Therefore, water must constantly be circulated. The water - or blood - in the bodies of the sick is usually stagnant. When blood stops flowing,*

the body starts to decay, and if the blood in your brain stops, it can be life threatening. We all have an important mission: To make water clear again, and to create a world that is easy and healthy to live in. In order to accomplish our mission, we must first make sure that our hearts are clear and unpolluted. If all the people of the world can have love and Gratitude, the pristine beauty of the earth will once again return."
~Masaru Emoto, The Hidden Messages in Water
(picture of water crystal on page 227)

A couple engaged in an experiment following Emoto's process by engraving the words "Love and Thanks" on their water glass and then shared how using this process helped them focus their thoughts and emotions on Gratitude. "It really works. I noticed how my drink of water feels so nourishing. We also express a lot more heartfelt Gratitude with each other."

Practice of Gratitude: How Do You Develop An Attitude of Gratitude?

A practice to create, cultivate, and deepen your cellular Pathways of Gratitude involves accessing the powerful feeling emotion of Gratitude by reconnecting and embodying it within your Being. Below we offer a guided meditation practice of Gratitude as a method to BE in the present feeling experience of Gratitude.

1. Find a comfortable sitting or standing position with your feet planted firmly on the ground. Rub your palms together in front of your heart space. Let your palms face each other and feel the flow of energy between your palms. In this position ... breathe and picture a time or place in your life or relations wherein a moment of Gratitude felt emotionally pure, clean, and positively warm and glowing from within. It could be your safe and peaceful place. It could be a time of beauty and awe. It could be a moment of specialness, a time of confidence. It could be being in nature, seeing the stars, sky, and sun, whatever it is now ...be with that in this present moment. Breathe... savor and cherish it. Breathe... fill Gratitude with color; make it bigger, fuller, and more radiant. Breathe it deeply into your heart center. Feel the warm glow of Gratitude within your heart and radiate Love and Thanks. Be Present NOW to the presence of Gratitude. Remember the Gratitude you feel now. See it, feel it all the way within and into your heart...all the way into the marrow of your bones. Feel Gratitude in your spine, into your backbone. Let Gratitude fill every cell of your being. Be one with Gratitude. Breathe Gratitude. Remember this now. Remember now in your cells. Now recorded in your cellular memory, you can remember and access this inner feeling state of Gratitude no matter what is happening around you. Breathe Gratitude. Breathe.

2. Sometimes people may not remember experiences of Gratitude, but may access a felt experience, in the present, of Gratitude, after a process of working through any of the Pathways. Because the tendency for most people is to go quickly to the next task or what didn't happen, we slow down with them to take a pause, and breathe in their moment of Gratitude, to savor their present felt experience. We see energy light up in their eyes as they

stay with the Pathway of Gratitude. For many couples, this present pause is a replenishing, empowering moment of going into their inner well, where there are feelings of connection with their blessings. A shift of energy is the embodied feeling experience of Gratitude. In Being with the 'magic' and savoring and cherishing this feeling, they are reinforcing the inner Pathway of Gratitude to be embedded into their cellular memory.

It is within our cellular memory (our cells do remember) that the heartfelt multiplication of your ability for Gratitude resides, and that couples can access even when there are difficult things happening around you. Thus, tapping Gratitude within, (tapping is explained later in the chapter) positively shifts your energy, and therefore shifts your experience in the outer world and in your relationship.

Activities and Practices to Develop Gratitude

These activities help us to connect to Gratitude within. Track your felt sense process. The activities and practices in the next section will assist you as a couple to enhance Gratitude in your relationship. When following the activities and practices, notice the impact of how the receiver received and the giver gave.

1. Keep a couples' journal or log of Gratitude. You can text it, put it on Facebook or Tweet it.

2. Start your morning and/or end your day with a Gratitude meditation.

3. Create a daily practice of sharing highlights of what you are grateful for that day. You can do this while walking, exercising together or sharing an activity together.

4. Thank each other for the simple things that occur throughout the day that each of you appreciate in the moment. This is the gratefulness habit. This is a very powerful practice.

5. Sift, sift and sift so you can notice, find and feel the present 'golden nugget' for which you can be grateful.

6. Notice what happens within you and around you when you thank your plants or pets with love...and when you thank all of nature and the universe.

7. Breathe, hum, sing, dance, draw, pray or meditate thankfulness. This is an energy shifter.

8. Go within and thank yourselves for how you have expressed Gratitude to your partner. Appreciate yourself for what you've noticed. Express this to your partner and you will notice your partner agreeing with it!

> **Reflection Exercise**
> We invite you to take a moment to reflect upon your own relationship(s) and your experience(s) of Gratitude, both the positive and the negative and record them.
>
> Notice the circumstance(s) of what was happening and how you are now experiencing Gratitude. Notice your body senses, emotions, your energy, your thoughts, your actions and others. Notice the energy between you and the field (environment). Notice what impact (positive and negative) these experiences have on you today and in your relationship with each other.

Practice the skills of Pathways A - F as you bring yourself to the Present Moment of sharing your reflections with each other by sitting: either facing each other; side by side; or if you are in different places, find a comfortable time with intention to sit for this meditation.

9. Deepen your Gratitude with the practice of a Gratitude Meditation: (either alone or together with your partner)

Take some clearing breaths. We invite you to take this moment to transport yourselves into Pathway G of Gratitude and be in the present wherever you are. Take this moment and name: what you see present, hear present, feel present, smell present, and thank their presence.

Go inward and thank your organs, heart, lungs, liver, spleen, and kidneys. Go outward and thank the sky, sun, moon, earth, waters, air, and the universe. Go through your life's journey appreciating your experiences, challenges, uncertainties, awareness, discoveries, feelings, growth, and possibilities.

Go to your relations and invite them into your mind's eye or your heart and thank your loved ones, family, friends, teachers, and those who have nurtured and helped you and those who you have helped as well as those who have created difficulties. Go to your compassion, wisdom, strength, creativity, and empowerment.

Go to the sacred place of silence within as you savor and cherish this moment, feeling the vibration of Gratitude within. Let Gratitude expand within your heart, and radiate down to your feet and extend like roots into the earth...lengthening and extending you to the sky, expanding through and around you. Feel well-being; let joyfulness radiate in your heart.

Let the waters of Love and Gratitude fill you and nourish you abundantly in harmony. Let thankfulness glow into your soul. Sing thanks in your heart with your Spirit and receive the amazing grace of awesome joy, transcending, and flowing with Infinite Love. Celebrate with affirmation, presence, Oneness, and peace.

Notice your inner experience of your Gratitude Meditation. Journal about this experience. Now, from within your heart of Gratitude, share by taking turns giving and receiving your experience of Gratitude, and share with each other. Notice where in your experience (heart, mind, being, or spirit) you are receiving? And from where are you giving?

10. Cherish and savor your experience of Gratitude within you and as you listen, feel yours and your partner's Gratitude. Notice its impact on your energy, as well as on your couple's energy.

11. Deepen the energetic flow of Gratitude to be embodied in your couples' core heart center, experience Gratitude's vibration multiplying and growing in your couple's relational field through your energetic expression for giving and receiving *'Gifts'* of Love and Gratitude.

    We call this energetic expression for giving and receiving the **'FIVE Ts'**:

    - *Gift of Time* - being in each other's presence, giving and receiving love and gratitude
    - *Gift of Touch* - in caring, healing, empathic, connective, heart-felt touch
    - *Gift of Talking* - in communications of love and gratitude
    - *Gift of Tasks* - in caring things we do for and with each other
    - *Gift of Token* - expressions symbolizing felt thoughts of love and gratitude

12. Knowing what yours and your partners *Gift* channels are for giving and receiving expressions of Love and Gratitude is a 'language' art and skill process in Pathway G. As you attend, acknowledge your awareness and appreciation of the <u>Gift given</u> and the <u>Gift received</u>, as the moment of Grace enriches both the intention of the giver and the impact on the receiver of the *Gift*. The *Grace* of Gratitude transforms Love's expressions beyond thought, word, and action. Its vibrations transforms the relational energetic field and magnetizes Gratitude blessings

When any of the Pathways, A-F are coupled with Pathway "G", the journey through that Pathway gains a quality of wonder, inner ease, and peace. The challenges of each Pathway become touched by the Spirit of Gratitude for the blessing that is unfolding.

One Couple's Awareness

Charles: "Twenty-five years ago to this day, I am grateful for the miracle of our meeting. I believe that Spirit orchestrated it because it was by 'accident' and at the lowest time in my life. I am so much a better person for your presence in my life."

Rose: "What amazed me was how you kept on thanking me. That has really stayed with me. I love it that you thank God for finding me. I felt special and loved. Then the thanks stopped. I complained about us and the lack of appreciation. Then I realized that I missed feeling Gratitude and missed the miracle of our meeting. We have done a lot of work and growing though the years and once even almost lost each other. Now that I choose to focus on Gratitude, even those things you do, like your sometimes critical tone has now become the sound you make when stressed. I am amazed that focusing on the Gratitude in my heart for you, that I am able to talk things through with you instead of becoming reactive and defensive when I hear that particular tone you make that I take as critical. Now I am thankful and believe that you really notice my intelligence and my essence. I can let you tease me about taking myself so seriously and laugh together. I am truly grateful for how much we have grown."

"That for me is what I am most grateful for...and each day, yes I am thankful, for us in my life."

The couple's awareness of being in Pathway "G" allows them to draw upon their learning experiences and manifest their dreams. We can choose to be connected energetically with Gratitude, where the landscape is filled with hidden and obvious, and sometimes disguised blessings. In the pathways of your relational journey affirming Gratitude, opens the door of your connection to the CORE where the Heart of Divine Love lives. We find that even through the shadows of our adversities and life's challenges, Gratitude and Grace are Present in the perceptual shift to see Life's miracles.

Have you observed that when you acknowledge a difficult situation that your partner is having or sharing, that they feel seen, heard, and affirmed?

A husband who was struggling with the adversity of his wife's illness had this to say:

"When my wife was diagnosed with terminal cancer, I was filled with the terror of her dying. She begged me to give her the gift of courage and the belief that we both will overcome this. Her courage was really mine to receive."

"I know this is very hard for you to be with. Thank you for coming with me to the doctors and being there through all the therapies."

"It would have been easier for me to numb myself through all this. But I owe it to myself and to us to give time to be in here with you. Feeling is not my strong suit. I suppose your illness made me realize, how much I have taken for granted. And how much I feel so very thankful and somehow have not expressed it. This intervention by the universe is for me to heal the other kind of cancer."

"Gratitude is healing our cancer."

Giving and Receiving

A significant aspect of Pathway "G" the Pathway of Gratitude and Grace, is that it teaches us the cycle of giving and receiving. When we are elevated to grateful giving and grateful receiving, the transformational processes of healing love becomes enhanced.

Imagine you are present observing couples and partners expressing the following statements with each other.

> "I am grateful that I am able to share my difficult thoughts and feelings without you blaming me or yourself or trying to fix me. Thank you for listening."

> "I am grateful that I slowed myself down, enough to receive your sharing. I am thankful for your patience because I really get it now - that being with you is what matters and not fixing what is difficult for me."

> "I am grateful for learning this way of giving and receiving. I feel really warm and good about us."

> "I am feeling even more Gratitude, for now I am able to receive your way of giving your care in the things you do provide."

Pathway G *links us to our Inner Self, our Soul-full relatedness*, our communion with each other, and with the Universal Source of All Grace, which sometimes comes as disguised blessings.

> "My grandfather reminded us to celebrate failures since he says there are really no failures in life…only blessings coming in disguise. I thanked his wisdom to this day even as he has been gone now for a long time; the blessing of his teaching is an enduring diamond for us."

> "I did not expect you to take my job loss as an opening for what is to come. Your faith gives me hope. Thank you."

> "I am grateful for being open to wonder what Goodness is on its way to you…to us. Thank you for including me in taking things over and for not going through this difficulty alone."

> "I believe that there is only good in us in facing this together. Man, I get it…it's the process not the fix; it's the learning that will be valuable, like the wisdom your grandfather left with you. What a gift! I should feel badly that I lost my job, but…it

does not feel that horrible. This is amazing to me. It's not what I expected. Thank you for you."

The Pathway of Gratitude is the *'glue' that links time, space, and our interconnectedness*. This is where our **intentions** and prayers to the Divine and Universal Source are in the ever-present moment.

Even when things are hard, if couples share Gratitude, they can hang in there together. Gratitude is the stance of being in the process so that you can deal with the other side as well. It doesn't mean that if you are grateful, that you don't have problems and pains. You can be in pain and groaning. One doesn't necessarily exclude the other.

> "Last night, I had an amazing dream where I went from room to room in the house of my grandparents, looking for the treasure. I am amazed that when I met my grandfather, he said the treasure is in my heart. I woke up feeling so grateful and bursting with so much love and joy. I saw my wife preparing breakfast, and I felt my heart treasuring her. I took her hand and looked into her soulful eyes and said, "I treasure you". She received me with a smile and said, "Me too." I know we can weather our bumps, big or small, and celebrate our successes, especially the small, seemingly insignificant ones." ~PB

The Pathway of Gratitude involves a conscious focus on gratefulness, even through the mundane and difficult things. It involves sifting through the 'dust and dirt, to harvest, take, and thank the gold'. It involves a trust that Gratitude connects us to our unfolding grace, whether we are aware or not, of the fullness of the blessing, and of the experience.

> "I remember my mother telling me, how grateful she is that she hung in there with my unfaithful father. It took so long before I began to understand where she was coming from and my anger transformed into respect for the strength of her belief. As she told me that these last years of my father's life were the happiest for her, I cried to hear her say, 'I had the best of the beginning and the best of the ending...it made the in-between worth it'. I was so angry with her for what seemed to me as her unwillingness to do anything about her unhappiness. Now, I am grateful that I am really able to hear her unconditionally. I wish it did not take this long and difficult journey to see my parents for who they are. I have transformed from within and I am grateful for how I have you to share all this with."

The Pathway of Gratitude takes life and all the relational bumps and adversities to be part of the 'University of Life'.

> "When I was going through my lowest time, you gave me something to hang on to, in saying that in the end, the journey will make sense. In choosing Gratitude, we gain inner control of our present moments, even as life brings things that 'grate in its fullness'. Now I realize what a pun this is!"

We observed couples who make a shift in their stuckness, when one or both of them accesses the Pathway of Gratitude in negotiating Pathways A to F. They drew upon resources within the present for themselves. Their expressions of Gratitude unfolded them to the next present steps of their process. The positive love hormone, 'oxytocin' impacted their emotional-mental and spiritual movement in their evolving perceptions and in their physiology leading them to the higher purpose of their relational life.

> "This may seem so ironic. Today as I look back, I am grateful to my ex-husband for being such an ass...at least that was the way I looked at him then. He challenged my sense of worth and unwittingly helped me find the angry 'bitch' in me. That is what propelled me to discover my gifts and develop my talents."

The Pathway of Gratitude is the multiplier of 'the loaves and the fishes', to see in the grain of sand, the amazing splendor of the beach and the ocean. When we learn this, we open ourselves to receive the bounty of grace and blessings.

> "When we look back to what we had to overcome, from being poor, with no jobs, and homeless, we were so very thankful for the recycled clothes and food, for the people who took us in and opened their doors for us. We made a feast and rejoiced at whatever food was offered and savored every morsel of it. We thanked nature, the air, the sun, the water, the cows, the farmers, the bakers, the cans and bottles found in the trash, and the grocer who exchanged the bottles for cash. We gave Gratitude time and time again and today we are truly grateful to have that memory bank of treasures filled with the miracles of Gratitude and Grace. Because of having to go through this experience, it has strengthened our relationships."

Finally, the Pathway of Gratitude is a process that involves an inner preparation for co-creating the giving-receiving process of Healing Love. We like to think of it as the climate and container for giving and receiving of 'The Gifts' of Grace.

This inner preparation involves grounding with nature and the earth, feeling our feet on the ground, receiving with our breathing in and exhaling to fill our inner and outer spaces with fullness and light. In centering into our heart space and aligning to connect with the heavens and expanding to the Universe, we breathe in the Grace of Gratitude.

Let us stretch Gratitude to the altitude of the Universe, aside from what we have described as an attitude, to become embodied in our thought, senses, emotion, and actions; to align with the energetic flow of the Grace of Gratitude.

The practice involves conscious breathing in, inhaling Gratitude, and letting Gratitude be felt in your whole being, feeling grateful that the 'gift' or blessing asked for is now received.

When one can ground with nature and the earth and center to that quiet place within, we are able to be calm in the midst of the stress and turmoil. We then connect with giving and receiving with heartfelt Gratitude and allow ourselves to be touched by Grace.

Examples of Gratitude - The Grace That Enhances Our Relationship

The life journey of relationships is like the tides of the ocean. There are high tides and low tides that impact the inter-connective fields of living. As we appreciate what stood out in our couples' journey, gratefulness is the **strong spiritual thread** that weaves the soulful 'gems' from challenges that seemed to be overwhelming.

Example 1:   We experienced a financial crisis that brought on difficult decisions in order to deal with mounting external consequences. Giving is so much easier and automatically feels good. With the loss, we have become so humbled by the stress of survival. We live each day focusing on one step at a time, grounding and centering to release fear and worry, and claim Gratitude for breathing, nature, and being alive. We were taken to balance with slowing down, to notice and allow receiving, to replenish, and savor, to empty excess, and create open spaces to re-fill in our sacred inner spaces of being.

Example 2:   Around the 7th year of our marriage, we had a huge fight that shook the foundations of our relationship. It escalated to a point that we questioned whether we could go past our impasse. We each felt the deep pain of not understanding and being understood. It seemed our values were at opposite ends. As we allowed ourselves to take space, the heat of our anger melted and we were each able to connect with positive memories for which we were each grateful. We were not going to 'throw out the baby with the bathwater'. Rather, we experienced Gratitude for the huge fight that revealed to us what we each valued. That brought us to face what matters and consciously take the Pathways for Healing Love that eventually became our calling.

Example 3:   Around our 21st year of marriage, we shared what we were grateful for but we also examined what we were unhappy about: the pain we experienced by how we handled our differences and the automatic survival strategies that we still were hanging onto. In coming together we each acknowledged our part and our contribution to our impasse. This paved the way for us being able to hear and listen with 'new' ears. We thanked each other for our on-going tenacity for coming back to our 'fight' for our different realities. Allowing ourselves to see with 'new' eyes, inner truths came, as Grace brought new light to our differences. We expressed our intentions for healing love and focused on our process of giving and receiving; of hearing and listening; and, of sharing with truth and love. We also acknowledged our Gratitude and our courage to delve into BEEHMSSS™ discovery of our deeper selves; of reaching beyond to tap universal and energetic realms to work through seeming incomprehensible obstacles to become open to Grace for mutually satisfying and transforming resolutions.

Present Day Challenges Couples Are Having Being In an Attitude of Gratitude

We have been revisiting Pathway G because we were noticing how couples would complain that they felt emptied out. Many have had adversities brought about by the downturn of the economy. Some couples noticed the stress of the economy impacting their relationship due to the difficulty of finding jobs or meaningful work. Their worries would take over and they would release their stress on each other in different ways, or act out; thus causing more stress on their relationship. Some focused on doing more with less time for relaxation or even enjoying each other.

One couple, Barb and Jason, argued about their' lack of time and scrambling for work to make ends meet'. They complained that they had minimal physical intimacy and felt depressed that their friends and family are all going through hard times. So, even though they felt badly, they felt worse about the guilt they imposed on themselves that "they should not feel badly at all or even complain because they should be grateful that "they still had their health" even though they could not afford to get sick because they would have no way to take care of it. Stressed, exhausted, and irritable, they dismissed each other's attempts at gratefulness. Their stress recycled into their quickness to point out each other's faults. They mirrored each other sinking lower into their chairs, shoulders slumped down, breathing shallowly, and thereby co-creating their further depletion.

When we affirmed their difficult situation and noticed that they mentioned feeling grateful about their health, we asked them to tell us more about that. They began to talk about themselves being health focused. He would run and she took long walks. This they did separately as it helped them get away from each other and they had more time to deal with their frustration. With no more work, they had more time to exercise but could not afford gym fees. They expressed resentment that they could not go out and have fun with their friends as it cost money that they did not have. They have been economizing and eating at home more but arguing at the same time. She had begun planting vegetables in their backyard and resented that he was not even noticing it and being grateful. He countered that she should be grateful that he did not comment on how much she spent to get those plants, when we do not have that kind of money to spend.

The challenge this couple had was that they were putting their frustrations and their gratefulness in the same pot. And so, neither was being heard and valued. We asked them to notice that they had two pots: one pot contained their frustrations and the other pot contained their Gratitude. We acknowledged with them that both pots are valid. We asked them to notice which pot they were focusing on, so that they would be on the same page with each other.

> Jason then stated, "I know I am frustrated because I feel like I am always the one begging for our intimate time together. It used to be our time after the kids went to bed and I was grateful that we did that regularly. But now, I do not know what you are grateful for. I think you resent me for not having a regular job, even though I do a lot more in our home now."

> Barb chimed in, "Me too...we used to share our Gratitude together...it is as though we have forgotten."

Jason and Barb noticed their co-created challenge as to how they together tended to take their frustration pot and pour the contents of it over their 'Gratitude Pot'.

Differentiating Between Your Frustration Pot and Your Gratitude Pot: Processes to Resolve These Challenges

1. <u>Involves activating the neural Pathways of Gratitude from within and being clear as to which pot they were *digging or filling in*.</u>

   "Remember a time of Gratitude and your experience of feeling good, warmed, and joyful. Describe the context. What is happening? What did you see, hear or feel? What are you experiencing now in this moment as you remember this in your body? Breathe. Savor that pleasurable and joyful feeling of Gratitude. Breathe. Remember feeling Gratitude all the way into your cells. Increase it in your inner Gratitude Pathway from the center of your heart and mind and as you exhale, see Gratitude flow as crystalline waters to circulate and nourish your Being."

2. <u>Involves knowing the difference between 'being in and with Gratitude', versus, doing or making a 'should' of Gratitude.</u>

   Try saying this statement to your partner: *"I <u>am</u> grateful for......"* and notice your inner experience. Notice the impact on your partner.

   Now say, *"I <u>should</u> be grateful for......"* or *"You should be grateful for......"* and notice what happens to your energy or inner experience. Note the impact on your partner.

3. <u>Involves how we give, how we receive, and how we co-create giving and receiving.</u> We find that sometimes couples wait for the other to do and that they let their behavior be determined by the other. It takes one in the couple system to genuinely shift their energy to claim and embody their sacred space within, and go to their heart space with a stance of Gratitude to shift the energy. It is even better when both are able to shift their energy and be in a co-creative stance of Gratitude.

   "I am shifting myself (moving internally or externally as in changing ones sitting position) to embody Gratitude in my heart space."

   "I am sitting on my frustration pot right now and I am grateful that I can choose, for now to be frustrated for about 10 minutes."

   "I am grateful that I can differentiate between my frustration pot and my Gratitude pot. It makes my energy clearer and our communications cleaner with each other."

This requires making a conscious effort to go to a place of Gratitude within, being there a moment and speaking to each other from this space. When you can take a moment and shift to this space, you will notice that you speak much more from a space of Gratitude rather than from your usual reaction.

4. <u>Involves a discipline of keeping Gratitude clear and clean, and not muddying it with countering or 'negative statements'</u>, such as: "I will feel grateful if you will…" and "Not like when you…" Most likely the statement that will be reacted to is the countering statement, and the first statement will be missed. An example of this is:

> **Barb:** "I am thankful that you prepared dinner so that I did not have to make dinner after a hard day at work. **But,** it would be better if the vegetables were a bit crispier."

The challenge is to stay with the first statement.

> **Jason:** (picking up on the <u>But</u> statement) "Somehow I feel criticized. Are you criticizing me?"

> **Barb:** "I want to share what I feel very grateful for. And, I want to also be able to share what I prefer without it coming out as criticism or being ungrateful. That would feel like a truer expression from me."

> **Coach:** "Experiment with using the word '<u>and</u>' rather than '<u>but</u>'."

> **Barb:** "I am so thankful that you prepared dinner for me. I feel cared for after a hard day's work - <u>and</u> I do love my vegetables crispy."

> **Jason:** "OK, I love that you noticed that I prepared dinner as it was my taking care of you and next time I will make crispy vegetables for you."

5. <u>Involves how you ground, center, and notice when you go off center.</u> When there is a hidden agenda of manipulation, of 'fixing' the other or of criticism, the energetic frequency is mixed. Check your 'pots' for clarity.

> **Jason:** "Somehow, I am leery when you tell me you are thankful, because I get this strange feeling that I am being set up for something. Is there an agenda behind your thanking me?"

> **Barb:** "I am thankful that you are a better parent than I am. I see you so perfect that I am the one who is the loser. Not really clear why I am frustrated for feeling this way and sometimes I resent you for not supporting me.

> **Jason:** "I notice you thank me for parenting, and then you went into the frustration pot."

> **Barb:** "I am in the frustration pot, when I feel unsupported. That's the way I deal with my frustration. I just criticized myself. I would rather talk about my frustration if that is OK with you.

Appreciating the Universal Law of Giving and Receiving

The Universe operates through a dynamic exchange of giving and receiving as reflected in the flow of energy in all of life. While nature operates in balancing the cycle of giving and receiving, your relational life can only be in balance when giving and receiving are in balance. Every interpersonal relationship is built on this flow of life. When you are <u>always</u> the <u>giver</u>, you act against this principle just as much as when you are <u>always</u> the only one who is the <u>receiver</u>. This basic truth is without exception everywhere where people deal with people.

In our willingness to be in balance, giving graciously and receiving gratefully, Gratitude and Grace becomes the energizing power that keeps the blessings of Divine Love flowing and enhancing our partnerships.

Giving and Receiving Exercise

We would like to invite you to explore an exercise with each other of Giving and Receiving in the present.

This is a **non-verbal exercise with no words exchanged during part of this exercise**. The purpose of the exercise is to gain awareness of your non-verbal 'giving and receiving' experience and to enhance awareness of 'intention and impact' in the experience of giving and receiving.

Please follow these instructions.

Setting up the exercise:
1. Together, choose small, neutral, and safe items in your house, such as an envelope, plastic cup, ball, crayons, card, etc. totaling ten (10) items.
2. Sit facing each other on chairs or on the floor.
3. Place the neutral item(s) you chose in the center between the two of you.
4. Select three (3) items each and place the 4 that are left off to the side. (they serve as extras if you choose to use them)
5. Now each of you take a notepad and pencil and place beside you for you to jot your thoughts and feelings.
6. Determine how many rounds you want to do. Each round has 3 exchanges of 'giving and receiving' and could last anywhere between 1-3 minutes.
7. Select who is **Person A** and who is **Person B**.

Round 1: The first round of exchange(s): (non-verbal)

Person A as the Giver: Choose any of your items to give **non-verbally** in any sequence to **Person B** by placing the item in his or her hand. Then **Person B as the Receiver,** notice your experience of receiving. After each Round, Person A and Person B, note your experience(s) (thoughts, feelings of giving, and receiving) on the notepad beside you.

> **Person A**: Choose from the following and do in any sequence without telling B. As you Give, pay attention to your experience of <u>how you hand</u> the item <u>as you give</u> and how <u>you intend</u> for B to receive it.
>
> - Think of a pleasant thought and <u>put that pleasant thought on the item</u> and give to **Person B.**
>
> - Think of a person (parent, teacher, coach) who gave you a meaningful experience, feel that meaningful experience now, and let the item symbolize the meaningful experience as you give it to **Person B.**
>
> - Think of **Person B** and his or her most 'divine' quality that you appreciate and are grateful for. <u>Place how you feel on the item</u> you choose and give to **Person B**.

Person B, as the receiver: Notice from the following items below **what** and **how** you are receiving each of the items from **Person A**. You may choose from any of the following below:
- Something pleasant
- Something meaningful
- Something 'divine'

Round 2: The second round of exchanges: (non-verbal)

Switch places - Person A becomes the Receiver and Person B is the Giver. Follow the instructions above for 1-3 minutes <u>non-verbally</u>. After Round 2, note your experience(s) as the giver and as the receiver on your notepad.

Round 3: The third round of exchanges: (non-verbal)

Follow the above this time being **both the giver and the receiver** in your exchanges, <u>non-verbally</u> giving your item(s) and receiving the other's items and noticing your experience as you are giving and receiving in an exchange circle of:
- Something pleasant
- Something meaningful
- Something 'divine'

Process Dialogue of the Giving and Receiving Exercise: (verbal)

Reflect on your experience together by sharing:

1. <u>What stood out</u> for you as the <u>Giver</u>?

2. <u>What stood out</u> for you as the <u>Receiver</u>?

3. <u>What did you notice</u> about each other's <u>Intention</u> of Giving and Receiving?

4. <u>What did you notice</u> about each other's <u>Impact</u> of Giving and Receiving?

5. **When did you notice** and **how did you notice** whether there was a match between what is <u>given </u>and what is <u>received</u>? What helped?

6. **When** there was a <u>mismatch</u> between what is <u>given</u> and what is <u>received</u>, how did you make adjustments non-verbally and in your dialogue?

Continue your reflection by practicing the Reflection Exercise on the next page, and <u>deepen your sharing dialogue</u> of your giving and receiving. Share you insights, awareness, and discoveries together.

In closing at the end of the exercise, share with each other what you learned in doing this exercise together and express your Gratitude. Then Pause…..and feel your Gratitude.

Reflection Exercise: Giving and Receiving

Let us take a moment and practice this reflection exercise on Giving and Receiving.

Giving:

1. Think of a pleasant, enjoyable experience where you are <u>giving</u>. Notice your present experience now as you bring <u>your giving</u> experience to mind. Journal or draw it.

2. Now think of a stressful experience where you are giving and having difficulty, not enjoying being in the position of giving. Journal or draw it.

3. Which one is a familiar experience of giving? What is the difference for you between the two experiences you described?

4. What is going on for you when you think about giving? What are you experiencing presently in your relationship in terms of giving and receiving? How would you have preferred yourself to be? How did your intention and the impact of your giving match or not match? How are you feeling now and what are you noticing?

Receiving:

1. Think of an experience of <u>receiving</u> where you had a pleasant and enjoyable experience. What are you noticing? What is it in the giving that you noticed yourself receiving?

2. Now think of an experience where you received and explore where it was difficult or stressful. What is it in the receiving that it is difficult for you to receive?

3. Do you notice a difference in your experience of giving and receiving? In your relationship with yourself and with your significant partner – describe your dance of giving and receiving.

4. What is it that you would like to experience and transform? What would make your receiving and giving satisfying and nourishing? What would you shift in yourself to participate in energetically co-creating giving and receiving with Gratitude?

The Skill of Giving and Receiving

Giving is generally valued. One who is fully giving is viewed as generous and is given praise and deemed honorable. Giving and receiving, like yin and yang, are complimentary energies linked together in the natural flow of life. Similarly, inhaling (receiving life force) and exhaling (giving life force) in breathing is the natural flow of Life Force energy. If one favors an aspect of the flow of our life force energy, their breathing system becomes out of balance and dis-ease happens.

Developing Receiving Skills

Learning and developing the skill of receiving and giving, begins with gaining awareness of how you receive and how you give. Notice what beliefs, thoughts, emotions, actions, and reactions are involved with receiving and giving. At times, we may have constructed walls and obstacles as a creative adjustment to block painful receiving.

It is valuable to receive, for it is in receiving when gratefulness abounds. It is in the art of our receiving that we are able to give with Healing Love.

In our work with couples, we find that the common difficulty is in the inability of couples in a relationship to truly receive...grace in their hearts. Their objections to receive are unexamined beliefs that 'it is selfishness, vulnerability, weakness', and other negative connotations, thus creating receiving love in relationships difficult.

> **When true heartfelt receiving is blocked, true heartfelt and gracious giving is blocked, and this becomes your subjective 'truth' and reality**.

We find that allowing ourselves to receive in ways that allows for replenishing, recharging of our life force, and receiving Universal blessings and grace, connects us to the Universal Source.

The practice, which we describe below, helps us in developing our 'receiving, spiritual muscles'.

Developing Your Receiving Muscles

Receive what life wants to give you. For example, nature gives sunlight, ground to stand on, trees to lean on, water to nourish, and air to breathe. All of this is FREE. Take the time to receive what life IS giving you. Receiving is both where we begin and where we end. Breathe in and experience receiving an affirmation or compliment, slowly taking it in. Exhale and notice where affirmation stays and what you release.

A. To be able to receive material, spiritual, and psychological gifts from those who offer them, learn to receive in small ways first. Receiving takes practice in noticing what you are receiving. To get started: start noticing your receiving and be with the pleasure of living in a world where people are kind, complimentary, and considerate. Before acting by doing a ritual 'thank you', BREATHE in, what you are receiving and take it to your cells. Feel the grace all the way within. BE genuinely grateful within.

B. Observe and be discerning of <u>how</u> you receive. For example, we choose what we take in. Someone is giving you their impression in a complimentary fashion. You notice that you are uncomfortable receiving a compliment even though you may secretly prefer that to criticism. Take your time and pause with it slowly breathing in the compliment. You do not need to give back a compliment. Experiment with saying, "I am taking that in."

222

C. Another way to practice your receiving muscles is to sift the 'gold' from the 'mud'. How is this done? For example, you partner is giving you advice to fix a situation that concerns you. You do not care for the advice ... that is the 'gray'. Exhale the gray and if it reminds you of 'old stuff'...release the mud as you exhale the gray. Sift the gold, "I am taking in how you really thought about me and all the effort you put into figuring the situation out. I am receiving your care and attention. And I am sifting through what you are advising me to do as I am not ready for any action. I really want to just share with you and receive your listening to me."

Receiving is an art and takes practice.

Developing Your Giving Muscles

Developing your **Giving** muscles involves a conscious inner process of *attending* to _how_ and _what_ you are giving and *how* and *what* you __intend__ to give. This is important because the origination of giving in a relationship emanates from our awareness or lack of awareness of our inner self process.

In a relationship, let us assume that we are always giving, both our intended and our unintended: our existence, our habits, our presence, our attention or inattention, our deeds, our thoughts, our diseases, and our health, etc. IT JUST IS. In our significant partnerships there are those aspects of Giving that enhances, heals, deepens, and transforms our relationship. And there are those aspects of Giving that diminishes, wounds, and recycles stuck interactions.

As you choose conscious awareness Giving, you begin to be aware of your *felt sense of receiving* in order to attend and respond with your ability for giving, whether that be of presence, time, listening, sharing, connecting, problem-solving, nurturing, appreciating, supporting, affirming, and giving of your receiving. You give by your willingness to be influenced by how and what your partner wants to receive, rather than what you assume they should receive. You learn to take responsibility for what you are giving, **and be open to 'your giving of your receiving' and the impact of your actions on your partner**. Therefore Giving and Receiving becomes a mutual learning process of an energy exchange that can replenish, revitalize, and rejuvenate.

Developing your Giving and Receiving Muscles

The receiving and giving practice is an evolving conscious steps process before it becomes part of your natural way of being. AS we receive, we learn to give by how we receive. The flow of loving is enhanced and deepened. Give thanks for your receiving and be amazed at how the love is growing between you. **Give thanks for your giving of your receiving**.

By opening to receiving with Gratitude, you ease any blocks in your heart to feel love. And as your heart become full, giving is an easier process. Begin unblocking with small steps and open the flow of the Universe. Notice what is abundantly here, practice receiving others Gratitude, acknowledgements, appreciations, and affirmations.

A. Be present to different types of feedback -- compliment, gift, presence, attention, suggestion, observation, action, help, and information. Be present in Gratitude. Say to yourself: "As I am open to receiving, I create a container for receiving blessings of grace within me."

B. Pause to take it in...Breathe. Inhale. Let Divine and Universal energy be present.

C. Listen to what is being said, similar to listening to music, noticing its rhythms, tones, and vibrations from an observer's place. Listen and attune to the core music from the Heart of Divine Love.

D. Feel the love and support behind it.

E. Let your partner know that you've connected with heart of his/her words and action.

F. Give voice to your thanks. The key here is remaining conscious of intention to take in and absorb the content and feelings you are being offered. Give yourself permission to receive the intention of the gesture and acknowledge the discomfort you are experiencing, whether you choose to verbalize it or not. Imagine a kind grandmother gently saying to you afterward: "See, that was not so bad? Was it?"

'Massage' your giving and receiving muscles with the Practice Healing Dialogue (refer to Pathway D). As you integrate the spirit of giving and receiving into your healing relationship, you reveal yourself to the Divine Love within. This transforms your prior troubled relationship into a conscious Divine partnership. In being spiritually 'naked', all your many different parts are becoming embraced by both of you. As you embrace yourselves, you both help each other to come to your wholeness. You feel your whole self accepting your many different parts. You feel that in your partnership, you are traveling through life's journey with a kindred spirit.

This spirit of your practice of healing dialogue--wherein you naturally move between giving and receiving, helps your relationship improve and you sensitize to attuning and resonating to each other as being unique individuals, with your personal histories and ways of being, joining in valuing, and respecting each other's views and preferences. Through the spirit of giving and receiving in dialogue, you make visible what is *in your unfolding process of experience* and the quality of your divine connection. Thus, together, your inclusion is a spiritual receptive action of your oneness with the universal divine relationship of authentic love.

In essence, *Gratitude* loops <u>all</u> the Pathways together. Each of the Pathways involves the circle of receiving and giving.

- ☼ Pathway A – Receiving and Giving Affirmation
- ☼ Pathway B – Receiving and Giving of your Being presence as well as Balancing with yourself and each other
- ☼ Pathway C – Receiving and Giving of your Connection, Resonance and Attunement
- ☼ Pathway D – Receiving and Giving in Dialogue through your Developmental journey of Discovery
- ☼ Pathway E – Receiving and Giving of your Evolving in Learning from Experience
- ☼ Pathway F – Receiving and Giving of Freedom and Response-ability

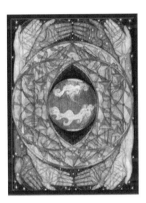

Summary Highlights of Pathway "G": Pathway of Gratitude and Grace

1. The Pathway of Gratitude is a powerful and energetic Pathway. When it is the cornerstone of the couple's journey, it allows them to be open to the *Present - Here and Now,* to receive life's blessings, which are presented as the Universe's gifts that are wrapped in many colors, and with multi-dimensional human experiences of our body-mind-soul-spirit.

2. The Pathway G fosters learning how Gratitude is a vital attitude, emotion, and an inner state of being. When it is an embodied experience, it emanates from one's heart and it creates a more satisfying and lasting relationship. It takes the couple beyond themselves and beyond their relationship to the unified field of Divine Love where they feel blessed.

3. When couples are on Pathway G, they can feel that Gratitude is missing in their lives or feel its overflowing energy. When couples feel Gratitude is missing, it is important to notice how this powerful energy has been thwarted, convoluted, or misunderstood.

4. The challenges in Pathway G often originate in past experiences that create a *'block'* in the universal flow of and to Gratitude. Those with such blocks are unable to truly receive the blessings that are in Pathway G. At times making a detour through Pathways A to F helps to savor being in Pathway G. At other times, accessing Pathway G and practicing the processes therein, helps movement through the other Pathways. Together these Pathways work together in the transformational journey of the couple.

5. The Pathway of Gratitude is the strengthening and deepening Pathway that helps their relationship last and transforms them together. The practice involves communicating in a ratio of at least 5 to 1 - 5 positives of energy, communications, expressions, and actions to 1 negative.

6. Learn to receive by letting your heart awaken to the transforming power of Gratitude by being receptive to life's abundance. Developing your receiving muscles is an inner process of Gratitude as a state of mind, to see life and resonate with life's gracious abundance. The more you receive with Gratitude the more the flow of things come to you to be grateful for. As you focus on Gratitude, your capacity to receive increases by what you focus on.

7. Pathway G is the 'glue' that links time, space, and our interconnectedness. This is where our intentions and prayers to the Divine and Universal Source are in the ever-present moment.

8. The Pathway of Gratitude involves a conscious focus on gratefulness, even through the mundane and difficult times. With an attitude of Gratitude, all the relational bumps and adversities are taken as part of the **University of Life,** and that in the processes to the end,

the journey will make sense. Gratitude harvesting involves sifting through the 'dust and dirt' to gather, reap, and give thanks for the gold.

9. Present day challenges involve differentiating between our frustration pot and your Gratitude pot, so as to be aware of tendencies to take your frustration pot and pour the contents of it over your Gratitude pot.

10. The Universe operates through a dynamic exchange of giving and receiving as reflected in the flow of energy in all of life. While nature operates in balancing the cycle of giving and receiving, your relational life can only be in balance when giving and receiving are in balance. As the couple's healing relationship is built on this flow of life, they demonstrate their willingness to enhance their giving and receiving inner 'muscles' through conscious evolving processes of the Pathway A to F practices.

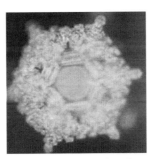

Love plus Gratitude

Photo: Masaru Emoto
"The Hidden Messages in Water"
(Emoto quote on pages 205 - 206)

In closing this chapter, we would like to share with you our Couple's Gratefulness Prayer

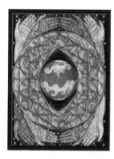

A Couple's Gratefulness Prayer

Oh...to greet the morning today, breathing in light, air and life,
Oh...to feel our bodies awakening with feeling and movement,
Oh...to see you beside me, your presence affirms my being,
My being is filled with Gratitude for living...

Oh...to see the smiling, laughing, crying, faces of children,
Oh...to hear the barking of dogs, the chirping of birds, the music all around,
Oh...to touch, to speak, to embrace, to make meals and create spaces,
My heart is filled with Gratitude for loving...

Oh...to share stories of struggling, surviving and overcoming,
Oh...to listen, to share and be moved with the courage of your spirit,
Oh...to witness our unfolding days, months and years becoming,
My soul if filled with Gratitude for giving...

Oh...to ache and pray with you in your yearning,
Oh...to allow light to warm darkness with graceful blessings,
Oh...to embrace experiencing the Pathways of living,
My spirit is filled with Gratitude for receiving...

Oh...to Being and Doing,
Oh...to Living and Loving,
Oh...to Giving and Receiving,
Our Daily Gratitude practice for God's Graces,
Are our Love's Heart, Soul, and Being.

~Phil & Lalei
© 2009

PATHWAY H: PATHWAY TO A HIGHER PURPOSE OF LOVE
A SACRED PATHWAY OF SPIRIT CENTEREDNESS

"True marriage serves as a spiritual device for perfecting the full expression of souls and freeing them into God...through restoration, realization, of their divine nature assisted by the companionship of their ideal helpmate."
~Paramahansa Yogananda

Introduction

Many people get caught up and lose themselves in the mundane stuff of survival, in and of itself. Some who feel they have 'arrived', live pleasant and/or content lives. And...on an inner level, some continue on, in their evolution, in search of a Higher Purpose to their life and their relations. They take their inner journey of soul and spirit.

As your relational life journey awakens you to your Higher Purpose, individually and as a couple, your transformational processes move to a higher plane of consciousness. With your willingness to delve into this sacred Pathway, quantum shifts can happen for you, and your journey together may reflect a spirit centeredness in the evolving present of your Higher Purpose of Love. The dynamic living process of your commitment develops into genuine love. Healing vibrates to deeper levels wherein Divine love, your Spirit awareness, brings you to align with your Higher Purpose perspective and to witness the awesome workings of Spirit in the multidimensional aspects of your life experience.

Pathway H Defined: The Higher Purpose of Love and Marriage

We would like you to consider that your relationship is a journey of transformation that includes your daily life together, as you move through the cycles of seasons. Consider the unforeseen matters of your adventure together: its complexities, challenges, and adversities. Consider that each of you have your own life purpose, whether you are aware of it or not. Consider the thrust your soul journey has for coming to your own awakening. Consider how you were drawn together to partner for each other's transformation through your Healing Love relationship. Consider that Pathway H is the sacred path of seeing Spirit in the disguise of daily life and centering with Spirit-awareness to be at the heart of your life journey together. And, finally consider that the unfolding of your deeper connection lies in the *healing* transformation of your human love to embrace the divine lover that resides within each of you and in both of you.

Now BREATHE and be in this moment. Notice what your inner experience is.

As you delve deeper into the Higher Purpose of your life and relationship, individually and together, you open to the universal spiritual laws for your meaningful life journey of love. You become interested in co-evolving your Higher Purpose together. You support each other's goals, dreams, and aspirations. You face with truth and honesty the Higher Purpose of your challenges and difficulties, as well as your blessings. The Higher Purpose becomes a part of your daily life. Your challenges and difficulties can be perceived as a perplexing expression of Divinity. Personally and together you can feel peace in the midst of chaos while your shared intimacy deepens into a true healing partnership of love.

The Value of Pathway H

> *"It is the perception of divinity wherever we go, in whatever we perceive – in the eyes of a child, in the beauty of a flower, in the flight of a bird. When we begin to experience our life as the miraculous expression of Divinity – not occasionally, but all the time – then we will know the true meaning of success and of love."*
> *~Deepak Chopra*

As a couple goes within together, they co-create their relationship or marriage with the divine view of themselves as a partnership of healing love by bringing light and love to the world. With a Higher Purpose consciousness the couple connects with that which is larger than themselves, the universal energetic field (called by many names such as God, Buddha, Nature, Mother Earth, Tao, Spirit, Allah, Krishna, Jehovah, the Universe, the Force, the Source, Energy, the One, the All). This spiritual base gives the couple a grounded foundation. Pathway H has us cultivate inner virtues such as patience, kindness, compassion, faith, hope and trust by beginning to heal the wounds of the heart. In Pathway H, couples get a new perspective, one of positive belief that their life and relationship journey is meant to be filled with the amazing grace of unfolding miracles.

For many couples finding themselves in Pathway H can come at any time in their personal soul journey. This can be initiated by a triggering or significant event. Or it can be a seemingly gradual development based on a particular problem, dilemma or issue. A member of the couple will ask "What was that about? Why now? Why is this happening to me/us? What is the meaning? I know there is a purpose, but what is it?"

Pathway H is pivotal for personal and relational healing. During a couple's relationship there will be chances to explore the Higher Purpose of one's life and your relationship. Some couples will consciously take Pathway H and multi-dimensionally explore it while others will succumb to numbing oblivion.

As couples examine, reflect and embrace their Higher Purpose together, they will open to receive the gifts of Spirit - multidimensional conscious awareness of their partnership that will unfold and deepen into unconditional love throughout their lifetime. Those who welcome the opportunity to heal their hearts, learn to appreciate the significant role they play in each other's fulfillment of their life's Higher Purpose.

Instructions for Guided Reflection or Meditation Exercise

Let us start with this guided reflection exercise or meditation to help you begin to connect with your divine Higher Purpose and the Higher Purpose of your relationship.

Then take some quiet time alone to complete the sentences below.

Then turn and face your partner. Sit in this present moment together and feel your presence and your partner's presence.

Afterwards take some quiet time alone to complete the sentences on page 234 after the Reflection Exercise and writing your **first thought or feeling** as it comes to you.

Reflection Exercise
The Divine Higher Purpose of Your Relationship

Imagine yourself among the star-studded night sky as a star. Imagine yourself at a time beyond your birth or your death, in the heavens, looking towards the earth rotating through time and space.

As a star, you are One with love, peace, beauty, and joy in all of creation. And as you see Earth, your parents, your family or caretakers, and the world around you, a yearning for something embeds in your heart. You cannot define it. But you want what is missing. It is a quality in some kind of knowing for that missing piece... to understand, to love, to be loved, to matter, to serve, to create, to contribute...to be a part of some cause... for peace, for justice and fairness...for compassion...

High in the quiet of the universe your soul self becomes embraced as one with Spirit in the universal energetic field of light. Your soul self receives your Higher Purpose for your earth journey as it is encoded by Spirit within your soul. Your soul convenes with other soul beings that you are to meet again below the speed of light. You understand the Higher Purpose for your earth journey. Peace fills your soul. You are listening to the music, resonating with your Higher Purpose within your whole being. Spirit fills your soul with joy, peace, and love of God. You feel so one with Love.

Your soul-self is escorted by angels who descend below the speed of light to earth. Your spirit remembers this portal of ascent and descent. Gathering elements of space, air, fire, water, and earth form your earth body's field, the blueprint of your soul's earth journey.

You enter a time zone, culture and family. You are born on earth at a specific time where all the planets are in relational position to highlight your uniqueness.

Notice who is present: your mother, father, siblings, relatives, etc. Notice the circumstances and events, the stage is set for your life journey. You are the star for the unfolding of the Higher Purpose of your life. Your Higher Purpose is encoded within your heart. Your intellect has protected you from remembering until now. Encoded within your heart is your Higher Purpose.

The shroud of layers of your culture, family, history that has been embedded within your tissue, muscle, and your automatic habits slowly begins to lift. Somehow you have felt some kind of knowing that something essential has been missing in your life. You yearn for your missing purpose, your connection with THAT something larger.

You are moved by knowledge as you search for something better, someone to follow. You want safety, to love and be loved, to matter and make a contribution, you want to discover your possibilities and have a meaningful, purposeful life.

Your life journey of relationships brings you now to your choice of your present significant relationship.

[continued next page]

[Reflection Exercise continued]

See your significant relationship (your spouse, partner, friend etc) in your mind's eye.

Do you recognize that indescribable feeling when you met?
Do you feel a connection, an expansion...delight...safety?
Do you feel peace, hope or faith?
Do you feel alive, vital, and joyful?
Would you say you were 'in love'?

Now, how has love transformed you? How has your commitment to love stretched you?

Do you see yourself moved to be of service, to attend, listen, and be present? Do you feel supportive and compassionate? Do you feel in tune and resonate?   Do you choose to extend yourself, to empathize, to empower, to speak your truth, to nurture your spiritual growth, as well as your partner's?

Do you choose to be loving to yourself and to your partner, even as loving feelings may not be present? Do you choose to take the path less travelled, the inner pathway of commitment, and a sacred covenant to the Higher Purpose of Love?

Imagine universal, divine love in the center of your relationship.
Visualize and be with this. Sit with yourself. Quiet your mind. Exhale and release all of your breath, all the way to the ground to the bottoms of your feet.
Sit together. Quiet your minds. Breathe and exhale.
Let yourself empty your mind as you exhale. Release...Exhale...Release...Exhale...

Breathe in Spirit.
Breathe in universal awareness of that something greater than the both of you.
Bring the vastness of the universe and your connection to the Source.
Breathe in Divine Love...to your Heart.
Breathe in Divine Love to your whole Being.
Breathe in Divine Love into your Higher Purpose.

You are a "spirit being", with the Divine Source of Love encoded as a signature in your cells. And in the present NOW, you have chosen each other as your partner on earth for your Higher Purpose of Love.

Now as you come back to earth, see yourself bring with you the vastness of the universe and your connection to source. As you make your way back to land on earth and in this time and place, now here, in your bodyself...fill every cell of your being with the light of love. Breathe now and feel your Self present within now - here.

Let yourselves be in a quiet neutral place as you connect your feet to the ground and your crown to the sky. Let sky and earth meet in your heart space.

Listen to spirit be within you. Listen...Breathe...Listen...Breath of Spirit within.

Together with your partner call in Divine Love to guide you. (If you are doing this meditation alone, think, imagine, call the higher self of your partner in your mind's eye to be NOW present and join your higher selves together in prayer) **"We pray that the Higher Purpose (of our life journey, this challenge, our struggle) be revealed in the light of Divine Love and Universal Wisdom. We pray that our perspectives be awakened, enlightened, and healed."**

Now in your journal, complete the following sentences in the flow of your stream of consciousness. Write your **first thought or feeling** as it comes to you.

My Higher Purpose is **to** _____.

My Higher Purpose is to **be** _____.

My Higher Purpose is to **give** _____.

My Higher Purpose is to **receive** _____.

My Higher Purpose is to **learn and evolve in** _____.

With _____ (partner's name) our Higher Purpose is **to** _____.

With _____ (partner's name) our Higher Purpose is to **be** _____.

With _____ (partner's name) our Higher Purpose is to **give** _____.

With _____ (partner's name) our Higher Purpose is to **receive** _____.

With _____ (partner's name) our Higher Purpose is to **learn** _____.

Then turn and face your partner. Sit in this present moment together and feel your presence and your partner's presence.

When you are ready, you may share with each other:
- your experience of the meditation
- your responses to complete the statements
- your experience of sharing and listening to each other

Together, experiment by *LINKING and* utilizing the word "AND". Take turns to listen within your heart as you hear each other use *LINKING* statements. Notice your embodied experiences in yourself, in the other, and in your relational field. PAUSE.......BREATHE.......BE.........

Challenges of Pathway H

When life is going well, it may seem easier to be grateful for our blessings and enjoy the favors of these blessings. It is easy to see what we are doing right, to feel that we are on the right path, and to believe in oneself and each other. This ease can become routine. Without tending to our conscious awareness, we eventually can take things for granted. In the best of circumstances we can go into excess, lose our balance, take the next promotion, go for more things to accumulate, etc. As we get busier with stuff, we lose our center and our sense of having a higher purpose.

Then adversity strikes, correction happens, the storms come and your relationship is impacted by an inner or outer crisis... and your relationship is thrust into Pathway "H". All else seems to defy understanding and the relationship is shocked by what occurs, even with the best of intentions, goals, and plans. Even doing good things and following all 'shoulds' it seems at times, from our human perspective that life does not spare us from life's ups and downs.

The Challenge of Meaningless To-Do's

A couple, Kate and Alex, described how their vacations in relaxing spiritual places, puts them in touch with their Higher Purpose. Away, they reconnect and feel affirmed in their love for each other and the ideals and values they both hold for a purposeful life together. When they return home to the 'reality' of their daily lives, whatever connections they had quickly evaporates. They are disappointed at their loss of perspective as the stress of the many 'meaningless to do's', take over until their next vacation.

Kate and Alex joined in affirming their intention of living their Higher Purpose marriage. They examined their stressful hectic lifestyle. They became aware of the ironic value of their escalating complaints as a spiritual signal of their splitting off from their spiritual practice that keeps them grounded in the Higher Purpose of their relationship.

With conscious choice, Kate and Alex first began with co-creating a 10-minute container for their complaints and made a daily, then weekly appointment on it. They reframed their complaints as a signal to focus on what they are being called to learn through Pathways A to G.

They faced the challenge of their meaningless to do's, by incorporating a daily 'mini vacation' practice and assigned a sacred place in their garden for the summer and a place in their house for the winters. With intention, they individually and together made daily visits to their sacred sanctuary where they meditated, reflected, and prayed for the realization of their Higher Purpose of Love in their vital and lasting marriage.

The Challenge of a Meaningless Loss or Tragedy

We worked with a couple who questioned how such a horrible thing could have happened to them. They had trusted in divine protection and allowed their son to go on a church mission to Africa. While there, he was mysteriously killed. They were devastated. They questioned and blamed themselves and each other. They became obsessed about what happened and questioned their faith. They were very angry with God. Their pastor referred them for couples counseling, as their relationship was in crisis brought on by their deep grief over their loss.

During one of their sessions, they spoke of their anger with God and wondered if they could ever find any peace because they felt so trapped in their pain and anger. They could not even talk with each other about their anger because they feared causing each other even more grief.

We listened and listened and prayed silently in our hearts. We acknowledged their sorrow, pain and fear. We validated their 'anger' with God. During our session we said to them: "You both have a relationship with a compassionate God. We truly believe God can handle your anger.

Your anger is valid. You trusted in God's protection of your son. How would you like to talk together with God as if God was sitting on this chair right now?"

"I am not able to talk. I would be screaming at Him. How could you allow this!" the mother's voice came through her wail of deep agony. Tears turned into heaving sound of sobs, deep from within.

The father, whose eyes were brimming with tears, reached out for his wife's hand for the first time during this whole event. They both sobbed deep from their belly while holding each other.

"How could He allow this? Our son did not harm anyone. He went there to help. This makes no sense."

"He was a good son. This is so very painful."

After their storm of tears, there was a long calm and the couple held each other's hand tightly. The moment was weighted with a deep and sacred sorrow. There were no words. We sat with them as they sat with each other.

The silent prayer in our hearts was to hold them in our mind and in our hearts, as we raised their sorrow to the Universal Presence, asking for compassion and ease, feeling with full trust and surrender to the process in the Power of Pathway "H" the Higher Purpose of the 'seemingly incomprehensible' loss of this couple to be held in Healing Love.

When all else fails, we realize that turning to prayer or being held in prayer, comforts us in the darkest moments of a couple's life journey.

The Challenge of Life's Call to Stretch Us into Love

Many times the Higher Purpose of a couple's relationship does not become apparent until their greatest challenges appear – a terminal illness, death, affairs, tragedy, catastrophic adversities, etc.

We knew a couple, Ninoy and Cory Aquino, whose relationship was tested to the maximum in this material world. Phil knew Ninoy Aquino, the husband, personally as they were political prisoners together during the Marcos regime. Aquino was a passionate lover of freedom for his countrymen and a staunch critic of the Marcos dictatorship that held the Philippines hostage. Though knowing the threat of assassination was strong, after three years of exile in the USA, Ninoy, felt the compelling love of God and country, and knew that it was he who held the hope of the people, so he returned to the Philippines. An upheaval of great proportions occurred upon his return to Manila in 1983. He was assassinated as he descended the steps of the airplane at the Manila airport for the entire world to see.

Cory Aquino (Ninoy's wife) passed away on August 1, 2009. She endeavored to bring integrity and healing back to the country. There were seven coup attempts against her and every time they were miraculously quelled. Her love and caring inspired and held the hope of the Philippine people. The re-awakening of a country out of apathy was a daunting healing process. It was her alignment with the Holy Spirit for guidance and her religious devotion that gave her inner peace and the strength to forge courageously in waters for which she had no experience or training, and to fulfill her Higher Purpose of love of freedom and to serve her country in the capacity for which she was elected.

In reflecting on their contribution as a couple, the Aquinos, seemed to combine heaven and earth together and exemplified a Higher Purpose beyond the material world. They aligned with the power of the Holy Spirit in a non-violent revolution harnessing "people power" by being armed with prayers and yellow flowers to disarm tanks and guns, and unseating a dictatorship of twenty years.

The Challenge of the Impact of Living with a Higher Purpose

We attended a conference where the participants, who represented the global community, gathered together, both for their own personal healing and well-being, and for the healing and transformation of the world. It was an uplifting, inspiring, and enlivening weekend. Participants felt love energies vibrating in the air and discussed how they would like to take their experience and radiate it at their home and work environments.

A number of the people in the workshop were in partnerships (marriage, long-term relationships, etc). Some discussed the impact of their experience and how their partners had various feelings of support or non-support for their attending the workshop. They wondered how to handle the 'perceived' threat to the security of their relationship that may be felt by their partner. Because of this discussion, participants were able to return home and share their concerns with their families, spouses and friends. They spoke of the Higher Purpose for which they had initiated their own healing process in loving themselves.

We also discussed at this workshop that when someone goes to reclaim him or herself and to feel a sense of wholeness, the other partner may feel some sense of confusion or fear knowing that the other person will not be the same. The choice to grow or heal on one hand can be very expansive and moving; on the other hand it can shake up their ways of relating with each other.

What do you do if one partner does not grow or proceed with their 'own' healing? What do you do if one of the partners resists change for themselves? Because you are a relational system, when one begins to heal, a change in the system or the partnership inevitably happens whether the other makes changes or not. For example, if you attend to your growth and healing and the other does not, how you re-enter into your home environment can be met with support and/or resistance. It is wise to slow down in making changes, particularly to 'make' the other change, and instead be with wisdom in acknowledging the present situation that is benefiting your partnership, while having the courage to continue with your personal growth and healing.

It is often when one grows, transforms or heals, that they may feel they are outgrowing their partner and then feel a need for their partner to make changes. The more one pushes for the change they want in their relationship, the more the other pushes for things to be the same.

Most couples tend to orient to their healing individually. While this is important, the impact on the whole couple relationship cannot be overlooked. One couple, Rose and Ron, individually took care of their own well being as they each sought their own counsel. They decided and took personal responsibility; one was for their weight issue, and the other for their issue with carrying the weight of responsibilities.

In looking at their health patterns, they acknowledged that weight was also a couple's issue. "I would like to believe that taking care of my well-being will be of service to us. We want to bring our new knowledge, our new being into our partnership, but that can be difficult because we related to each other through our dis-ease and stress."

In approaching their healing, they became cognizant of their Higher Purpose to lovingly reclaim the health of their bodies their thinking, their emotions, and their spirit. They noticed very different results occurring because of this new awareness. They then joined together in their conscious awareness of what their parts are in co-creating the sabotage of their present healing relationship and of the 'old' weight patterns they revert to when they feel threatened, shamed, or angry. Together they harnessed the supports and to intentionally surround themselves with en-lightening their Self-Other Loving, in a healthy and healing community that affirmed their Higher Purpose to Heal with Love, to themselves and to each other.

The Higher Purpose of Relationships

Let us explore the Higher Purpose of a relationship and how this is connected to our own life purpose. This is very important to look at first.

Here is an example: One partner spoke of how his spouse went ahead on a retreat for self-discovery and professional development. He was aware of his own fear of losing 'the most important person in my life' while in some funny way, he supported his partner's courage to take the leap. Though he felt threatened by his partner's actions for change, it propelled him to examine what really matters in his own life. "In supporting my partner to go for what matters for him, it was my way of giving me permission to have the courage to live authentically. My Higher Purpose has become evident to me...to be loving and accepting of myself...the way God has made me with all my gifts and all my flaws. That is the journey of our partnership since our families judge us and want to change us." Together the impact for us is we now serve others courageously in our professions as we have become authentic and unconditional in our acceptance of being alive and vital in our Present. We now love in a whole and healthy way, and have our own family community who see us healthy and whole."

Another has shared what moved him to take the steps to grow. When his wife came home from a workshop she was joyous, excitedly talking about the new wonderful friendships she had made, that felt nourishing to her spirit. She brought to light what was missing in our relationship. She decided: "Our relationship is unhealthy for me and I cannot stand how we are any longer."

He proceeded in telling us, "The more she continued going to workshops and seminars, the more I tried to stop her. I tried everything that I knew and it seemed that the wedge grew even more between us. We used to enjoy going out to bars together. Even our mutual friends noticed a change in her. What really was the clincher was when she said that she loved me so much that she was willing to set me free to do what I wanted and that for her sake she had to continue to heal herself and being with me was becoming unhealthy for her right now. I knew it was not the right motivation when I started to seek help for myself. It was hard, because to be honest, it was to win her back. But now I am grateful for her determination. My jealousy then, was because I wanted what she found within herself.   I understand the fullness of why I fell in love with her. Even though we met in a bar and drank together, deep down within we were numbing ourselves from life's pains. We dreamed of growing, healing, and being better. She did something about it. I came up with more excuses. It must have been her deep love that brought me to check myself in to treatment. I could not lose the most important person in my life. We were meant for something greater and I was holding us back."

Living in accordance to a Higher Purpose is a dynamic and a living process. Your personal healing and well-being and the healing and well-being of your relationship together, depends on a dynamic practice of recommitment and devotion to something larger than each one individually and together. We see it as the Higher Purpose of Healing Love: **to love one another as you love yourself with the love of the Divine above all**. This is an over-arching purpose that links your goals, dreams, aspirations, your process of healing, and your evolution to be coming to your Wholeness and Oneness.

Why Partners Come Together

Generally, partners come together because they fill what is 'missing, incomplete or lacking' in themselves through the other. An opportunity for becoming healing partners presents itself to them through their challenges, so they can support themselves and the relationship to become whole persons with a greater capacity for love. It is like reclaiming the Divine or connecting with the Source of one's Higher Power within.   It is about helping each other to come to their wholeness. Everyone is always searching for the divine lover within; we look to the other to fill that hole. The flip side of this is to feel that wholeness, to become whole ourselves.

This was poignantly demonstrated to us by a couple, Arlene and Bill, who were dealing with the many issues related to his terminal cancer. He had just a few months to live. They determined together that he was to die in the love and comfort of their home. She decided that this was all-important for both of them to share every precious moment together. It was amazing for us to be with them, the depth of their love and their Gratitude was palpable. The journey of their life, their amazing challenges and growth of spirit, their celebrations of themselves and each other, the love of their family and community, and the affirmation of their Higher Purpose of love of each other was evident to all. They talked of him going ahead home to Spirit. There was an atmosphere of prayerful peace that was with them. This couple recommitted themselves in their love to each other and to be in love in accordance to their Higher Purpose.

Arlene spoke as Bill lay on the hospital bed. They created a room in their home for comfort with music, familiar smells, presence of loved ones, and spiritual supports created a climate of peace. "We remember our sacred covenant. Telling our visitors, we are marrying unto death do us part. Thank you for coming to pray and meditate with us. Since the doctors said nothing can be done, I could not see Bill staying in hospital. I am glad we decided to let him be at home. Every moment is special as we live one day at a time and one breath at a time." In the midst of the sound of the oxygen-supplying machine, Bill made sounds in synchrony with Arlene's sharing. Arlene holding Bill's hand... "This is beyond words. So much healing has been happening in our whole family. We wonder if the Higher Purpose of this is for us to witness all the love that is all around us. We still pray for a miracle, that Bill will be able to get up and all the cancers will be gone. We know only God can cure. And if the Higher Purpose of this present process is to love deeply and to be present to the miracle that is so subtle, then here we are both. God is the center of our love." Arlene continued, holding Bill's hand, "I am so grateful to God for our deep love and I know our souls will love each other beyond. We recommit to love each other through this journey."

A Formula for Healing: The Practice of Co-Creating Miracles

The Pathway of Higher Purpose brings us to providing you with our formula for healing. **It is based on *H-O-P-E* (<u>H</u>onesty, <u>O</u>penness, <u>P</u>ractice <u>E</u>ncouragement).** When couples are able to face life, knowing that whatever happens that they have an-awareness of a Higher Purpose and that in the end, good will ultimately come to them as they live consciously.

There is a story by an ancient elder who talked about the struggle between hope and despair. "I feel as if I have two wolves fighting in my heart. One wolf is vengeful, angry, and violent and the other is loving and compassionate." His disciples asked, "Which wolf will win the fight in your heart?" The holy elder said, "It depends on which one I feed."

When you practice *H-O-P-E* you 'feed' yourself. This is a spiritual practice on your life's journey together. Focusing on your Higher Purpose helps partners take a leap of faith, to step out of false securities, and allow the healing partnership with your Higher Self to transform and deepen into the process of love.

Honesty: Honoring the Truth Process

Hope involves getting better in the inside of oneself, rather than hoping for things to get better on the outside, like the situation or your partner. Your inner practice of honesty is within yourself and with one another. Honesty can be a challenge when dishonesty is used as protection and when honesty is used as a weapon. Honesty involves sharing one's own inner and subjective experience and an honest attending to each other's 'truth' (thoughts, feelings, sensations, images, process etc) without negating the other. As long as two people continuously recommit to each other in terms of honesty, there is hope that their relationship can thrive and be vitally alive.

Openness: Trusting the Discovery Process

Partners are open to the discovery process and become authentic within themselves and with one another. They uncover the inner landscape and discover the higher purpose of their relational challenges and possibilities. They notice that when their energy is tied up in their secrets, addictions, or unhealthy beliefs, their relationship becomes depleting and 'dis-eased'. They open beyond survival and protection, facing their fears with a safe coach, counselor, spiritual director or support group helps ease the intensity of its hold. Their shifts free up energy for healing interactions that heal.

Practice: Processing Inner Experience and the Power of Prayer

Couples practice their commitment, whether alone or together to be constant in their processing of their internal and subjective experiences. That involves how they perceive what is happening with one another by checking with one another, talking with one another, and communicating with one another. It also involves engaging in the power of prayer to release stuckness, and to surrender feelings of powerlessness to the Higher Power. It is also helpful practice to have a coach or group to facilitate your processing interactions of inner experiences and/or to pray with. As couples learn **how** to learn from experience, they harness life's crisis as opportunities in their evolutionary process with one another and discover their practice disciplines bringing them to new realms of being and experiencing. Beyond finding solutions, processing involves a deep respect of awareness and an ability to face their dilemmas and to allow time, energy, and support for healing.

Encouragement: Supporting Presence (Energy+Courage+Mentoring)

Couples choose to adopt an encouraging presence and stance that is grounded, rather than judgmental, critical or fixing. One of the biggest challenges for couples is to be encouraging. When their words and actions are dissonant, like using 'blame and criticism', this can become the unwitting killer to the energy of encouragement. This practice involves the intentional focused energy of support and courage to sift through the 'stuff' to see and notice positives and to be able to co-mentor together to make it through and grow.

This whole process is not only a skill; it is the art of their couples' sacred heart. Aligning energetically with Spirit, one or both, elevates to their Higher Purpose to co-create an energy of hope. Hope is fed and cultivated in their spiritual life and expands to the spirit of their relationship, something that is larger than the both of them together.

On the following page is the Reflection Exercise: **Your *HOPE* Practice**. Sit quietly, reflect, and answer each *HOPE* question.

Reflection Exercise: Your *HOPE* Practice

Honesty: Honoring the Truth Process
1. What I honestly think about (issue, dilemma, situation) is _____
    _____
2. I feel emotionally_____ about what I think _____
    and my body (sensations) feels _____
    as I imagine _____
3. I would feel better inside when I honestly and truthfully _____
4. I stop myself from being honest and truthful within myself by _____
    _____
5. Right now, the truth within my heart is _____

Openness: Trusting the Discovery Process
1. I would like to be open to _____ and I am having
    difficulty being open because _____
2. When I open _____, I _____
3. I trust/mistrust that I would respond to our openness with _____
    _____
4. Right now, I am truthfully opening to _____

Practice: Processing Inner Experience
1. Check the following and indicate how often (daily, weekly, monthly etc).
    Affirm your practice and give examples.
    I/We process my/our inner experiences including sharing the above by:
        Journaling ( ) _____
        With my partner ( ) _____
        With my friend(s) ( ) _____
        With my coach ( ) _____
        In prayer ( ) meditation ( ) exercise ( )_____
2. My/Our experience of practicing processing inner experience is _____
    _____
3. I am/We are discovering _____
    _____

Encouragement: Supporting Presence
1. I/We provide encouragement when I/we _____
    _____
2. I/we are gaining courage to _____
    _____
3. I/We can be mentors to one another as I/we _____
    _____
4. I/We are amazed _____

Higher Purpose of Health and Healing

When you begin on the path of healing, you will begin to discover the deeper and higher purpose of conditions that brought you together. Here is an example of a couple, Jennifer and Justin, who found their deeper purpose of conditions.

Jennifer started to bump against the idea that her sense of worth was dependent on her husband's continual affirmation of her. She recalls growing up with a 'steady diet of what she needs to improve' and rarely any affirmation. She married Justin, who does not give his wife any affirmation. Jennifer's use of comfort food increased as she felt insecure about her worth.

In his family, Justin received lots of criticism that he never did things right. Jennifer and Justin recognized they have a mutual hook, an attraction to each other. They loved to eat and drink together. They did this for a good many years until they discovered that their son has a life threatening allergy and a great sensitivity to many foods.

Their son's recovery process created 'a push' to heal for the whole family. The more they healed, the more they had to relate in a new way. The more they transformed, the more they found that their family's old ways did not work for them.   Their love recovered through toughness, compassion, and the support of their healing community. They co-created a healthy family by reclaiming their wholeness consciously. Because they loved their son, they consciously as a couple, sought their own recovery by examining and becoming aware of their family's habits, both healthy and unhealthy. Extended family gatherings became difficult for them, as it challenged their Higher Purpose of health and healing as an expression of their conscious love.

Changes Upon the Path of Healing

The path of healing for a couple involves being in environments that can support their positive growth, health, and healing. As one or both members of the couple choose their own inner changes, something can shift, even though their original or external environment may or may not change.

You may notice that your family's unhealthy habits and repetitive patterns have become uncomfortable for you. You might notice that they may not know how to be with your choice of healing and wellness.

While working together on your changes, it is important to be part of a circle or group of couples who are on the path of healing. This is mutually supportive and encourages the couple to stay on their path, to notice and validate their changes that they intentionally want to make.

An Example of a Couple on Pathway H

Sally and Joseph shared how they are adult children of alcoholic parents and family and how they met in 12-step circles. They shared how together they have been sober for more than 25 years combined.

> "We want to be an example to our children because we don't want to pass on our family disease of addiction to our children, if we can help it. We want them to have options. However, the individual has to be willing to change, for it is easier to try to make our children change, rather than changing ourselves."

Sally recognizes her inclination is to be lazy and continue the family patterns around their addiction. Sally acknowledged:

> "My Higher Purpose is to develop my spirituality and love in a healthy way. My actions will speaker louder than my words when I tell my children about how the disease affected us as children. It was so hard to go through my own healing and deal with the pain of watching my beloved father die of alcoholism, to see my brother go to prison with a DUI, and that my mother is a passive enabler."

She and her husband made a decision to go on the path of inner healing themselves. Aware of her inner psychic pain, Sally engaged in a holistic process of healing, "I want to grow in all my possibilities. I feel good in caring for myself this way. I am growing in body-mind and spirit and I am being really loving to myself. Sally's process has created a shift between her and her husband who unbeknownst to her was also an alcoholic.

Sally shifted from being the 'fixer and rescuer' to gaining awareness of her own participation in creating the problem situation. Sally asked for her healing group to pray for her and her husband.

> "Those were such difficult times and many times I was so close to getting a divorce, but every time I was about to do it, my husband's endearing qualities would show up and I could not do it at all. I had to learn to be tough and speak my truth. As I took charge and faced my own shadow, I lost weight and felt good about myself. I felt the courage to speak my truth with my husband, about how our marriage was dying and how I was grieving."

Joseph, her husband didn't like the fact that she was getting better, because it threatened their marriage. Another crisis brought things to a head, where her husband had to make a very critical decision and bring himself to treatment. It was not easy for them initially. He had jeopardized his career. There was an intervention that occurred. Sally said to him, "It is really up to you, because I cannot be in this situation anymore."

He decided and started on his journey of healing. His healing and her healing brought them to a different level, where they had to get to know themselves and each other as healthy people.

They discovered skills as a couple that they had not learned from their relationship models. Part of their continuing sobriety, involved their relational dynamics of sobriety. Becoming healthy in terms of their spiritual life meant being in support groups that examined addictive thinking and provided supports for healthier ways of relating.

They expressed Gratitude for the critical happenings in their life. "If those things had not happened, we would not have gone in this direction, to be in search of our dharma or Higher Purpose in their life, individually and as a couple."

Sally and Joseph spoke of how they were really meant to be together because alone neither one of them would have been able to overcome the 'weight' of their family patterns of addiction and to discover their spiritual purpose. Joseph affirmed, "Sally has my deep Gratitude, for she really is my better half. She always held a view of me in my best and true self. She knew my dreams, my interests, my frustrations, and supported me throughout, even though I abandoned myself. It was when she with all the passion of her truth and love for me that I realized I really needed help and that I was letting her hold the Higher Purpose for which we committed our love together many years ago." They also went on to help many who were recovering their Spiritual Self and help them lead meaningful lives.

They would come regularly for their own counseling to stay on course in their program of self-care, which in the later years became like tune-ups of affirming their journey.

Deriving from Sally and Joseph's example, we have noticed several common elements in a couple's journey through Pathway H:

- Foremost, they both felt there was a Higher Purpose for their lives and they were in search of their unique talent or contribution with the support of the other. Their shared Higher Purpose helped them create meaning and a shared value system that connected them throughout their life journey.

- They were in a search to discover their true Self, perhaps initially in unconscious and unhealthy ways. Later a crisis became the portal to an opening in consciousness to help discover their unique gift or contribution. They say they had to hit rock bottom or face their "dark shadows" and wished there was an easier way.

- They admired each other with affection and noticed each other's unique talents that may have been hidden from them. They each felt truly seen in loving and tender ways. For instance, Joseph noticed Sally's amazing expressions in her art and was touched by her spirituality. "Your art is so soulful." Joseph would say. "He wanted to use my art for greeting cards in his office. He said I see with amazing eyes. That always melts my heart to feel seen." As Sally sees how Joseph noticed and affirmed her spirit and helped her see that for herself, in reciprocity, he too felt very affirmed and seen in his soul.

Sally noticed how Joseph made possible avenues for people to flourish, by finding them jobs. Sally loved how he could help people see their talents and find employment. Joseph took his ability for granted as he saw it only as a job.

- They created their shared meaningful vision and life purpose together. This impacted their 'hanging in there' that in spite of their challenges; they nurtured their fondness and respect for their different gifts.

- They supported each other as friends in a community on their recovery journey. They learned they were part of something greater than themselves. They turned toward each other especially when things were difficult and had to take individual steps. They acknowledged feeling the importance of their relationship with a supportive community and a relationship with a Higher Power.

- They valued each of their expressions in being of service to their relationship which is evident in their ability to influence each other, even in tough core issues where resistance could be met. Working with their Higher Purpose served as a guide for them to benefit humanity as examples of their commitment to love and accept their self and each other.

A Search for Meaning in Living an Extraordinary Life in an Ordinary World

Reflection Exercise: Our group of couples pondered the following questions in their search for a Higher Purpose or meaning. This became especially important in the wake of the intensification of natural disasters and noticing how couples fared when confronted with them.

We welcome you to ponder this as well.

- Is it possible to live a meaningful life or an extraordinary life without a crisis, catastrophe, challenge or adversity? How do you derive meaning from adversity or crisis?

_____

_____

- If this were the last year of your life, how would you live it? How would you be with each other in your relationship? What would bring meaning for you?"

_____

_____

- How can you live your ordinary life in extra-ordinary ways?

_____

_____

- How would you describe your relational life now? Are you having a pleasant life personally and together? What makes it pleasant? Unpleasant?

  _____

  _____

- Are you having a 'good enough' life personally and together? What makes it a 'good enough' life personally? Together?

  _____

  _____

- Are you having a 'meaningful life' personally and together? What makes it a 'meaningful life' personally? Together?

  _____

  _____

- How can I/we keep ourselves connected to our Higher Purpose, and live meaningful lives, when our unmet needs can distort our love?

  _____

  _____

Couples Group Reflections

Here are some highlights from a couples group and their shared reflections:

- We found the search for meaning and living in accord with a Higher Purpose seems to fluctuate. They shared that It might be easier to be connected to their Higher Purpose as a member of a community that has a joint mission or vision, something larger than self or as a couple, something that makes this world better, like a life focus on peace, freedom, or love.

- Some members talked about enhancing other people's lives, like alleviating suffering, helping in times of crisis and coming together. Other members talked of living by example, in other words - by walking their talk.

- Couples discussed and gave examples that fit them. One couple shared how their pleasant life afforded them their comforts and met their needs for a home, material pleasures of life and connections with family and friends. Other couples talked of having a good life when they felt they were in the flow and groove of expressing their strengths, felt empowered in their relationship, have wonderful communications, are able to be real with one another and feel the support to flourish in what they to do. These couples appreciate the goodness of their life, beyond having material things, even though material things do help bring pleasure to their good life.

- Couples pondered the Higher Purpose of the healing dilemma, wherein their unmet needs of childhood carry their complementary core wounds, which are made more intense with the unprocessed expectations bestowed upon their spouse or partner.

- Couples peeled the layers of their existence that when all else is 'gone' and when we are at our barest minimum, stripped of things, as what may happen in natural disasters, we ask will our divine humanity's goodness accept ourselves and each other at our barest selves?

- So what are the extra-ordinary things that can be external or internal? A way to think of the Higher Purpose of a relationship is to ponder "If I only had a day, month, year to live, how would I/we be now with you/us?" These were some of the extraordinary things that sound ordinary that these couples came up with. You can add to the list.

  ➢ take the dream vacation that they promised each other
  ➢ complete the bedroom floor that you have asked for so long ago
  ➢ forget the bedroom floor, as in the scheme of things, enjoying our time together is more important
  ➢ sit and be with nature
  ➢ appreciate what is present together
  ➢ spend more family time with the children
  ➢ support each other in visiting nana in the nursing home
  ➢ be in the present with whatever is and infuse it with divine love
  ➢ live now, with peace and love, choosing joy and gratitude

Guidelines to Build a Healing Relationship with a Higher Purpose

No matter what two people bring into the relationship, there are certain conditions for the healing process in Pathway H.

1. Be part of a healing and supportive community.

2. Have a supportive group, coach, or counselor for your personal and collective wellbeing.

3. Nurture your appreciation, affirmations, admiration, and positive view of each other. Commit to building each other up by noticing the positives. Choose to nourish your relationship with affirming practices. Otherwise, it is easy to fall into the one of the biggest pitfalls of a couple - as time passes you can take each other for granted. This is dangerous - like weeds it can be menacing. Think of the relationship like a beautiful flowering plant that needs regular watering.

4. Learn how to affirm each other as <u>human beings</u> rather than as <u>human doings</u> (Pathway A). This is especially helpful when you may not agree on what you are talking about. Affirming each other helps to stay connected when disagreeing. People work on trying to

agree, but usually in the process of agreeing, one or both parties feel disempowered, or someone feels as if they have to lose themselves in order to agree. There is a difference between affirming and agreeing. The skill here is to be in an affirming stance towards each other's spirit, soul, and being, as well as to oneself, and to be able to be free within to agree and to disagree.

5. Learn to overcome your 'deadlocks' or polarizations in perceptions by focusing on your Higher Purpose where you can join. Learning involves how to be open to the other's experience as their subjective reality or way of perceiving, without creating unhealthy competition for whose reality is right or whose reality wins. From this place the couple learns how the other sees the situation, thereby widening their perspectives in holding multiple realities and in developing empathy for themselves and each other even when compromise or agreements cannot be reached. By joining in connection and alignment with their Higher Purpose, they access empathy for their experience and tolerance for their differences.

6. Harness the Power of Prayer to learn the Higher Purpose of recurring relationship dilemmas, to open in wonder and understanding and to **be for-giving and for-receiving** of healing energy for one another. Focusing on your Higher Purpose as a couple co-creates options and possible choices.

7. Enhance and harness your strengths as couples as you maintain your own identity in your sustainable relationship. You are able to influence and be influenced by each other, to yield and accommodate, to negotiate and give and take, to learn to respect yourself and each other and in consciously affirming your awareness of the higher dimensions of your Higher Purpose.

8. Learn the skill and process of forgiving. Forgiveness is one of the most misunderstood skills for a couple. It is a process of forgiving oneself and another with radical acceptance of the situation for what it is and accepting life's terms, instead of counting points and building resentments. This also involves compassion and empathy for the struggles and sufferings, and often of choices not taken and the regret thereof.

9. Appreciate the life path each of you were born to live and the life path the combinations of your energies were brought to have and to fulfill together. We find other non-traditional or metaphysical modalities have been helpful to discover their Higher Purpose, such as astrology, numerology, meditation, hypnosis, spirituality etc. While together as a couple, you may join with a focus to dedicate your meaningful lives to love and to service, and the inner path that each takes. **The strength of your Higher Purpose is seeing yourselves bringing <u>your</u> higher purposes <u>together</u> and by living in true alignment with the universal energy of love.**

10. Foster the attitude of Gratitude by acknowledging and appreciating the small and present moments of your daily life, as you orient yourselves to the vital flow of the inter-connective pathways that your Higher Purpose brings to your relationship.

11. Nurture your spiritual life allowing prayer and meditation to be a practice which helps you stay connected to that which is greater than the two of you.

12. Evolve into your couple's divinity. As your Higher Purpose with divine love becomes radiant and creative in expression, you will know true inner joy. You experience your life personally and together, filled with grace and miracles. You experience your extra-ordinary life in the ordinary divinity of the present.

"The path of the co-creator is to be awakened spiritually within, which then turns into your own deeper life purpose, which then makes you want to reach out and touch others in a way that expresses self and really evolves our communities and our world. Certainly, we can't do that unless we activate ourselves first. That's why, for me, emergence is the shift from ego to essence. That is so important."
~Barbara Marx Hubbard, Emergence: The Shift from Ego to Essence

Summary Highlights of Pathway "H": Higher Purpose of Love

1. With a Higher Purpose consciousness the couple connects or reconnects with the Source of All Love. This spiritual base gives the couple a grounded foundation. Pathway H has us cultivate inner virtues such as patience, kindness, compassion, faith, hope, and trust by beginning to heal the wounds of the heart. In Pathway H, couples get a new perspective, one of positive belief that their life and relationship journey is meant to be filled with the amazing grace of unfolding miracles.

2. Pathway H can come at any time in their personal soul journey. This can be initiated by a triggering or significant event. Or it can be a seemingly gradual development to a crisis of a particular problem, dilemma or issue. Many times the Higher Purpose of a couple's relationship does not become apparent until their greatest challenges appear – a terminal illness, death, affairs, tragedy, catastrophic adversities, etc.

3. As couples examine, reflect and embrace their Higher Purpose together, they will open to receive the gifts of Spirit - multidimensional conscious awareness of their partnership that will unfold and deepen into love throughout their lifetime. Those who welcome the opportunity to heal their hearts, learn to appreciate the significant role they play in each other's fulfillment of their life's Higher Purpose.

4. *Living in accordance to a Higher Purpose is a dynamic living process.* Your personal healing and well-being and the healing and well-being of your relationship together, depends on a devoted dynamic practice of recommitment to the Higher Purpose of love: **to love one another as you love yourself with the love of the Divine above all**. This is an over-arching purpose that links your goals, dreams, aspirations, your process of healing, and your evolution to becoming to your whole Self.

5. The Pathway of Higher Purpose **is** center **based on *H-O-P-E (Hope, Openness, Practice, Encouragement).*** When couples are able to face life, knowing that whatever happens that they have Spirit centered-awareness of a Higher Purpose and that in the end, the 'why' of it all will make sense.

6. The path of healing for a couple involves being in environments that can support their positive growth, health, and healing. As one or both members of the couple choose their own inner changes, something can shift, even though their original or external environment may or may not change.

7. No matter what two people bring into the relationship, there are certain conditions for the healing process in Pathway H. We provide Twelve Guidelines in the Healing Process in Pathway to a Higher Purpose:

Twelve Guidelines in the Healing Process in the Pathway to a Higher Purpose

1. Be part of a healing and supportive community.

2. Have your own coach for your personal and collective well-being.

3. Nurture and nourish your positive view of each other.

4. Be in an affirming stance towards each other's spirit and soul being and be free to agree and disagree.

5. Overcome 'deadlocks' or polarizations, widen perspectives to see your multiple realities and attend to where you can join, with empathy and appreciation of differences.

6. Focus on your Higher Purpose in co-creating options and possible choices.

7. Enhance and harness your strengths as you learn to respect yourself and each other by deeply affirming the higher dimensions of your Purpose together.

8. Learn the skill and process of forgiving one another with radical acceptance of the situation for what it is and accepting life's terms.

9. Appreciate the life path each of you were born to live and the life path the combinations of your energies were brought to have and fulfill together.

10. Foster the attitude of Gratitude by acknowledging and appreciating the small moments of your daily life, and orient yourself to your connection to the vital flow of abundant blessings that your Higher Purpose brings to your relationship.

11. Nurture your spiritual life allowing prayer and meditation to be a practice which helps you stay connected within to that which is greater than the two of you.

12. Evolve into your couple's divinity. As your Higher Purpose with divine love becomes radiant and creative in expression, you will know true inner joy. You experience your life together, filled with grace and miracles. You experience your extra-ordinary life in the ordinary divinity of the present.

And in the end of it all, may you appreciate with Gratitude and Divine Love, the choices for your soul's journey with a Higher Purpose together.

253

Closure and Summary
of the Pathways A to H

Now you are at the end of *Eight Pathways of Healing Love: Your Journey of Transformation* at the pace you have taken to work your way through it.

Congratulations!

You may affirm your expanded knowledge and gained awareness. You may acknowledge your widening perspective and appreciate your learned tools. You may feel appreciative for your practices of the dialogue process and skills in Pathways A to H. You may also be experiencing greater mutual self-other support and feeling a freedom to be more fully yourself while being response-able to each other. You may be feeling a deepening of your love and noticing your personal transformation, as you become a witness to your relationship's evolving process. You may be feeling shifts and changes that though you may not be able to articulate it yet, you feel yourselves resting in the safety of something larger and grander than the imperfections that either one of you have and hold.

Celebrate yourself and each other. Celebrate this moment. Savor it. Feel it. You owe it to yourselves as the journey of relationship stretches you to new heights and depths, breadth and limitations that your soul and being can reach. Stay and breathe in the present moment. Pause in this present place and take note. (You may journal it individually...and then share it or you may dialogue together.)

What am I (are we) appreciating as we come to the closure of this Book?

_____

_____

What stood out for me (us) in our journey utilizing this Book?

_____

_____

What am I/we learning that is New? Useful? Helpful? Inspiring? Affirming?

_____

_____

What regrets do I/we acknowledge? What feels unfinished for me/us are?

_____

_____

How will I/we continue our journey as a healing partnership?

_____

_____

What pathway stands out for you at this time in your journey?

_____

_____

What am I (are we) celebrating right now? Feel Gratitude for?

_____

_____

As for us...

We are grateful for this closure with you. We appreciate that good closures affirm the journey you have chosen to take with us through this Book. It includes all the experiences that were a part of this journey.

While you have completed the **Eight Pathways of Healing Love: Your Journey of Transformation** together, you are both acknowledging what you have finished. At the same time it is also valuable to acknowledge what is unfinished. As mentioned in Pathway E, acknowledging what is unfinished is a way of closing without going into 'fixing' or working on it at the moment. This is a way of affirming your next steps.

With intentions for good closure, we support healing relationships in their feeling a sense of completion for a unit of work, such as completion with this Book, and that helps relationships to be open to what may be new and evolving in your relationship.

As our closure for the **Eight Pathways of Healing Love: Your Journey of Transformation**, we acknowledge that writing this Book has been a heart-soul-being process that has taken us longer in the writing process than we anticipated. It has been a challenge to put into writing our own couple relationship journey and our work with the many relationships that the Universal network has sent for us, to coach, to counsel, and to facilitate in their journey, in a way that condenses the multidimensional complexities of human relationships and the transformational journey of love.

As we write this closure page, we feel ease with heartfelt peace, closing, and ending with the **Eighth Pathway**, even though we had initially intended to write all Ten Pathways in one book. Ending with eight feels 'right' for now. The infinity symbol in the number eight represents for us the abundance of surrendering this book to the Higher Power. We pause with the infinite source of healing love feeling the infinity vibration of eight as it unfolds the co-creative power of couples' conscious practice of deepening love to align with and embody divine love. This opens us to the unfolding process of the Ninth Pathway of Healing Love (which is currently in its conscious evolving process and we are currently writing). When the time is right and according to universal intelligence, the Ninth Pathway of Healing Love book will be complete. Subsequently, the Tenth Pathway of Healing Love will evolve unto itself.

A word of caution...

Closure is important, as it is human nature to want things to be finished. In other words, when we think the work is done, we want it done. In the relationship journey, like the seasons, things move on. This does not lend to complacency or to taking things for granted as though you have completed a task that the 'change' should be a 'done deal'...permanently or perfectly.

The journey of transformation in a relationship is an <u>on-going process</u> of evolution. With greater awareness, know that sometimes your relationship can be confusing and frustrating even though you are trying your best. Even with your commitment to be a healing partnership you may feel downhearted when it seems that you are back to square one or that things are not working the way that you would like it to.

Sometimes you may find yourselves struggling within yourself as you slip into old patterns of reactions with each other, particularly in stressful situations.

We know.

The *'relational journey of healing love'* is a continuous process throughout your life. Now you wonder how and why it is that having more awareness can increase one's sensitivity to bumpy and difficult interactions.

Perhaps it is because you are more conscious and more aware of the old ways. You also have more options to choose to see those bumps as opportunities to practice your skills, to shift your energy, to choose your responses, and to dialogue rather than debate. Yes! It is work. Or it can be to **play-work (plark)** in any of the **Eight Pathways**. We have often *plarked*, consciously giving ourselves opportunities to transform and together see our relationship as our laboratory for experiencing deepening love. We have opened ourselves to experiences to transform physically, emotionally, mentally, energetically, interactively, heart-fully, soulfully, and spiritually in this amazing field of possibilities. You can, too.

Soon you may notice how those seemingly familiar places of feeling 'stuck' do not seem to last as long. Also, you notice how the gripping intensity of your automatic reactions has transformed to feel more ease, more space for wiggle room, and for possibilities to explore. You are shifting your energy even though it seems as others are doing more of their same stuff.

Plarking through the practices in the Pathways, you find and co-create your own art of your healing relationship. There is no prescription of how you have to do things or be like other couples. Rather than using this Book as giving you more 'shoulds', you become accepting of your 'imperfections' as human beings and appreciate your growth as the unfolding process of the divine love presence within.

Funny it is! You can feel your heart lightening. The cosmos around seems to be shifting because you are orienting to notice more healing relationships within yourself, each other, and all around. You notice that how you look at the situation and how you respond reflects your inner evolution.

To summarize, your significant love relationships give you cues as to what is yearning to be healed and what Pathway is waiting to be awakened in your journey of relationship. When you really listen to your words, feelings, and experiences and examine where you are stuck, the Pathways of Healing Love shows you how being stuck becomes an opportunity to heal and transform, and how your relationship is the vehicle for a healing partnership of deepening love. To really listen to the heart and soul of our loved one's repetitions of what they want to go beyond, the blame, the criticism, and painful exchanges of unconscious love interactions, we find the cues that are invitations in the **Pathways of Healing Love**. For the healing partnership, which is committed to conscious healing love, the transformational process of the relationship journey opens to great possibilities of discovery of the divine love presence within oneself, the other, and the field.

Behavior and Thematic Word Cues

Here are some behavior and thematic word cues to be aware of as to which Pathway your relationship may be in. Often what makes couples stay stuck is the recycling of the critical aspect. Imbedded in the cue of the critique of the crisis, is the opportunity to take what the relationship is 'being invited' to consciously heal, evolve, and transform through the **Eight Pathways of Healing Love.**

Pathway A: Pathway of Affirmation and Awakening invites the healing relationship to move from unawareness to awareness with affirmation in a body-mind-spirit foundation. This nourishes and supports the healing and growth of their significant relationship for whenever we affirm something it gives it energy and life. In a significant relationship the intention of the affirmation draws to us what we experience.

Behavior cue:	Affirming is the Draw
Some word cues:	"I just need you to appreciate me."
	"It's like I do not exist...don't feel included...don't feel I matter."

Pathway B: Pathway of Being and Balance involves an invitation to gain awareness of the multiple ingredients of seemingly discordant, diverse, and polar aspects of yourself and your partner's needs in the struggle and the quest for being in harmony and balance.

Behavior cue:	Relating is the Journey
Some word cues:	"This is not fair." "What about my needs."
	"I have lost me. It is all about you. Where's the balance?"

Pathway C: Pathway of Connection and Communication invites you to become aware of your multi-level ways of connecting and communicating. This attunes your intentions with impact, gains practice skills that facilitate sharing, support, working through conflict, and appreciating differences, as well as, enhancing embodied connections that foster a couple's growth and transformation.

Behavior cues:	Awareness is the Beginning
Some word cues:	"I am feeling misunderstood. We are not connecting."
	"We need to communicate better."

Pathway D: Pathway of Development and Discovery reinforces the evolution of the couple's soul: both individually and together. In their repetitive patterns of being stuck lies the opportunity for dialogue that fosters discovery, development, healing, and transformation.

Behavior cues:	Wondering is the Choice
Some word cues:	"I notice all of my relationships end up this way."
	"This is getting old. Why are we doing this again?"

Pathway E: Pathway of Evolving - Learning How to Learn from Experience invites the couple to appreciate how to co-create their learning partnership. Experience is the 'teacher' and their relationship journey is the school of life so together they can appreciate their cycle of an interactive cycle of experiencing as their soul's journey into evolving their divine love connection.

Behavior cues:	Presence is the Healing
Some word cues:	"What am I supposed to learn from this experience?"
	"What direction do I take so to avoid making this mistake?"

Pathway F: Pathway of Freedom and Responsibility invites couples to explore the creative tension and the depths of freedom and responsibility to find in its paradoxical nature, how their spirit of devotion to their Higher Purpose allows them to experience the vitality of responsibility and the freedom of unconditional love.

Behavior cues:	Allowing is the Opening
Some word cues:	"I need some space to express my authentic self."
	"This responsibility feels limiting. Where's the freedom?"

Pathway G: *Pathway of Gratitude and Grace – Giving and Receiving* allows the couple to experience the powerful vibrations of giving, receiving and authentic Gratitude to deepen and strengthen their love. This unfolds then to the flow of Universal blessings even when they are disguised in challenge and adversities.

Behavior cues:	Thankful Loving is Empowering
Some word cues:	"We made it through the hard times."
	"It was very difficult. It's amazing that we're together."

Pathway H: *Pathway to a Higher Purpose of Love – A Sacred Pathway of Spirit Centeredness* awakens the couple personally and together to the quantum shift in the higher plane of consciousness, where their life journey together reflects a dynamic living process in the evolving present to the Higher Purpose of Love.

Behavior cues:	Healing is becoming Whole
Some word cues:	"I hope this will make sense in the end."
	"We have to believe there is a Higher Purpose."

Where there is Faith, there is Love,

Where there is Love, there is Peace,

Where there is Peace, there is God,

Where there is God, there is Bliss.

~ Sri Sathya Sai Baba

Epilogue

A few years ago, I started on a *Journey of Healing Love* with Lalei and Phil, to help them to crystallize their thoughts, and write about how they support couples to go deep into their relationships. Little did I know the impact that this book would have on my own personal journey...

When Lalei and I were getting to know each other, and tapping into her intuitive radar, she said to me that by the time this book came into fruition, I would find a man who would be my compliment and that I would be able to have a deep, meaningful, soulful, loving, and intimate relationship with him.

In assisting Lalei and Phil to write this book, I found myself deeply immersed in learning the Pathways. I began to notice what Pathway I would be in with the various men I was dating. Unfortunately, I didn't feel with any of them this willingness and commitment to brave through the terrains (which at times felt like they were filled with landmines) of the Pathways.

Lo and behold after a great deal of exploration and discovery, and just as Lalei said, I have been given the sweet gift of sharing my life with a wonderful man. I am not your average gal, so finding another so unusual, intense, intelligent, spiritual, and funny was more than a tall order.

So here I am today, writing about how her words came to pass and finding myself in a relationship where we brave the terrains of the Pathways daily.

I marvel often at the sweetness of intimacy. Knowing what I do about the Pathways, I can get a birds-eye view of how we now seem to be weaving back and forth with Pathways A, B and C. I am also reminded when my sweetheart and I want to throttle each other, when we find that we are either triggering each other or challenged because we are communicating like we are from two different planets (the Mars/Venus metaphor is quite apropos...) that we can breathe, re-center, step-back, and return to our original commitment, allowing ourselves to drop back into our hearts and remembering that:

"Love is when you can be your true self with someone,
and you only want to be your true self because of them."
~Terri Guillemets

Warmly From My Heart,
Marci* Lebowitz
Word Designer

About the Authors

Philip Belzunce, Ph.D. and Lalei Gutierrez, Ph.D. have over 50 years of combined experience in working with individuals, couples, families, and groups. Philip and Lalei are holistic and energy psychologists and are certified professional life coaches specializing in relationships, diversity, and wellness. Both are board certified polarity practitioners. They teach, train, lead workshops, and host seminars for groups, companies, communities, and organizations, both locally and internationally.

Their extensive experience and knowledge, personally, relationally, and professionally integrates mind-body-soul-spirit energetic-systemic and diversity processes for the whole person and the whole relational system. **Eight Pathways of Healing Love: Your Journey of Transformation** is their gift to couples and all types of relations.

They are contributing authors to a best-selling book, *Overcomers Inc. –True Stories of Hope, Courage and Inspiration* (2009), wrote the instruction manuals, *Polarity Therapy in Significant Relationships* and *Polarity Exercises for Partners,* contributed a chapter entitled, *Developing Cultural Competence Through the Use of Self* in the Handbook of Diversity Management that is used in universities and by diversity professionals. They also wrote a children's book, *Once Upon a Doggie,* a lighthearted book that teaches us through a puppy's discovery about who he is and how he gives back to our world. Philip has written books that address cancer issues: *Heart Shadows,* which is a novel of a couple's journey dealing with cancer and laying out for us the levels of insight, awareness, and forgiveness that can arise during life's challenges, and *What Really Matters is the Heart,* which journals the grieving process of loss from the author's firsthand experience of his own process of grief and how we are guided into the windows of healing and how we can embrace the grieving process.

You can learn more about their work and contributions at their websites:
www.phillalei.com
www.spiritcenteredcoaching.com

Philip and Lalei are available for lectures, conferences, speaking engagements and personal coaching in person and via telephone or Skype. They can be reached through their websites: www.phillalei.com, and www.spiritcenteredcoaching.com or by phone at 216.712.6192 EST.

References & Suggested Readings

Ackerman, Diane. ***A Natural History of the Senses,*** 1991
  A Natural History of Love, 1995

Adler, Felix. ***An Ethical Philosophy of Life,*** 2010

Adrienne, Carol and James Redfield. ***Purpose of Your Life: Finding Your Place in the World Using Synchronicity, Intuition, and Uncommon Sense,*** 1999

Alexander, Skye. ***The Pocket Encyclopedia of Healing Touch Therapies: 136 Techniques That Alleviate Pain, Calm the Mind, and Promote Health,*** 2010

Andrews, Frank. ***The Art and Practice of Loving,*** 1992
  The Art and Practice of Loving: Living a Heartfelt Yes, 2010

Arroyo, Stephen. ***Astrology, Psychology, and the Four Elements: An Energy Approach to Astrology and Its Use in the Counseling Arts,*** 1978

Balswick, Jack O. and Judith K. Balswick. ***A Model for Marriage: Covenant, Grace, Empowerment and Intimacy,*** 2006

Beattie, Melodie. ***Journey to the Heart: Daily Meditations on the Path to Freeing Your Soul,*** 1996

Belzunce, Philip Ph.D. ***What Really Matters Is the Heart,*** 1998
  Heart Shadows, 1999

Braden, Gregg. ***The Divine Matrix: Bridging Time, Space, Miracles, and Belief,*** 2009
  The God Code: The Secret of Our Past, The Promise of Our Future, 2004

Braybrooke, Marcus. ***Learn to Pray: A Practical Guide to Faith and Inspiration,*** 2001

Brothers, Barbara Jo (ed.). ***Couples and Body Therapy,*** has been co-published simultaneously as Journal of Couples Therapy, Volume 10, Number 2, 2001

Brown, Brene. ***The Gifts of Imperfection: Let Go of Who You Think You're Supposed to Be and Embrace Who You Are,*** 2010

Brown, Emily M. ***Affairs: A Guide to Working Through the Repercussions of Infidelity,*** 1999

Buber, Martin. ***I and Thou,*** 1971
  The Ten Rungs and The Way of Man, 2006

Caldwell, Christine Ph.D. ***Getting in Touch: The Guide to New Body-Centered Therapies,*** 1997

Campbell, Susan. ***The Couple's Journey: Intimacy as a Path to Wholeness,*** 1987

Carroll, Cain et al. ***Partner Yoga: Making Contact for Physical, Emotional, and Spiritual Growth,*** 2000

Chapman, Gary, Ph.D. ***The Four Seasons of Marriage,*** 2007

Chia, Mantak. ***Healing Light of the Tao: Foundational Practices to Awaken Chi Energy,*** 2008

Chopra, Deepak. ***Perfect Health: The Complete Mind/Body Guide***, 2001
Reinventing the Body, Resurrecting the Soul: How to Create a New You, 2010
The Seven Spiritual Laws of Yoga: A Practical Guide to Healing Body, Mind and Spirit, 2005
The Path to Love: Spiritual Strategies for Healing, 1998

Clunis, Merilee Ph.D. and G. Dorsey Green, Ph.D. ***Lesbian Couples: A Guide to Creating Healthy Relationships,*** 2004

Cohen, Gabriel. ***Storms Can't Hurt the Sky: A Buddhist Path Through Divorce,*** 2008

Cox, Louis and Fran Cox. ***A Conscious Life: Cultivating the Seven Qualities of Authentic Adulthood,*** 1995

Dale, Cindi. ***The Subtle Body: An Encyclopedia of Your Energetic Anatomy,*** 2009

Draper, Maureen McCarthy. ***Nature of Music: Beauty, Sound and Healing,*** 2001

Dyer, Wayne W. ***The Power of Intention: Learning to Co-create Your World Your Way,*** 2010

Eden, Donna , David Feinstein, and Caroline Myss. ***Energy Medicine,*** 1999
Energy Medicine: Balancing Your Body's energies for Optimal Health, Joy and Vitality (Updated and Expanded) 2008

Eggerichs, Dr. Emerson. ***Love and Respect: The Love She Most Desires, The Respect He Desperately Needs,*** 2004

Eigen, Rebecca and Ann Bugh. ***The Shadow Dance and the Astrological 7th House Workbook (Marriage, Partnership and Open Enemies: ie., The Shadow is Us All),*** 2009

Einstein, Albert. ***Sidelights on Relativity,*** 2011

Emmons, Robert A. ***Thanks! How the New Science of Gratitude Can Make You Happier,*** 2007
Words of Gratitude Mind Body & Soul, 2001

Emoto, Masaru. ***The Hidden Messages in Water,*** 2005
Messages of Water and the Universe, 2010

Estes, Clarissa Pinkola. *Untie the Strong Woman: Blessed Mother's Immaculate Love for the Wild Soul,* 2011
   Seeing in the Dark: Myths and Stories to Reclaim the Buried, Knowing Woman, 2010
Women Who Run with the Wolves, 1996

Firestone, Robert W. and Joyce Carlett. *Fear of Intimacy,* 1999

Friedlander, John, and Gloria Hemsher. *Psychic Psychology: Energy Skills for Life and Relationships,* 2011

Gaynor, Mitchell L. *The Healing Power of Sound: Recovery from Life-Threatening Illness Using Sound, Voice, and Music,* 2002

George, Mike. *Discover Inner Peace: A Guide to Spiritual Well-Well-Being*, 1999

Gerber, Richard. *A Practical Guide to Vibrational Medicine: Energy Healing and Spiritual Transformation,* 2001

Gerner, Christopher K., Ph.D. *The Mindful Path to Self-Compassion: Freeing Yourself from Destructive Thoughts and Emotions,* 2009

Gibran, Kahil. *The Prophet,* 1965, 1995
The Collected Works (Everyman's Library) , 2007

Gilbert, Roberta M. *Extraordinary Relationships: A New Way of Think about Human Interactions,* 1992

Glass, Lillian, Ph.D. *He Says, She Says: Closing the Communication Gap Between the Sexes,* 1992

Goldman, Daniel. *Emotional Intelligence,* 2010
   The Brain and Emotional Intelligence, 2011
   Social Intelligence: The New Science of Human Relationships, 2007
   Leadership" The Power of Emotional Intelligence, 2011

Gordon, Lori Heyman. *Passage to Intimacy,* 2001

Gottman, John M. *Ten Lessons to Transform Your Marriage: AMERICA'S LOVE LAB EXPERTS SHARE THEIR STRATEGIES FOR STRENGTHENING YOUR RELATIONSHIP,* 2007
   Why Marriages Succeed or Fail: What You Can Learn From the Breakthrough Research to Make Your Marriage Last, 1994

Gottman, John et al. *Raising An Emotionally Intelligent Child The Heart of Parenting,* 1998

Grigg, Ray. *The Tao of Relationships: A Balancing of Man and Woman,* 1988

Gurdjieff, G.I. *Life is Real Only Then, When I Am (Compass),* 1999

Hannaford, Carla. ***Playing in the Unified Field: Raising and Becoming Conscious, Creative Beings,*** 2010
> ***I Thought It Was Just Me (but it isn't): Telling the Truth About Perfectionism, Inadequacy, and Power,*** 2007

Harley, Willard F. Jr. ***His Needs, Her Needs: Building an Affair-Proof Marriage,*** 2001

Hawkins, David R., M.D., Ph.D. ***Power VS Force: The Hidden Determinants of Human Behavior,*** 2000

Hay, Louise. ***Letters to Louise: The Answers Are Within You (Updated Edition),*** 2011

Heller, Susan, and Paula Singer. ***The Power of Two: Secrets of a Strong and Loving Marriage,*** 1997

Helmering, Doris Wild. ***Sense Ability: Expanding Your Sense of Awareness for a Twenty-First Century Life,*** 2000
> ***Building Emotional Intelligence: Techniques to Cultivate Inner Strength in Children,*** 2008

Hendricks, Gay Ph.D. and Kathlyn Hendricks, Ph.D. ***Conscious Loving: The Journey to Co-Commitment,*** 1992

Hendricks, Gay. ***Conscious Living: How to Create a Life of Your Own Design,*** 2001

Hendrix, Harville. ***Getting the Love You Want: A Guide for Couples, 20th Anniversary Edition,*** 2007
> ***Keeping the Love You Find: A Personal Guide,*** 1993

Hendrix, Harville Ph.D. and Helen Hunt, Ph.D. ***Receiving Love: Transform Your Relationship by Letting Yourself Be Loved,*** 2004

Hicks, Esther, and Jerry Hicks. ***Ask and It is Given: Learning to Manifest Your Desires,*** 2005

Hillman, James. ***The Soul's Code: In Search of Character and Calling,*** 1997

Horner, Althea. ***Being and Loving,*** 1999
> ***Being and Loving: How to Achieve Intimacy with Another Person and Retain One's Own Identity,*** 2005

Huang, Chungliang Al. ***Mentoring: The Tao of Giving and Receiving Wisdom,*** 1995

Hubbard, Barbara Marx. ***Emergence: The Shift from Ego to Essence,*** 2012

Kasl, Charlotte Sophia. ***If the Buddha Married: Creating Enduring Relationships on a Spiritual Path,*** 2001

Kayser, Karen. ***When Love Dies: The Process of Marital Disaffection,*** 1993

Kelly, Matthew. *The Seven Levels of Intimacy: The Art of Loving and the Joy of Being Loved,* 2007

Kennedy, Randall. *Interracial Intimacies: Sex, Marriage, Identity, and Adoption,* 2003

Korte, Kim. *The Perfect Heart: Creating and Maintaining Love/Life Balance,* 2011

Kortsch, Gabriella, Ph.D. *Rewiring the Soul: Finding the Possible Self: How Your Connection to Yourself Can Make All The Difference,* 2011

Kramer, Kenneth. *Martin Buber's I and Thou: Practicing Living Dialogue,* 2004

Krystar, Phyllis. *Sai Baba: The Ultimate Experience,* 1994

Laing, R.D. *Politics of Experience,* 1983

Lawrence, D.H. *Complete Poems (Penguin Twentieth-Century Classics),* 1994

Lee, Robert G. and Gordon Wheeler. *The Voice of Shame: Silence and Connection in Psychotherapy (Gestalt Institute of Cleveland Book Series),* 1997

Lerner, Harriet Goldhor. *The Dance of Intimacy,* 1990;
The Dance of Anger: A Woman's Guide to Changing the Patterns of Intimate Relationships, 2005

Lewis, Dennis. *Free Your Breath, Free Your Life: How Conscious Breathing Can Relieve Stress, Increase Vitality, and Help You Live More Fully,* 2004

Lyod, Alexander, Ph.D. *The Healing Code,* 2010

Madonik, Barbara. *I Hear What You Say, But What Are You Telling Me?: The Strategic Use of Nonverbal Communication in Mediation,* 2001

Markova, Dawna, Ph.D. *No Enemies Within, The Creative Process Discovering What's Right About What's Wrong,* 1994

Marshall, Jeanne. *Affirmations: A Pathway to Transformation: Empowered Development by the Day, by the Month , by the Year,* 1996

Martin, Wilhelm. *The Parent's Tao Te Ching: Ancient Advice for Modern Parents,* 1999

Martin, William et al. *The Couple's Tao Te Ching: Ancient Advice for Modern Lovers,* 1999

McTaggart, Lynne. *The Field, The Quest for the Secret Force of the Universe,* 2008
The Bond: Connecting Through the Space Between Us, 2011

Meindl, Anthony. *At Left Brain Turn Right: An Uncommon Path to Shutting Up Your Inner Critic, Giving Fear the Finger & Having an Amazing Life,* 2012

Millman, Dan. *The Life You Were Born to Live: A Guide to Finding Your Life Purpose,* 1993
Everyday Enlightenment: The Twelve Gateways to Personal Growth, 1999
The Laws of Spirit: A Tale of Transformation, 2001
Way of the Peaceful Warrior: A Book That Changes Lives, 2006

Moore, Thomas. *Soul Mates,* 1994
Care of the Soul: A Guide for Cultivating Depth and Sacredness in Everyday Life, 1994
The Soul of Sex: Cultivating Life as an Act of Love, 1999

Moss, Richard. *Inside-Out Healing: Transforming Your Life Through the Power of Presence,* 2011
The Mandala of Being: Discovering the Power of Awareness, 2012

Moss, Rober. *Conscious Dreaming: A Spiritual Path for Everyday Life,* 1996

Murakami, Kasuo, Ph.D. *The Divine Code of Life,* 1997

Murata, Sachiko. *The Tao of Islam: A Sourcebook on Gender Relationships Islamic Thought,* 1992

Murdock, Maureen. *The Heroine's Journey - Woman's Quest for Wholeness,* 1990

Myss, Caroline. *Anatomy of the Spirit: The Seven Stages of Power and Healing,* 1997
Why People Don't Heal and How They Can, 1998
Energy Anatomy, 2001

O'Donohue, John. *Beauty: The Invisible Embrace,* 2005

Ornish, Dean, M.D. *Love and Survival: The Scientific Basis for the Healing Power of Intimacy,* 1998

Otto, Herbert. *Ways of Growth: Approaches to Expanding Awareness,* 1996

Page, Susan. *How the One of Your Can bring the Two of You Together: Breakthrough Strategies to Resolve Your Conflicts and Reignite Your Love,* 1997
Why Talking is Not Enough: Eight Loving Actions That Will Transform Your Marriage, 2007

Peck, M. Scott. *The Road Less Travelled: A New Psychology of Love, Traditional Values and Spiritual Growth,* 1998

Pert, Candace. *Molecules of Emotion: The Science Behind Mind-Body Medicine,* 1999

Pittman, Frank. *Private Lies: Infidelity and the Betrayal of Intimacy,* 1990

Prager, Karen J. *The Psychology of Intimacy,* 1995

Reginster, Bernard. ***The Affirmation of Life: Nietzsche on Overcoming Nihilism,*** 2006

Richards, Shaeri. ***Dancing with your Dragon: The Art of Loving your Unlovable Self,*** 2011

Richio, David and Kathlyn Hendricks. ***How to Be an Adult in Relationships: The Five Keys to Mindful Loving,*** 2002

Rilke, Rainer Maria. ***Letters to a Young Poet,*** 1993, 2001, 2009
    Rilke on Love and Other Difficulties: Translations and Considerations, 2004
    A Year with Rilke: Daily Readings from the Best of Mainer Maria Rilke, 2009

Salsberg, Sharon. ***Lovingkindness: The Revolutionary Art of Happiness (Shambala Classics),*** 2002

Schwartz, Richard and Jacqueline Olds. ***Marriage in Motion: The Natural Ebb and Flow of Lasting Relationships,*** 2002

Seashore, Charles and Edith Whitfield Seashore. ***What Did You Say? The Art of Giving and Receiving,*** 1992, 1996, 1997

Seligman, Martin, E.P., Ph.D. ***Authentic Happiness: Using the New Positive Psychology to Realize Your Potential for Lasting Fulfillment,*** 2002

Shafia, Louisa. ***Lucid Food: Cooking for an Eco-Conscious Life,*** 2009

Shapiro, Rabbi Rami. ***The Sacred Art of Lovingkindness: Preparing to Practice (Art of Spiritual Living),*** 2006

Shem, Samuel, et al. ***We Have To Talk: Healing Dialogues Between Men and Women,*** 1999

Siegmann, Johanna. ***The Tao of Tango,*** 2006

Sills, Franklin. ***The Polarity Process: Energy as a Healing Art,*** 2001

Spring, Janis Abrahms and Michael Spring. ***After the Affair: Healing the Pain and Rebuilding Trust When a Partner Has Been Unfaithful,*** 1997

Stevens, Ramon. ***Conscious Life: Creating Your Reality,*** 1991

Stone, Randolph. ***Health Building: The Conscious Art of Living Well,*** 1999

Tao Te Ching: The Art and the Journey. Translated and Illustrated by Holly Roberts, Ph.D.

Taylor, Sandra Anne. ***Quantum Success: The Astounding Science of Wealth and Happiness,*** 2006

Tolle, Eckhart. ***The Power of Now: A Guide to Spiritual Enlightenment,*** 2004
    Stillness Speaks, 2003
    Practicing the Power of Now: Essential Teachings, Meditations, and Exercises From the Power of Now, 2001

Trine, Ralph Waldo. *In Tune With The Infinite: Fullness of Peace, Power and Plenty,* 1910

Trungpa, Chogyam. *The Myth of Freedom and the Way of Meditation (Shambala Library),* 2005
   Transcending Madness: The Experience of the Six Bardos (Dharma Ocean Series), 1992
   Cutting Through Spiritual Materialism (Shambala Library), 2008

Ucik, Martin. *Integral Relationships: A Manual for Men,* 2010

Vissell, Joyce & Barry Vissell. *The Heart's Wisdom: A Practical Guide to Growing Through Love,* 1999

Wallace, Dee. *Conscious Creation: Directing Energy to Get the Life You Want,* 2011

Weiss, Brian. *Many Lives, Many Masters,* 1988, *Messages from the Masters,* 2000

Welwood, John. *Journey of the Heart: The Path of Conscious Love,* 1996
   Love and Awakening: Discovering the Sacred Path of Intimate Relationship, 1997
   Perfect Love, Imperfect Relationships: Healing the Wound of the Heart, 2007

Weshons, John. *One Soul, One Love, One Heart: The Sacred Path to Healing All Relationships,* 2009

Wheeler, Gordon. *Beyond Individualism: Toward a New Understanding of Self, Relationship, and Experience,* 2000

Wilber, Ken. *Integral Psychology: Consciousness, Spirit, Psychology, Therapy,* 2000
   Integral Vision: A Very Short Introduction to the Revolutionary Integral Approach to Life, God, the Universe, and Everything, 2007

Wilber, Ken, et al. *Integral Life Practice: A 21st-Century Blueprint for Physical Health, Emotional Balance, Mental Clarity, and Spiritual Awakening,* 2008

Williamson, Marianne. *Return to Love: Reflections on the Principles of "A Course in Miracles",* 1996

Yogananda, Paramahansa. *The Yoga of Jesus, Understanding the Hidden Teachings of the Gospels,* 2007
   The Second Coming of Christ: The Resurrection of the Christ Within You (2 Volume Set), 2008
   Scientific Affirmations: Theory and Practice of Concentration, 1958

Zerof, Herbert G. *Finding Intimacy: The Art of Happiness and Living Together,* 1978, 1981

Zi, Nancy. *The Art of Breathing: Six Simple Lessons to Improve Performance, Health and Well-Being (Book and Video),* 1994

Zukav, Gary. **Seat of the Soul,** 1990

Zukav, Gary and Linda Francis. **Heart of the Soul: Emotional Awareness,** 2001

Eight Pathways of Healing Love

Eight Pathways is also available in paperback and Kindle at Amazon and as individual e-books or whole book that can be downloaded at eightpathways.com:

- Introduction
- Pathway A: Pathway of Affirmation and Awakening
- Pathway B: Pathway of Being and Balance
- Pathway C: Pathway of Connection and Communication
- Pathway D: Pathway of Development and Discovery
- Pathway E: Pathway of Evolving in Experience
- Pathway F: Pathway of Freedom and Responsibility
- Pathway G: Pathway of Gratitude and Grace
- Pathway H: Pathway to a Higher Purpose of Love

The *Pathways of Healing Love* series is continually evolving for your transformational journey. Please check back with us for more discoveries on the *Pathways - for your continuing Journey of Transformation*.

- ❖ Pathway I
- ❖ Pathway J
- ❖ Pathway K
- ❖ Pathway L

 **Like Us** and Follow Us on Facebook

Philip and Lalei are available for life changing lectures, seminars, conferences, speaking engagements and personal coaching either in person and via telephone or Skype. They can be reached via their websites:

www.phillalei.com
www.spiritcenteredcoaching.com
or by calling 216.712.6192 EST

Other books available by Philip Belzunce and Lalei Gutierrez:
- Heart Shadows
- What Really Matters Is The Heart
- Overcomers, Inc. – True Stories of Hope, Courage and Inspiration
- Once Upon A Doggie
- Pairs Polarity in Significant Relationships - Becoming Aware of Our Interpersonal Elements
- Pairs Polarity in Significant Relationships - Meditations, Exercises, and Stretches

Notes

Notes

Notes

6165144R00149

Made in the USA
San Bernardino, CA
03 December 2013